AMERICA'S
TEST KITCHEN

ALSO *by* AMERICA'S TEST KITCHEN

The Chicken Bible
The Complete Plant-Based Cookbook
How Can It Be Gluten-Free Cookbook Collection
The Complete One Pot
Meat Illustrated
Cooking for One
The Complete Summer Cookbook
Bowls
Vegetables Illustrated
The Side Dish Bible
Foolproof Fish
100 Techniques
Easy Everyday Keto
Everything Chocolate
The Perfect Pie
How to Cocktail
Spiced
The Ultimate Burger
The New Essentials Cookbook
Dinner Illustrated
America's Test Kitchen Menu Cookbook
Cook's Illustrated Revolutionary Recipes
Tasting Italy: A Culinary Journey
Cooking at Home with Bridget and Julia
The Complete Diabetes Cookbook
The Complete Slow Cooker
The Complete Make-Ahead Cookbook
The Complete Mediterranean Cookbook
The Complete Vegetarian Cookbook
The Complete Cooking for Two Cookbook
Just Add Sauce
How to Braise Everything
How to Roast Everything
Nutritious Delicious
What Good Cooks Know
Cook's Science
The Science of Good Cooking
The Perfect Cake
The Perfect Cookie
Bread Illustrated
Master of the Grill
Kitchen Smarts
Kitchen Hacks
100 Recipes: The Absolute Best Ways to
 Make the True Essentials
The New Family Cookbook

The America's Test Kitchen Cooking School Cookbook
The Cook's Illustrated Baking Book
The Cook's Illustrated Cookbook
The America's Test Kitchen Family Baking Book
America's Test Kitchen Twentieth Anniversary
 TV Show Cookbook
The Best of America's Test Kitchen (2007–2021 Editions)
The Complete America's Test Kitchen TV Show
 Cookbook 2001–2021
Toaster Oven Perfection
Mediterranean Instant Pot
Cook It in Your Dutch Oven
Vegan for Everybody
Sous Vide for Everybody
Air Fryer Perfection
Multicooker Perfection
Food Processor Perfection
Pressure Cooker Perfection
Instant Pot Ace Blender Cookbook
Naturally Sweet
Foolproof Preserving
Paleo Perfected
The Best Mexican Recipes
Slow Cooker Revolution Volume 2: The Easy-Prep Edition
Slow Cooker Revolution
The America's Test Kitchen D.I.Y. Cookbook

THE COOK'S ILLUSTRATED ALL-TIME BEST SERIES
All-Time Best Brunch
All-Time Best Dinners for Two
All-Time Best Sunday Suppers
All-Time Best Holiday Entertaining
All-Time Best Appetizers
All-Time Best Soups

COOK'S COUNTRY TITLES
Big Flavors from Italian America
One-Pan Wonders
Cook It in Cast Iron
Cook's Country Eats Local
The Complete Cook's Country TV Show Cookbook

FOR A FULL LISTING OF ALL OUR BOOKS
CooksIllustrated.com
AmericasTestKitchen.com

PRAISE *for* AMERICA'S TEST KITCHEN TITLES

"The book's depth, breadth, and practicality makes it a must-have for seafood lovers."
PUBLISHERS WEEKLY (STARRED REVIEW) ON *FOOLPROOF FISH*

"Another flawless entry in the America's Test Kitchen canon, *Bowls* guides readers of all culinary skill levels in composing one-bowl meals from a variety of cuisines."
BUZZFEED BOOKS ON *BOWLS*

Selected as the Cookbook Award Winner of 2019 in the Health and Special Diet Category
INTERNATIONAL ASSOCIATION OF CULINARY PROFESSIONALS (IACP) ON *THE COMPLETE DIABETES COOKBOOK*

"Diabetics and all health-conscious home cooks will find great information on almost every page."
BOOKLIST (STARRED REVIEW) ON *THE COMPLETE DIABETES COOKBOOK*

"This is a wonderful, useful guide to healthy eating."
PUBLISHERS WEEKLY ON *NUTRITIOUS DELICIOUS*

"*The Perfect Cookie*. . . is, in a word, perfect. This is an important and substantial cookbook. . . . If you love cookies, but have been a tad shy to bake on your own, all your fears will be dissipated. This is one book you can use for years with magnificently happy results."
THE HUFFINGTON POST ON *THE PERFECT COOKIE*

Selected as one of the 10 Best New Cookbooks of 2017
THE LA TIMES ON *THE PERFECT COOKIE*

"The sum total of exhaustive experimentation . . . anyone interested in gluten-free cookery simply shouldn't be without it."
NIGELLA LAWSON ON *THE HOW CAN IT BE GLUTEN-FREE COOKBOOK*

"True to its name, this smart and endlessly enlightening cookbook is about as definitive as it's possible to get in the modern vegetarian realm."
MEN'S JOURNAL ON *THE COMPLETE VEGETARIAN COOKBOOK*

"If you're a home cook who loves long introductions that tell you why a dish works followed by lots of step-by-step hand holding, then you'll love *Vegetables Illustrated*."
THE WALL STREET JOURNAL ON *VEGETABLES ILLUSTRATED*

"A one-volume kitchen seminar, addressing in one smart chapter after another the sometimes surprising whys behind a cook's best practices. . . . You get the myth, the theory, the science, and the proof, all rigorously interrogated as only America's Test Kitchen can do."
NPR ON *THE SCIENCE OF GOOD COOKING*

"The 21st-century *Fannie Farmer Cookbook* or *The Joy of Cooking*. If you had to have one cookbook and that's all you could have, this one would do it."
CBS SAN FRANCISCO ON *THE NEW FAMILY COOKBOOK*

"Some 2,500 photos walk readers through 600 painstakingly tested recipes, leaving little room for error."
ASSOCIATED PRESS ON *THE AMERICA'S TEST KITCHEN COOKING SCHOOL COOKBOOK*

"The go-to gift book for newlyweds, small families, or empty nesters."
ORLANDO SENTINEL ON *THE COMPLETE COOKING FOR TWO COOKBOOK*

"Some books impress by the sheer audacity of their ambition. Backed by the magazine's famed mission to test every recipe relentlessly until it is the best it can be, this nearly 900-page volume lands with an authoritative wallop."
CHICAGO TRIBUNE ON *THE COOK'S ILLUSTRATED COOKBOOK*

"It might become your 'cooking school,' the only book you'll need to make you a proficient cook, recipes included. . . . You can master the 100 techniques with the easy-to-understand instructions, then apply the skill with the recipes that follow."
THE LITCHFIELD COUNTY TIMES ON *100 TECHNIQUES*

THE
ultimate
meal
prep
COOKBOOK

ONE GROCERY LIST.
A WEEK OF MEALS.
NO WASTE.

AMERICA'S TEST KITCHEN

Library of Congress Cataloging-in-Publication
Data

Names: America's Test Kitchen (Firm), author.
Title: The ultimate meal-prep cookbook : one
grocery list. a week of meals.
  no waste / America's Test Kitchen.
Description: Boston : America's Test Kitchen,
2021. | Includes index.
Identifiers: LCCN 2020044424 (print) | LCCN
2020044425 (ebook) | ISBN
  9781948703581 (paperback) | ISBN
9781948703598 (epub)
Subjects: LCSH: Quick and easy cooking. |
Make-ahead cooking. | LCGFT:
  Cookbooks.
Classification: LCC TX833.5 .A4456 2021
(print) | LCC TX833.5 (ebook) |
  DDC 641.5⁄2--dc23
LC record available at https://lccn.loc.
gov/2020044424
LC ebook record available at https://lccn.loc.
gov/2020044425

AMERICA'S TEST KITCHEN

21 Drydock Avenue, Boston, MA 02210

Printed in Canada

10 9 8 7 6 5 4 3 2 1

Distributed by Penguin Random House
Publisher Services
Tel: 800.733.3000

Pictured on front cover

Meal Plan 15 (page 148)

Front cover photography and food styling by
Steve Klise

Editorial Director, Books **Adam Kowit**

Executive Food Editor **Dan Zuccarello**

Deputy Food Editor **Stephanie Pixley**

Executive Managing Editor **Debra Hudak**

Senior Editors **Valerie Cimino, Leah Colins,
Sara Mayer, Russell Selander**

Associate Editor **Camila Chaparro**

Test Cooks **Samantha Block, Sarah Ewald**

Editorial Assistant **Emily Rahravan**

Design Director **Lindsey Timko Chandler**

Deputy Art Director **Katie Barranger**

Designer **Molly Gillespie**

Photography Director **Julie Bozzo Cote**

Photography Producer **Meredith Mulcahy**

Senior Staff Photographers **Steve Klise,
Daniel J. van Ackere**

Staff Photographer **Kevin White**

Additional Photography **Carl Tremblay and Joseph Keller**

Food Styling **Catrine Kelty, Steve Klise,
Chantal Lambeth, Kendra McNight, Ashley Moore,
Christie Morrison, Marie Piraino, Elle Simone Scott,
Kendra Smith, Sally Staub**

Photoshoot Kitchen Team

  Photo Team and Special Events Managers **Allison Berkey**

  Lead Test Cook **Eric Haessler**

  Test Cooks **Hannah Fenton,
  Jacqueline Gochenouer**

  Assistant Test Cooks **Gina McCreadie, Christa West**

Senior Manager, Publishing Operations **Taylor Argenzio**

Imaging Manager **Lauren Robbins**

Production and Imaging Specialists **Tricia Neumyer,
Dennis Noble, Amanda Yong**

Copy Editor **Elizabeth Wray Emery**

Proofreader **Vicki Rowland**

Indexer **Elizabeth Parson**

Chief Creative Officer **Jack Bishop**

Executive Editorial Directors **Julia Collin Davison and
Bridget Lancaster**

CONTENTS

WELCOME *to* AMERICA'S TEST KITCHEN

This book has been tested, written, and edited by the folks at America's Test Kitchen, where curious cooks become confident cooks. Located in Boston's Seaport District in the historic Innovation and Design Building, it features 15,000 square feet of kitchen space including multiple photography and video studios. It is the home of *Cook's Illustrated* magazine and *Cook's Country* magazine and is the workday destination for more than 60 test cooks, editors, and cookware specialists. Our mission is to empower and inspire confidence, community, and creativity in the kitchen.

We start the process of testing a recipe with a complete lack of preconceptions, which means that we accept no claim, no technique, and no recipe at face value. We simply assemble as many variations as possible, test a half-dozen of the most promising, and taste the results blind. We then construct our own recipe and continue to test it, varying ingredients, techniques, and cooking times until we reach a consensus. As we like to say in the test kitchen, "We make the mistakes so you don't have to." The result, we hope, is the best version of a particular recipe, but we realize that only you can be the final judge of our success (or failure). We use the same rigorous approach when we test equipment and taste ingredients.

All of this would not be possible without a belief that good cooking, much like good music, is based on a foundation of objective technique. Some people like spicy foods and others don't, but there is a right way to sauté, there is a best way to cook a pot roast, and there are measurable scientific principles involved in producing perfectly beaten, stable egg whites. Our ultimate goal is to investigate the fundamental principles of cooking to give you the techniques, tools, and ingredients you need to become a better cook. It is as simple as that.

To see what goes on behind the scenes at America's Test Kitchen, check out our social media channels for kitchen snapshots, exclusive content, video tips, and much more. You can watch us work (in our actual test kitchen) by tuning in to *America's Test Kitchen* or *Cook's Country* on public television or on our websites. Download our award-winning podcast *Proof*, which goes beyond recipes to solve food mysteries (AmericasTestKitchen.com/proof), or listen to test kitchen experts on public radio (SplendidTable.org) to hear insights that illuminate the truth about real home cooking. Want to hone your cooking skills or finally learn how to bake—with an America's Test Kitchen test cook? Enroll in one of our online cooking classes. And you can engage the next generation of home cooks with kid-tested recipes from America's Test Kitchen Kids.

Our community of home recipe testers provides valuable feedback on recipes under development by ensuring that they are foolproof. You can help us investigate the how and why behind successful recipes from your home kitchen. (Sign up at AmericasTestKitchen.com/recipe_testing.)

However you choose to visit us, we welcome you into our kitchen, where you can stand by our side as we test our way to the best recipes in America.

facebook.com/AmericasTestKitchen
twitter.com/TestKitchen
youtube.com/AmericasTestKitchen
instagram.com/TestKitchen
pinterest.com/TestKitchen

AmericasTestKitchen.com
CooksIllustrated.com
CooksCountry.com
OnlineCookingSchool.com
AmericasTestKitchen.com/kids

Getting STARTED

"what's for dinner?" **Whether a family member is asking you or you're just silently asking yourself, if that question gives you a sinking feeling then you need this book. With the constant schedule juggling that we all do, meal planning and meal prep are invaluable skills to master if you want to avoid eating takeout every night.**

What's the difference between the two? Meal planning is the process of choosing recipes for the week ahead, while meal prep is the process of actually bringing those plans to fruition. This book comes to your rescue by showing you how to succeed at both.

While other meal-prep resources exist, many are rigid: If you don't follow their road map to the letter, you'll be thrown off course. Conversely, sometimes the information is just too vague to be a reliable guide. Or else the meal plans are geared toward a specific destination: meal planning to lose weight, for instance. With this book, we sought to create a wider, more flexible path down the middle that anyone could follow.

We've mapped out the meal planning for you with 25 weekly plans that include a menu, a grocery list and pantry list (both with plenty of substitution options), ingredient prep-ahead lists, and recipe make-ahead lists. We can't do the actual meal-prep kitchen work for you, though! And that's just as well, because that's the part you'll want to tailor to suit your ever-changing weekly schedule.

Our short grocery lists get you in and out of the store fast and our recipes inventively use up what you buy so that you avoid the unwelcome scenario of throwing food away at week's end. You can make the recipes in whatever order you want—or you can pick and choose individual recipes if you don't want to follow a full plan. And one meal every week is a pantry-friendly recipe that can be made without any additions to your weekly shopping list, so you can make it or skip it, as you like. Because takeout isn't *always* bad: Who doesn't sometimes succumb to that indulgence on a Friday night?

Our tested strategies will lower your what's-for-dinner stress level, save you time and money, and make it not only easy but also enjoyable to serve home-cooked meals bursting with fresh, modern flavors.

WINNING STRATEGIES
for MEAL-PREP SUCCESS

Efficient meal preppers take advantage of multiple strategies. Depending on your preferences and your available time in any given week, there are many different ways to customize meal prep.

PLAN INTENSIVE INGREDIENT PREP-AHEAD SESSIONS

Possibly the most valuable meal-prep habit to adopt is a "Sunday power hour," during which time you can get well ahead of the weeknight scramble by completing as much advance kitchen work as possible. You can prep fresh ingredients (such as produce and protein) for your week's meal plan ahead of time and also make recipe components in advance. For example, searing the chicken breasts, cooking the bulgur, and cutting the vegetables can all be done ahead of time for the Pan-Seared Chicken with Warm Bulgur Pilaf (page 153). To make this habit even more useful, try a "pantry power hour" after a grocery-store trip to restock your pantry. Slice an entire jar of artichoke hearts or roasted red peppers or chop a whole deli container of olives or can of chipotles in adobo, and then put them back into their jar or another container for refrigerator storage. You can even freeze some bulk-prepped pantry ingredients for longer-term storage, such as toasted nuts, citrus zest, chopped onions, and more (see page 14).

AVOID FOOD WASTE BY CROSS-UTILIZING FRESH INGREDIENTS

We designed these meal plans to use a limited number of ingredients in creative ways throughout the week. If you decide to experiment with creating your own plans, try to map out ways to efficiently use up what you buy at the grocery store while still keeping meals varied. For instance, in Meal Plan 2 we use all our purchased fresh spinach by quickly wilting some for Pan-Seared Chicken Breasts with Artichokes and Spinach (page 48) and also serving it as a salad green in Shrimp and White Bean Salad with Garlic Toasts (page 51). Likewise, when we ask you to buy herb bunches, we try to use them up in the plans. (Just in case, see page 14 for how to freeze fresh herbs and page 19 for how to dry them.)

STORE ASSEMBLED MEAL COMPONENTS TOGETHER

If prepped ingredients get cooked together, you can store them together. For example, potatoes, shallots, and carrots are roasted together on a baking sheet in Rib-Eye Steaks with Roasted Vegetables and Sage Butter (page 97), so after you prep those vegetables you can store them in one container in the fridge. For Spicy Pork Chops with Summer Vegetable Sauté (page 170), the prepped onion, squash, poblanos, and corn are added to a skillet all at once, so you can store them together after prepping. Our foil packet recipes, where the assembled ingredients become an entire meal, take this concept a step further (see page 17 for a list of these recipes).

MAKE ENTIRE MEALS AHEAD

We'd never knock meatloaf as a reheat-and-eat classic, but we've elevated the make-ahead meal concept with dishes such as Chicken Curry with Tomatoes and Ginger (page 80), Shiitake Mushroom Frittata with Pecorino Romano (page 91), Spinach-Stuffed Portobello Caps (page 99), and Italian Sausages with Balsamic Stewed Tomatoes (page 121). And be sure to look at page 20 for our simple tips for reheating food so that it tastes freshly made. (Hint: The oven is often—but not always—better than the microwave.)

MAKE BIG BATCHES OF STAPLES TO SERVE ALL WEEK

Cook a big batch of rice or other grains to store in the refrigerator for the week. They can bulk up recipes such as Garlicky Stir-Fried Pork, Eggplant, and Onions (page 186) or Spicy Beef Lettuce Wraps with Oyster Sauce (page 169). You can also stir in any leftover vegetables and top with a fried egg for an emergency instant meal. (See pages 34–35 for our white and brown rice recipes.) Whisk up a batch of Make-Ahead Vinaigrette (page 33) to use on the Simplest Salad (page 32), or mix a compound butter (page 34) to melt over Chicken, Sun-Dried Tomato, and Goat Cheese Burgers (page 225) or slather on crusty bread.

DOUBLE RECIPES FOR "FREEZER INSURANCE" OR INTENTIONAL LEFTOVERS

We tell you when a recipe doubles well for freezing. Soups and chili are often great choices, but most of our burger patties and the meatballs from Meatballs and Lemon Orzo with Mint and Dill (page 146) freeze great, too. This doubling principle also applies to meal components, even if you can't freeze them. For example, when you're prepping Skirt Steak with Pinto Bean Salad (page 57) for dinner, make a double batch of just the pinto bean salad. You can bring the extra for lunch and enjoy it on its own, over greens, or on top of those cooked grains you're stocking in the refrigerator.

ALWAYS HAVE A MEAL IN YOUR BACK POCKET

Keep your pantry stocked and you will always be able to pull together a last-minute meal when a weekday throws you a curveball. Our Pantry Meals chapter (pages 236–291) offers 30 meals that do not require a grocery-store run and can be made on a moment's notice, with no advance planning needed (although we do offer prep-ahead suggestions for those recipes, just in case you want to take advantage of that). In the section that follows, you'll see how a well-stocked pantry can deliver all these pantry meals to your table—and provide a major assist with the rest of the meals in the book.

A STOCKED PANTRY SAVES YOUR BACON

Having a wide array of pantry items at your fingertips is a sanity-saving necessity when it comes to meal prep. What qualifies an ingredient as pantry-worthy? We think they are easy-to-find, seasonless, shelf-stable ingredients that keep for a least a week but often longer. And a well-stocked pantry is more than just a cupboard or closet; it also includes items stored in the refrigerator or freezer.

Part of making the most of your stocked pantry is keeping it organized, fully utilizing your available storage space, and knowing how to make substitutions when necessary.

Marry like items: Having a pantry full of open or almost-empty boxes isn't efficient. If you are currently stocking multiple boxes of open pasta that take the same amount of time to cook, store them in one container. If your box of grains is nearly empty, transfer them to a smaller airtight container. You are both preserving their shelf life and opening up more space for less uniformly shaped foods (such as potatoes).

Practice FIFO (first in, first out): A good rule is that ingredients arriving in your kitchen first should be the first to leave. So store your most recently purchased pantry items at the back of the cupboard; and if you're marrying like items, check the expiration dates and make sure the items to expire first get a spot at the top of the container.

Store produce smartly: Make sure pantry produce items such as potatoes, onions, shallots, and garlic live in a cool, dark, dry spot with space between them.

This will slow down the sprouting process. If you want to get really serious, turn to an old trick from Maine and store your potatoes with an apple. The ethylene gas released by the apple, along with some other airborne compounds, will inhibit sprouting and keep your potatoes usable for up to 2 months.

In a pinch: Most cooking oils are interchangeable in recipes, so you don't need to keep five different bottles on hand unless you want to. If all you stock is extra-virgin olive oil, go ahead and stir-fry with it! We do make an exception for oils to drizzle over a finished dish, so if we finish a recipe by drizzling extra-virgin oil over it, we call for using that oil in the recipe itself. Likewise, while it's fun to stock different vinegars, they are often interchangeable in recipes. Throughout the book, we offer substitutions for a variety of pantry ingredients; also see page 15 for pointers on specific ingredient substitutions.

Now that you know *how* to store pantry items, turn the page to see our thorough list of *what* to store. You don't have to buy every single ingredient to make great meals; and likewise, there may be things that you consider pantry must-haves that aren't on our list.

CUPBOARD AND COUNTER

Pasta and noodles: Spaghetti or other long shape; penne or other short shape; ditalini or other small shape; orzo; couscous; egg noodles; soba noodles

Rice: long-grain white, brown

Other grains: farro, cornmeal, polenta

Panko bread crumbs

Canned beans: chickpeas, black beans, red beans, cannellini or small white beans

Dried lentils: brown and green

Tomato products: tomato paste, canned diced, crushed, and whole peeled tomatoes

Canned tuna

Canned coconut milk

Nut butters

Cooking oils: one neutral-tasting vegetable oil, extra-virgin olive oil

Finishing oil: toasted sesame oil

Vinegars: some combination of red wine vinegar, apple cider vinegar, balsamic vinegar, white wine vinegar, rice wine vinegar, and sherry vinegar

Wines: White wine or dry vermouth, sake or dry vermouth, Shaoxing wine or dry sherry, Madeira or dry sherry, mirin or sweet sherry

All-purpose flour, cornstarch

Sweeteners: granulated sugar, brown sugar, honey

Table salt, flaky sea salt

Dried herbs and spices: At a minimum, black pepper, cayenne, chili powder, cinnamon, cumin, curry powder, ginger, herbes de Provence, oregano, paprika, red pepper flakes, sage, tarragon, thyme

Fruit: apples, dried currants, dried figs, raisins

Potatoes: small red or white, Yukon Gold, sweet

Alliums: garlic, red and yellow onions, shallots

REFRIGERATOR

Dairy: butter, milk, heavy cream, plain Greek yogurt, regular yogurt

Eggs

Cheese: Parmesan or Pecorino Romano; cheddar or other firm cheese; feta or other soft crumbly cheese; cream cheese

Broth: chicken or vegetable broth

Jarred artichoke hearts packed in water

Jarred roasted red peppers

Canned chipotle chiles in adobo

Olives: black, green

Condiments and sauces: As with spices, the more the merrier: Asian chili-garlic sauce, barbecue sauce, fish sauce, hot sauce, maple syrup, mayonnaise, mustards (Dijon, whole-grain), oyster sauce, soy sauce, sriracha, tahini, Thai curry paste

Carrots

Celery

Citrus: lemons, limes, oranges

FREEZER

Bread: crusty bread, sandwich bread, pita, naan, hamburger buns, tortillas

Puff pastry

Nuts and seeds: almonds, cashews, peanuts, pecans, pine nuts, walnuts, sesame seeds, sunflower seeds, pepitas

Frozen produce: corn, edamame, peas, spinach

Bacon or pancetta

Shrimp

FROZEN ASSETS

We consider frozen shrimp and certain frozen vegetables to be invaluable pantry staples.

In general, seafood's high perishability means that a lot of the seafood you eat—even the "fresh" pieces you buy at the seafood counter—has been frozen. Most is frozen right at sea, so some argue that frozen seafood is even "fresher" than what's on display at the counter.

We particularly love bagged frozen shrimp, as it's easy to thaw exactly what you need. Extra-large shrimp (21 to 25 per pound) or large shrimp (26 to 30 per pound) are our go-to. Because peeled shrimp tend to be drier, we prefer to buy shell-on frozen shrimp and peel them ourselves. Be sure to check the label before purchasing: "Shrimp" should be the only ingredient listed. In an effort to prevent darkening or water loss during thawing, some manufacturers add salt or STPP (sodium tripolyphosphate). Our tasters found an unpleasant texture in salt-treated and STPP-enhanced shrimp; the latter also had a chemical taste.

We also stock frozen corn, peas, and edamame in our freezers. One of our most frequently used frozen veggies, though, is spinach. We found in recipe testing that we prefer a brand-name frozen spinach, such as Bird's Eye or Green Giant. These brands were more tender and flavorful than generic and store-brand choices, qualities that become important especially when using frozen spinach as a stir-in for recipes such as our Fusilli Salad with Artichokes, Spinach, and Sun-Dried Tomatoes (page 255) and Bulgur Salad with Spinach, Chickpeas, and Apples (page 252).

Discover more ways to make your freezer work for you in meal prepping on page 14.

INGREDIENT PREP SCHOOL

Most vegetables can be simply chopped a few days in advance and refrigerated in airtight containers, but some benefit from a little special handling to help preserve their flavor, texture, or color.

APPLES

Apples oxidize (turn brown) after cutting because enzymes and compounds stored separately in each cell of the fruit become available to interact with each other and with the air. Although oxidation doesn't affect taste, we store chopped apples in acidulated water in an airtight container in the fridge to prevent browning. Use about ¾ tablespoon lemon juice or vinegar per 1 cup water. Drain and pat apples dry before using them in a recipe.

CELERY

Celery doesn't turn brown after cutting, but it loses moisture and crispness rapidly. Wrap whole heads loosely in aluminum foil to prolong their crispness and life span. The foil allows ethylene gas (a ripening hormone) to escape while keeping moisture in. Store chopped or sliced celery in plain water in an airtight container in the fridge to keep it from drying out.

GREENS

Washing lettuce and hearty greens as soon as you get them home is not only good meal-prep practice, but it will also help prolong their freshness. Once you wash the greens, spin them dry in a salad spinner and then either store them right in the spinner (lined with paper towels to absorb excess moisture) or wrap them in paper towels and store them in a partially open zipper-lock bag in the refrigerator.

HERBS

We rely on fresh herbs to add loads of flavor to our prepped meals, but they spoil quickly. To extend their life, wrap the sprigs in a damp paper towel and store them in a partially open zipper-lock bag in the refrigerator. This storage method also works if you prep your herbs ahead by washing and picking the leaves and tender stems. Be sure to remove rubber bands or twist ties before storing herbs, since those will cause quicker spoilage.

EGGPLANT

Like apples, eggplant will oxidize after you cut it, but since it's such a sponge you can't store the pieces in water as you would apples or potatoes. Since the oxidation doesn't affect its flavor or texture, and since the eggplant pieces brown anyway when cooked, we usually prep our eggplant ahead and simply store it in an airtight container in the refrigerator.

ONIONS

Chop or slice onions and store them in a zipper-lock bag or airtight container in the refrigerator. Prepped onions also freeze well (see page 14), which is especially handy since they are so often needed in small amounts for a recipe. Because their odor is so strong, we think it's a good idea to store prepped onions in either zipper-lock bags or a dedicated storage container.

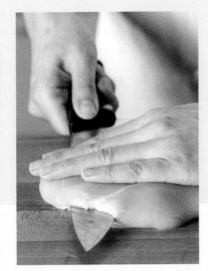

POTATOES

Cut potatoes will also oxidize, so we store sliced or chopped potatoes in water in an airtight container in the refrigerator to prevent browning. Unlike with apples, we don't use acidulated water, as the acid will firm up the potatoes' pectin too much and affect cooking times. We also suggest storing prepped potatoes for no longer than 1 day.

CUTLETS

You can purchase pre-cut chicken and pork cutlets, and they are undeniably a boon for busy meal preppers. However, they are often packaged in irregular sizes, meaning they will cook at different rates—decidedly not a boon. When we have time, we prefer to buy boneless chicken breasts and pork tenderloin and cut our own cutlets to ensure uniformity. You can then refrigerate or freeze your custom cutlets until ready to cook.

STEAK TIPS

As with cutlets, you can buy pre-cut steak tips (they are most often labeled sirloin steak tips), but again, they are often irregularly sized, posing the same problem of uneven cooking. We specify what size to cut steak tips into in the recipes (generally 2-inch pieces). If you see flap meat at your butcher counter, you can buy that instead and cut your own steak tips.

PREP *and* FREEZE

You can store many prepped ingredients in the freezer for at least a couple of months. Keeping these freezer-friendly staples at the ready will make your weeknight cooking even easier.

Bread: We like to keep crusty bread, sandwich bread, burger buns, pita, and tortillas on hand at all times, and the freezer keeps them fresh for us. For maximum freshness and ease of use, wrap portions tightly in plastic wrap and then tightly seal (with as little air as possible) in a zipper-lock freezer bag.

Canned chipotle chiles in adobo: Spoon out each chile, along with a couple teaspoons of adobo sauce, onto different areas of a baking sheet lined with parchment paper and freeze. Transfer the frozen chile mounds to a zipper-lock freezer bag for storage.

Cheese: Wrap hard and semifirm cheeses such as Parmesan and cheddar tightly in plastic wrap, seal in a zipper-lock freezer bag, and freeze. Thaw in the refrigerator before using in a recipe. And freeze Parmesan rinds as well; you can add them to simmering soups to enrich and deepen flavor.

Citrus zest: Remove the zest from the entire fruit. Deposit the grated zest in ½- or 1-teaspoon piles on a plate and freeze. Once the piles are frozen, store them in a zipper-lock freezer bag.

Fish: We recommend cooking fish within 2 days of purchase. But if it hasn't been previously frozen (ask at the counter), one of our favorite tricks is short-term freezing: After your weekend grocery run, simply toss it in the freezer for a couple of days and then enjoy it fresh at the end of the week. This allows you greater flexibility in planning the order of your meals.

Fresh herbs: Place 2 tablespoons chopped fresh mint, oregano, rosemary, sage, parsley, or thyme in each well of an ice cube tray and add water to cover (about 1 tablespoon), then freeze. Once frozen, transfer the cubes to a zipper-lock freezer bag or other freezer container. Add the cubes directly to soups, stews, or sauces.

Garlic: Peel the cloves, mince or press them through a garlic press, and place the minced garlic in a bowl. Add enough neutral-flavored oil to coat (about ½ teaspoon per clove), then spoon heaping teaspoons of the mixture onto a baking sheet and freeze. Transfer the frozen portions to a zipper-lock freezer bag. Thaw in the refrigerator (not at room temperature) or use directly from the freezer.

Ginger: Simply cut fresh ginger into 1-inch pieces and freeze in a zipper-lock freezer bag. Chop or grate directly from the freezer (no need to peel).

Onions: Freeze chopped onions in zipper-lock freezer bags in ¼-cup or ½-cup portions, and use directly from the freezer. We recommend using frozen onions only in cooked preparations, not in salads or salsas.

Wine: Measure 1 tablespoon wine into each well of an ice cube tray and freeze. Once frozen, store the wine cubes in a zipper-lock freezer bag or other freezer container.

SUBSTITUTE *with* CONFIDENCE

We've provided specific guidance in our meal plans on how to substitute both pantry staples and fresh ingredients. Sometimes it's a 1:1 sub (such as substituting canned cannellini beans for canned chickpeas). But sometimes it's less straightforward, as when you are substituting shallots for onions or frozen spinach for fresh spinach. Here's a quick guide for substitutions that we suggest regularly. And remember—just because you *can* substitute an ingredient doesn't always mean you *should*. Consider the overall flavor profile of your dish when making decisions.

A note on herb substitutions: We generally prefer fresh herbs to dried and often suggest alternative fresh herbs as substitution options in a given recipe. That being said, for sturdy herbs such as oregano, sage, and thyme, it's OK to substitute dried for fresh. We don't recommend substituting the dried version of delicate leafy herbs, such as basil, parsley, cilantro, tarragon, dill, and chives, because their flavor is inferior. If you do substitute dried herbs for fresh, you can add the dried herbs to the recipe at the same time that you would add the fresh herbs.

1 small onion = ¾ cup chopped

1 medium onion = 1 cup chopped

1 large onion = 1½ cups chopped

1 small shallot = 1 tablespoon chopped

1 medium shallot = 3 tablespoons chopped

1 large shallot = 4 tablespoons chopped

You need 4 large shallots or 5 or 6 medium shallots to substitute for 1 medium onion.

1 medium leek = 1½ cups sliced

1 medium vine-ripened tomato = 6 ounces cherry or grape tomatoes

1 lemon = 1½ limes

1 tablespoon citrus juice = 1 to 2 teaspoons vinegar (to taste)

1 portobello mushroom cap = 3 ounces cremini or white mushrooms

3 celery ribs = 1 fennel bulb

1 ounce fresh spinach = 1 cup = 1 ounce frozen spinach (in cooked recipe applications)

1 ounce fresh spinach = 2 ounces frozen spinach (in pasta salads or other uncooked recipe applications)

3 parts fresh herb = 1 part dried herb

1-inch piece fresh ginger = 1 tablespoon chopped = ¼ to ⅓ teaspoon ground ginger (to taste)

1 slice bacon = 1 thin slice pancetta (about 1 ounce) = 1 ounce salt pork

Pasta: When substituting different shapes, substitute by weight, not by volume.

Chiles: When substituting chiles, their heat level is more important than their volume when sliced or chopped. Add to taste and proceed with caution!

Jalapeño = 2,500 to 8,000 Scoville units

Serrano = 8,000 to 22,000 Scoville units

Thai chile = 50,000 to 100,000 Scoville units

Habanero = 150,000 to 575,000 Scoville units

the TEST KITCHEN'S TOP TIPS *for* MEAL PREPPERS

Make the A-list

For each meal plan, we provide you with a weekly shopping list, a list of pantry items (and amounts) you'll need for the week, and prep-ahead lists for both the whole menu and each recipe. But the most important list is one you must make yourself each week: the list that maps out your schedule for the days ahead to remind yourself of exactly what—and when—you'll be prepping.

Put a date on it

Everything you store should have a date on it; use whatever method works for you, be it freezer marker, permanent marker, masking tape labels, or something else. You might think you'll remember more or less when you stashed that double batch of meatballs for the Meatballs and Lemon Orzo with Mint and Dill (page 146) in the freezer, but time flies so trust us—you won't.

Bulk it up

Buy frequently used pantry items in bulk to minimize shopping. Those eye-poppingly large tins of extra-virgin olive oil are more cost-effective than smaller glass bottles, and the opaque tin maintains quality longer. Buying in bulk doesn't have to mean an overstuffed pantry, though. For example, a good-quality jarred concentrated chicken broth base takes up far less room than multiple bulky cartons of liquid, and the base keeps for a year in the refrigerator.

Develop labeling savvy

Sell-by dates on canned goods are about peak quality, not safety, and remembering this can help you minimize food waste. As long as the cans look good and have been stored well (in a dry pantry between 40 and 70 degrees), their contents should be safe to use indefinitely.

Keep it crunchy

Reserve crunchy or crisp toppings such as toasted nuts and seeds, croutons, and fresh herbs to add to your dishes just before serving; this will prevent them from turning soggy or limp. Likewise, store dressings or vinaigrettes separately and combine them with your vegetable salad or other food just before serving.

Roll with it

Freeze food in a way that makes it easy to use in the amount that you need and that prevents food waste. We like to roll individual slices of bacon or pancetta for freezing in a zipper-lock bag, so you can remove just the number of slices you want. Cut a crusty loaf of artisan bread into slices or chunks before wrapping and freezing for the same reason.

Spice things up—with variety

Beyond logistics, meal planning often fails because no one wants to eat the same thing multiple nights in a row. But if you use the same ingredient in creative ways during the week—as we do with butternut squash in One-Pan Roast Chicken Breasts with Butternut Squash and Kale (page 184) and Butternut, Poblano, and Cheese Quesadillas (page 187)—you'll hear compliments rather than complaints around the dinner table.

Bring TV dinners into the 21st century

If you can bake it in a foil packet, do it! Cod Baked in Foil with Leeks and Carrots (page 56), Foil-Baked Chicken with Sweet Potatoes and Radishes (page 112), Foil-Baked Cod with Black Beans and Corn (page 130), Cod Baked in Foil with Potatoes, Zucchini, and Sun-Dried Tomatoes (page 224), and Halibut and Creamy Coconut Couscous Packets (page 200) are far more delicious than anything you'll ever find in the frozen food aisle.

Flex your culinary muscles

Think of these recipes as guides rather than mandates. Don't hesitate to swap one herb for another, one nut for another, or one condiment for another. If the scallops don't look great at the fish counter, substitute shrimp in the Seared Scallops with Squash Puree and Sage Butter (page 98). If someone doesn't want pork cutlets, substitute chicken cutlets in the Parmesan-Crusted Pork Cutlets with Chive Smashed Potatoes (page 234).

MAKE THE MOST *of* YOUR MICROWAVE

We all know that the microwave can be a lifesaver for quickly reheating leftovers as well as meal components or entire meals that you've made ahead and refrigerated. But savvy meal preppers also turn to their microwave to streamline recipe prep, speed up cooking times, and make their dinner preparation easier overall.

PARCOOK DENSE, HARD VEGETABLES

In our Herbed Steaks with Lemon-Garlic Potatoes (page 178), we microwave 1-inch pieces of red potatoes for just 4 minutes to parcook them so that they need only a few minutes more to turn golden brown in the same hot skillet you use for the steak. For the Butternut, Poblano, and Cheese Quesadillas (page 187), we microwave ½-inch cubes of butternut squash all the way to tenderness in just 8 minutes before using them to stuff tortillas.

Bonus: You can make a plain whole baked potato this way, too: While the oven heats to 450 degrees, microwave 1 russet potato (poke holes in it with a fork first) until slightly soft, 6 to 12 minutes, then pop it in the oven to finish cooking for another 20 minutes.

MAKE QUICK GARNISHES THAT ELEVATE YOUR MEAL

For our Sun-Dried Tomato and White Bean Soup with Parmesan Crisps (page 240), we created a microwave rendition of Italian frico by shredding Parmesan, arranging it in neat piles on a large plate, and microwaving them until golden brown and crisped.

TOAST NUTS

Place chopped nuts in a shallow bowl or a glass pie plate in a thin, even layer. Microwave, stirring and checking the color every minute. When the nuts start to color, microwave them in 30-second increments until golden brown. You can toast larger batches of nuts this way and store them in the freezer (they'll stay crunchy for up to a month).

DRY LEFTOVER FRESH HERBS

We've designed our meal plans to use up the fresh herbs that you purchase on your weekly grocery run, but if you find yourself with some left over, dry them in the microwave and store for later use. Place sturdy herbs (rosemary, thyme, sage, oregano) in a single layer between two paper towels on the turntable. Microwave on high power for 1 to 3 minutes, until the leaves turn brittle and fall easily from the stems. Store in an airtight container for up to 3 months.

REHEAT *without* RESERVATION

Making food ahead of time is an important part of successful meal prep—as is planning for intentional leftovers. Paying just a bit of attention to the smartest way to reheat and serve these foods will legitimize your leftovers and ensure that they always taste freshly made.

PROTEINS

From burger patties and meatballs to skin-on or skinless chicken to breaded pork cutlets, place them on a wire rack set inside a rimmed baking sheet, cover with aluminum foil, and reheat in a 350-degree oven. The wire rack allows for better air circulation and more even heating.

SOUPS AND STEWY DISHES

Meals such as Tortellini and Vegetable Soup with Pesto (page 138) and Green Chicken Chili (page 152) are best reheated in a pot on the stovetop. In a pinch, you can use the microwave.

CASSEROLES AND SKILLET DISHES

Reheat dishes such as Cheese Enchiladas (page 290) and Chicken and Rice with Chorizo and Artichokes (page 105) in a baking dish covered with foil in a 350-degree oven.

PIZZAS, TARTS, AND QUESADILLAS

Reheat items such as Arugula Pesto and Potato Pizza (page 203) and Butternut, Poblano, and Cheese Quesadillas (page 187) on a rimmed baking sheet tented with foil in a 350-degree oven. Or reheat them in a loosely covered nonstick skillet over medium heat to crisp up the dough and melt the cheese.

RICE AND GRAINS

An uncovered dish in the microwave works best. Add a tablespoon of water to up to 4 cups of cooked rice or grains and heat until steaming, stirring once about halfway through.

PASTA

Casserole-style pastas such as Creamy Stovetop Macaroni and Cheese (page 259) and stewy pastas like Pasta and Chickpeas with Tomato and Parmesan (page 262) can be reheated in a covered baking dish in a 350-degree oven. We don't recommend reheating other pasta dishes.

Revive Flavor and Texture: An easy way to dramatically elevate reheated food is through seasoning, and we mean more than just salt and pepper. Refreshing reheated foods before serving with a drizzle of extra-virgin olive oil, a spritz of vinegar, or a squeeze of citrus juice enriches and wakes up any flavors that might have gone quiet with storage. Often, soups and stews thicken when refrigerated, so they benefit from the addition of a little water or broth during reheating to help return them to their original consistency. If you do add water, don't forget to taste and reseason, if necessary, before serving.

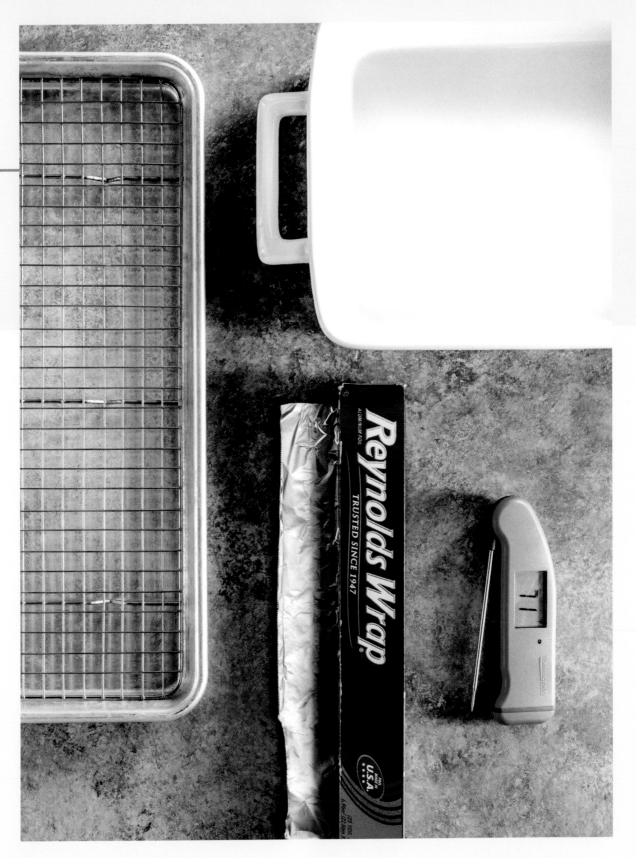

ANATOMY *of a* FRIDGE

While your freezer should always be set to the coldest possible setting, refrigerators have natural temperature zones that you should take advantage of when storing raw, prepped, and cooked food.

To avoid temperature fluctuations within these natural zones and to keep your refrigerator consistently cold, let cooked items cool on the counter before refrigerating or freezing them. Perishable foods should be refrigerated with 2 hours, and the food should be cooled to room temperature (70 to 75 degrees) before storing. This is often achieved within 1 hour of the food resting on the counter; you can transfer large batches of items such as soups or chilis to smaller containers to help them cool faster. (The food should then cool down to 40 degrees in the fridge within 4 hours to be considered in the "safe zone.")

Within the natural temperature zones of the refrigerator, we follow what's known as "swim-walk-fly," which is a top-to-bottom storage arrangement for the highest level of food safety. In this arrangement, ready-to-eat foods such as dairy and cooked proteins go on top. Uncooked seafood (stored on a bed of ice in a container) goes below, then whole cuts of uncooked meat and poultry, and finally, uncooked ground meats and poultry on the bottom. Store raw meats in bags or on plates to prevent any juices from dripping onto the shelves or other foods.

The refrigerator is also your best tool for safe, proper thawing. With very few exceptions (such as frozen nuts), defrosting should always be done in the refrigerator—not on the counter at room temperature where bacteria can rapidly multiply. Place food on a plate or in a bowl while defrosting to prevent any liquid it releases from coming into contact with other foods. And don't forget to plan ahead: Some foods can take up to 24 hours to thaw fully.

Even if your refrigerator has a built-in thermometer, we suggest you invest in a separate high-quality thermometer that tracks the temperature of your refrigerator and freezer over time and alerts you if their temperature veers out of the safe range (see page 27).

COLD ZONE (BACK, TOP TO BOTTOM)

The area of the shelves at the back of the fridge and the shelves at the bottom of the door are normally the coldest spots. What to store here: prepared foods, leftovers, meat, dairy, and fruit that is not prone to chilling injury, such as cherries and grapes.

MODERATE ZONE (FRONT, TOP TO BOTTOM)

The areas at the front of the refrigerator, top to bottom shelves, are more moderate in temperature. This also includes the top shelves of the door, which should be reserved for items such as condiments. What to store here: eggs, butter, and fruit that is sensitive to chilling injury, such as berries and citrus.

HUMID ZONE (CRISPER DRAWER)

The crisper drawer provides a humid environment that helps keep produce with a high water content from shriveling and rotting. If the humidity is too high, moisture can accumulate and hasten spoilage. The more cold air that is let in through the vents, the less humid the environment will be. What to store here: vegetables.

DOUBLE DOWN

These recipes are easily doubled for freezing in some significant fashion, whether it's the entire recipe, as for the Chicken Curry with Tomatoes and Ginger, or a major component of the recipe, as for the burger patties and meatballs.

Freeze an Entire Meal

Chicken Curry with Tomatoes and Ginger   (page 80)

Spicy Corn and Tomato Soup (page 83)

Beef and Bean Chili   (page 113)

Green Chicken Chili   (page 152)

Sun-Dried Tomato and White Bean Soup with Parmesan Crisps   (page 240)

5-Ingredient Black Bean Soup (page 242)

White Bean Soup with Lemon and Oregano   (page 243)

Red Lentil Soup with North African Spices   (page 245)

Cheese Enchiladas   (page 290)

Freeze a Meal Component

Skillet Turkey Burgers with Tomato and Arugula Salad   (page 40)

Ground Beef Tacos   (page 81)

Shrimp Burgers   (page 139)

Meatballs and Lemon Orzo with Mint and Dill   (page 146)

Ground Beef Stroganoff with Egg Noodles   (page 163)

Salmon Burgers with Asparagus and Lemon Mayo   (page 176)

Spiced Pork Lettuce Wraps with Avocado and Mango   (page 194)

Chicken Noodle Soup   (page 216)

Chicken, Sun-Dried Tomato, and Goat Cheese Burgers   (page 225)

Skillet Turkey
Burgers with
Tomato and
Arugula Salad
(page 40)

Meatballs and
Lemon Orzo
with Mint and
Dill (page 146)

Ground
Beef Tacos
(page 81)

Sun-Dried
Tomato and
White Bean
Soup with
Parmesan
Crisps
(page 240)

USE A HALF-GRILL FIRE FOR FAST WEEKNIGHT GRILLING

For the most efficient weeknight grilling with the biggest flavor payoff, high and fast is the way to go. A half-grill fire allows you to sear items such as pork chops or tenderloin quickly over the hotter side of the grill and then move them to the cooler side until the specified internal temperature is reached.

To build a half-grill fire in a gas grill, simply turn all the burners on high to preheat the grill for about 15 minutes; once heated, leave the primary burner on high and turn off the other burners. For a charcoal grill, bank the hot coals on one side of the grill and leave the other side empty.

To keep your food from sticking, don't forget to clean and oil the grate before starting to grill. After preheating the grill, scrape the cooking grate clean with a grill brush. Then, using tongs, dip a wad of paper towels in vegetable oil and thoroughly wipe the cooking grate before adding food.

ESSENTIAL EQUIPMENT
for MEAL PREP

The name of the game is storage when it comes to our most-wanted equipment for successful meal prepping. Beyond wraps and containers, you might also get a lot of use from a vacuum sealer. And to keep all that stored food in tiptop shape, keep a good thermometer in your fridge.

PREP IT

Plastic wrap, aluminum foil, and zipper-lock plastic bags are essential meal-prep equipment.

PLASTIC WRAP

For meal-prepping purposes, we prefer plastic wrap made from low-density polyethylene (LDPE); while it's less clingy than wrap made from PVC, it's impermeable and keeps food fresher longer. If you are trying to minimize plastic wrap waste, we suggest **Bee's Wrap**, a washable and reusable alternative to standard plastic wrap.

ALUMINUM FOIL

We find heavy-duty foil easier to work with and stock standard 12-inch rolls and extra-long rolls.

ZIPPER-LOCK BAGS

We use freezer-safe zipper-lock bags to hold prepped ingredients, since they are thicker and sturdier than standard bags and will protect food for a longer time in the fridge as well as the freezer. Smaller sizes can hold a variety of ingredients (and you can often wash and reuse the bags), while larger sizes can hold marinating meat and be used for freezing cutlets, burger patties, and more.

STORE IT

There's no getting around the fact that as a meal prepper you need plenty of reusable storage containers in a variety of sizes, from small ones to hold prepped ingredients to medium ones to hold single meals to large ones to hold a whole batch of chili or soup. Whether you choose plastic or glass containers is up to you. Plastic is lightweight and easy to transport, but it can stain, absorb odors, and warp, and it can't go into the oven. Glass containers can go from fridge to oven to table and don't stain, absorb odors, or warp, but they are heavier to transport and are breakable.

PLASTIC CONTAINERS

We found a clear winner when testing plastic storage containers: the **Rubbermaid Brilliance Food Storage Container** line. They are airtight, with strong, sturdy latches and flat tops that make for secure, compact stacking in the refrigerator and freezer. They are sold both in individual sizes and in sets. If you're looking for multiple identical containers for individual meal servings, we like the 3.2-cup size. The 4.7-cup will hold a baking sheet's worth of roasted vegetables, a big batch of rice, or a large portion of leafy greens, while the 9.6-cup will store a whole batch of soup or chili. And the 1.3-cup size is great for storing prepped ingredients and dressings.

GLASS CONTAINERS

Our favorite glass storage containers are **OXO Good Grips Smart Seal**, which also come in multiple sizes, from 8 cups down to 4 ounces, and are sold both individually and in sets. They have durable latches and airtight, leakproof seals. We like the rectangular containers for their efficient stackability and the larger round containers for their depth, which adds to their versatility. For multiple identical containers for individual meal servings, try the 3.5-cup rectangle or the 4-cup round, which are also good for storing roasted vegetables and cooked grains. The 7-cup and 8-cup sizes can store a full batch of soup. Smaller sizes, including the 1.6 cup and the 1 cup, are good for prepped ingredients, dressings, etc.

COUNTERTOP VACUUM SEALER

You'll get a lot of use out of this meal-prep helper. These machines remove air from customized storage bags before sealing them tightly, protecting the foods inside the bags from moisture loss or gain, whether they're stored for long periods in the freezer or at room temperature in the pantry. We recommend the **Nesco Deluxe Vacuum Sealer**, which is sturdy but relatively compact, with an easy-to-use display screen and a roll storage compartment with built-in slicer so you can easily cut the storage bags to size.

REFRIGERATOR AND FREEZER THERMOMETER

To keep all your stored food at its freshest for as long as possible, it's vital to know your refrigerator's and freezer's temperatures. Even if your refrigerator has a built-in thermometer, it's a good idea to set up an independent thermometer as backup. We like the **ThermoWorks RT8100 Fridge/Freezer Thermometer**, which is a single, fully programmable thermometer with two probes, one for the refrigerator and one for the freezer. An alarm alerts you when the temperature goes out of safe limits, and it keeps track of the duration as well as what the highest and lowest temperatures were during the monitoring cycle.

How to
NAVIGATE THIS BOOK

Learn why we chose these recipes and how they're interconnected

Serve the week's meals in whatever order works best for you

Make our suggested pantry recipe, choose a different one, or take a night off from cooking

For flexibility, pantry recipe ingredients are not included in Pantry Items list

Get in and out of the store fast with this shopping list organized by area

MEAL PLAN 02

Pan-Seared Chicken Breasts with Artichokes and Spinach
(page 48)

Quick White Wine–Braised Chicken and Potatoes
(page 49)

Flank Steak with Farro and Mango Salsa
(page 50)

Shrimp and White Bean Salad with Garlic Toasts
(page 51)

Choose a Pantry Recipe
(we suggest Garlicky Spaghetti with Artichokes and Hazelnuts, page 257)

WHY THIS MEAL PLAN WORKS

This plan offers creative ways to cross-utilize ingredients in quite varied recipes, ensuring you use them up before you forget they're in your refrigerator. For example, we love fresh baby spinach but often run out of ideas for getting through the container or bunch before the delicate greens turn slimy. This meal plan deploys 12 ounces between the pan-seared chicken and the shrimp and bean salad. And while crème fraîche may not be a typical item on your grocery list, it brings a deliciously creamy element to two chicken recipes with different flavor profiles—and it all gets used up.

GROCERY LIST

PROTEIN		Substitutions
☐ Boneless, skinless chicken breasts	4 (6 to 8 ounces each)	
☐ Bone-in chicken thighs	8 (5 to 7 ounces each)	
☐ Flank steak	2 pounds	
PRODUCE		
☐ Leeks	1 pound	Onions
☐ Baby spinach	12 ounces	Frozen spinach (for chicken); baby arugula (for shrimp and bean salad)
☐ Red bell pepper	2	Cherry or grape tomatoes
☐ Mango	1	1 large peach
☐ Cilantro	1 small bunch (enough for ½ cup chopped)	Parsley
DAIRY		
☐ Crème fraîche	1 cup	Sour cream

Every meal plan includes a "dashboard" that introduces the meals for the upcoming week and walks you through your grocery shopping list, the list of pantry items you need to have on hand to complete the plan, your ingredient prep-ahead options, and your meal-component make-ahead options. Here's an example.

PREP AHEAD

Halve potatoes

Trim leeks of dark green parts; wash and chop white and light green parts

Peel and slice carrots

Stem, seed, and finely chop bell peppers

Peel, pit, and chop mango

Finely chop red onion

Wash and pick cilantro

Thinly slice 3 garlic cloves

Grate lemon zest (1 tablespoon)

Juice lemons (5 tablespoons)

Thaw, peel, and devein shrimp

Trim and cut flank steak into 4 pieces

MAKE AHEAD

UP TO 3 DAYS	Boil farro for steak
UP TO 2 DAYS	Cook and assemble bean mixture for white bean salad
UP TO 1 DAY	Assemble mango salsa for steak
	Sear shrimp for white bean salad

PANTRY ITEMS

CUPBOARD & COUNTER

			Substitutions
☐ Farro	2 cups		Brown rice or pearl barley
☐ Cannellini beans	2 (15-ounce) cans		Small white beans or chickpeas
☐ Extra-virgin olive oil	½ cup		
☐ Ground cumin	1 tablespoon		
☐ Dried thyme	¾ teaspoon		2¼ teaspoons fresh thyme leaves
☐ Red pepper flakes	¼ teaspoon		
☐ Extra-small red potatoes	1½ pounds		Extra-small white potatoes
☐ Garlic cloves	6		
☐ Red onion	1		4 large shallots

REFRIGERATOR

☐ Unsalted butter	6 tablespoons		Oil
☐ Jarred baby artichoke hearts packed in water	2 cups (from two 10-ounce jars)		Frozen artichoke hearts
☐ Dry white wine	1¼ cups		Dry vermouth
☐ Carrots	4		
☐ Lemon	2		3 tablespoons white wine vinegar (for braised chicken and shrimp salad); 1 lime (for steak)

FREEZER

☐ Extra-large shrimp (21 to 25 per pound)	1 pound		
☐ Rustic bread	4 slices		

Do as much or as little as you like for the weekly ingredient prep

If your pantry is well stocked, you might not need to buy any of these items

Choose your options for making meal components (or an entire meal) ahead

How to PREP A MEAL

Active time tells you how long you'll spend prepping and hands-on cooking

FLANK STEAK *with* FARRO *and* MANGO SALSA

SERVES 4 | ACTIVE TIME 40 MINUTES

2 cups whole farro

1½ teaspoons table salt, divided, plus salt for cooking farro

1 mango, peeled, pitted, and chopped fine

1 red bell pepper, stemmed, seeded, and chopped fine

½ red onion, chopped fine

½ cup chopped fresh cilantro

3 tablespoons extra-virgin olive oil, divided, plus extra for drizzling

2 tablespoons lemon juice

1 teaspoon pepper, divided

1 (2-pound) flank steak, trimmed and cut into 4 equal steaks

1 tablespoon ground cumin

1. FOR THE FARRO Bring 2 quarts water to boil in large saucepan. Add farro and 1 tablespoon salt. Return to boil and cook until grains are tender with slight chew, 15 to 30 minutes. Drain farro well.

2. FOR THE MANGO SALSA Combine mango, bell pepper, onion, cilantro, 1 tablespoon oil, lemon juice, ¼ teaspoon salt, and ½ teaspoon pepper in bowl; set aside until ready to serve.

3. TO FINISH Meanwhile, pat steaks dry with paper towels and sprinkle with cumin, remaining ¼ teaspoon salt, and remaining ½ teaspoon pepper. Heat remaining 2 tablespoons oil in 12-inch nonstick skillet over medium-high heat until just smoking. Cook steaks until well browned and meat registers 120 to 125 degrees (for medium-rare), 5 to 7 minutes per side. Transfer to carving board, tent with aluminum foil, and let rest for 5 minutes.

4. Toss all but ½ cup reserved salsa with farro in bowl. Slice steaks against grain on bias. Serve steaks with farro and remaining salsa, drizzled with extra oil.

If you haven't prepped the whole plan's ingredients ahead, here's your prep for this recipe

PREP AHEAD

- Peel, pit, and chop mango
- Stem, seed, and chop bell pepper
- Chop red onion
- Wash and pick cilantro
- Juice lemon
- Trim and cut steak

MAKE AHEAD

- Refrigerate farro for up to 3 days
- Refrigerate mango salsa for up to 1 day

NOTES FROM THE TEST KITCHEN

- To make 4 equal-size steaks, cut the steak in half lengthwise with the grain, then cut each piece in half crosswise against the grain
- Sub brown rice or pearl barley for farro
- Sub 1 large peach for mango
- Sub 8 ounces halved cherry or grape tomatoes for bell pepper
- Sub 2 large shallots for red onion
- Sub parsley for cilantro
- Sub lime juice for lemon juice

Following some or all of the substitution options can give you a whole different flavor profile

SHIITAKE MUSHROOM FRITTATA
with PECORINO ROMANO

SERVES 4 | ACTIVE TIME 25 MINUTES

1 tablespoon oil

1 pound shiitake mushrooms, stemmed and cut into ½-inch pieces

¾ teaspoon table salt, divided

¼ teaspoon pepper

2 tablespoons water

2 scallions, white parts minced, green parts sliced thin

1 tablespoon sherry vinegar

½ teaspoon dried thyme

12 large eggs

2¼ ounces Pecorino Romano, shredded (¾ cup)

⅓ cup whole milk

1. FOR THE MUSHROOM MIXTURE Adjust oven rack to middle position and heat oven to 350 degrees. Heat oil in 12-inch ovensafe nonstick skillet over medium-high heat until shimmering. Add mushrooms, ¼ teaspoon salt, and pepper and cook, stirring frequently, until mushrooms are tender and spotty brown, 7 to 9 minutes. Add water, scallion whites, vinegar, and thyme and cook, stirring constantly, until no water remains in skillet, about 1 minute.

2. FOR THE FRITTATA Whisk eggs, Pecorino, milk, scallion greens, and remaining ½ teaspoon salt in bowl until well combined, then add to skillet and cook, using heat-resistant rubber spatula to stir and scrape bottom of skillet until large curds form and spatula leaves trail through eggs but eggs are still very wet, about 30 seconds. Smooth curds into even layer and cook, without stirring, for 30 seconds. Transfer skillet to oven and bake until frittata is slightly puffy and surface bounces back when lightly pressed, 6 to 9 minutes. Using rubber spatula, loosen frittata from skillet and transfer to cutting board. Let sit for 5 minutes, then slice and serve.

Options for make-ahead recipe components are highlighted so they're easy to follow

Choose whether to make recipe components— or sometimes the entire recipe—ahead

Recipes are complete meals, but you can add a simple salad or some crusty bread

PREP AHEAD

- Stem and cut mushrooms
- Mince scallion whites
- Slice scallion greens
- Shred Pecorino Romano

MAKE AHEAD

- Refrigerate sautéed mushroom mixture for up to 2 days
- Refrigerate frittata for up to 2 days

NOTES FROM THE TEST KITCHEN

- You will need a 12-inch ovensafe nonstick skillet
- Serve with Simplest Salad (page 32), if you like
- Sub portobello or cremini mushrooms for shiitakes
- Sub 1½ teaspoons fresh thyme for dried
- Sub Parmesan for Pecorino Romano

BUILDING-BLOCK RECIPES

The recipes in our weekly plans stand on their own, saving you the quandary of what to serve alongside. But if you want a green salad to go with a homey soup, a bed of rice for a stir-fry, or a simple flavored butter to slather on crusty bread, here are our go-to recipes.

SIMPLEST SALAD

serves 4

This incredibly simple green salad requires the bare minimum of ingredients, no measuring, no whisking, and (virtually) no thought. We like to rub the bowl with the halved and peeled garlic clove to add just a hint of flavor. Use whatever vinegar you have on hand or you prefer. Because this salad calls for so few ingredients, try to use interesting and flavorful leafy greens such as mesclun, arugula, Bibb, or romaine.

- ½ garlic clove, peeled
- 8 ounces (8 cups) lettuce, torn into bite-size pieces if necessary

   Extra-virgin olive oil

   Vinegar

Rub inside of salad bowl with garlic. Add lettuce. Slowly drizzle oil over lettuce, tossing greens very gently, until greens are lightly coated and just glistening. Season with vinegar, salt, and pepper to taste, and toss gently to coat. Serve.

MAKE-AHEAD VINAIGRETTE

makes about 1 cup

This versatile dressing will stay emulsified for a week in your refrigerator, and you can use white wine vinegar, balsamic vinegar, apple cider vinegar, or sherry vinegar, as you like. To keep the oil and vinegar from separating, we added mustard and mayonnaise, two natural emulsifiers. A little molasses stabilized the dressing and further prevented separation without lending a strong flavor. Cutting the olive oil with some vegetable oil ensured that our refrigerated dressing was always pourable.

- 1 tablespoon mayonnaise
- 1 tablespoon molasses
- 1 tablespoon Dijon mustard
- ½ teaspoon table salt
- ¼ cup vinegar
- ½ cup extra-virgin olive oil
- ¼ cup vegetable oil

1. Combine mayonnaise, molasses, mustard, and salt in 2-cup jar with tight-fitting lid. Stir with fork until mixture is milky in appearance and no lumps of mayonnaise or molasses remain. Add vinegar, seal jar, and shake until smooth, about 10 seconds.

2. Add ¼ cup olive oil, seal jar, and shake vigorously until combined, about 10 seconds. Repeat, adding remaining ¼ cup olive oil and vegetable oil in separate additions, shaking vigorously until combined after adding each and vinaigrette is glossy and lightly thickened, with no surface pools of oil. Season with salt and pepper to taste. (Vinaigrette can be refrigerated for up to 1 week; shake briefly to recombine before using.)

CLASSIC BASIL PESTO

makes about 1½ cups (enough for 2 pounds pasta)

Pesto is super versatile and it freezes very well. It's great with pasta, but you can also dollop it on cooked chicken or fish or use it as a sandwich condiment or a dip for crusty bread. If you're tossing the pesto with pasta, don't forget to add some pasta cooking water to achieve the proper sauce consistency. Pounding the basil helps to bring out its flavorful oils.

- 6 garlic cloves, unpeeled
- ½ cup pine nuts
- 4 cups fresh basil leaves
- ¼ cup fresh parsley leaves
- 1 cup extra-virgin olive oil
- 1 ounce Parmesan cheese, grated fine (½ cup)

1. Toast garlic in 8-inch skillet over medium heat, shaking skillet occasionally, until softened and spotty brown, about 8 minutes. When garlic is cool enough to handle, remove and discard skins and chop coarsely. Meanwhile, toast pine nuts in now-empty skillet over medium heat, stirring often, until golden and fragrant, 4 to 5 minutes.

2. Place basil and parsley in 1-gallon zipper-lock bag. Pound bag with flat side of meat pounder or with rolling pin until all leaves are bruised.

3. Process garlic, pine nuts, and herbs in food processor until finely chopped, about 1 minute, scraping down sides of bowl as needed. With processor running, slowly add oil until incorporated. Transfer pesto to bowl, stir in Parmesan, and season with salt and pepper to taste. (Pesto can be refrigerated for up to 3 days or frozen for up to 3 months. To prevent browning, press plastic wrap flush to surface or top with thin layer of olive oil. Bring to room temperature before using.)

GARLIC-HERB COMPOUND BUTTER

makes 8 tablespoons

Compound butters are a secret weapon in the meal-prepper's arsenal. Stirring seasonings into softened butter is an easy way to make a rich, flavor-packed condiment for meat, fish, and vegetables that can be refrigerated for several days or frozen for a couple of months. They are also a great way to use up small amounts of leftover herbs.

- 8 **tablespoons unsalted butter, softened**
- 2 **tablespoons minced fresh sage or** 1½ **teaspoons dried**
- 1 **tablespoon minced fresh parsley**
- 1 **tablespoon minced fresh thyme or** ¾ **teaspoon dried**
- 2 **garlic cloves, minced**

Whip butter with fork until light and fluffy. Mix in sage, parsley, thyme, and garlic and season with salt and pepper to taste. Wrap in plastic wrap and let rest to blend flavors, about 10 minutes, or roll into log and refrigerate. (Compound butter can be refrigerated in airtight container for up to 4 days or frozen, wrapped tightly in plastic, for up to 2 months.)

MUSTARD-CHIVE COMPOUND BUTTER

Omit sage, parsley, thyme, and garlic. Mix in 5 tablespoons whole-grain mustard and 3 tablespoons minced fresh chives after whipping butter.

WHITE RICE PILAF

serves 4 to 6

For stovetop white rice with distinct, separate grains and fluffy texture, we rinsed the rice of excess starch and then sautéed the grains in butter before covering them with water to simmer. Once the rice was cooked, we placed a dish towel under the lid to absorb excess moisture.

- 1 **tablespoon unsalted butter or oil**
- 1½ **cups long-grain white rice, rinsed**
- 2¼ **cups water**
- ½ **teaspoon table salt**

1. Melt butter in large saucepan over medium heat. Add rice and cook, stirring often, until grains begin to turn translucent, about 3 minutes. Stir in water and salt and bring to simmer. Reduce heat to low, cover, and continue to simmer until rice is tender and water is absorbed, 16 to 18 minutes.

2. Remove pot from heat and lay clean folded dish towel underneath lid. Let sit for 10 minutes. Fluff rice with fork, season with salt and pepper to taste, and serve.

BOILED BROWN RICE

serves 4 to 6

We cook stovetop brown rice differently than white rice. Boiling it in an abundant amount of water speeds up its cooking time (which is typically longer than white rice) and helps it cook more evenly.

- 1½ **cups long-grain brown rice**
- 1 **teaspoon table salt**

Bring 4 quarts water to boil in large pot. Add rice and salt and cook until tender, 25 to 30 minutes. Drain well and serve.

BIG-BATCH BAKED WHITE RICE

serves 8 to 10

Wanting a hands-off version of everyday rice, we turned to the oven. Be sure to rinse the rice before combining it with the water, or else the excess starch clinging to the rice will make it gluey. It's also important to use boiling water or the rice will take forever to cook through in the oven. For an accurate measurement of boiling water, bring a full kettle of water to a boil, then measure out the desired amount. Basmati, jasmine, or Texmati rice can be substituted for the long-grain rice. To halve this recipe, use an 8-inch baking dish; the baking time remains the same.

2⅔ cups long-grain white rice, rinsed

2 tablespoons unsalted butter or oil

1 teaspoon table salt

5½ cups boiling water

1. Adjust oven rack to middle position and heat oven to 450 degrees. Spread rice in 13 by 9-inch baking dish.

2. Stir butter and salt into boiling water and pour water over rice in baking dish. Cover baking dish tightly with double layer of aluminum foil. Transfer baking dish to oven and bake rice until tender and no water remains, about 20 minutes.

3. Remove dish from oven and uncover. Fluff rice with fork, scraping up any rice that has stuck to bottom. Cover dish with clean dish towel and let stand for 10 minutes. Serve.

BIG-BATCH BAKED BROWN RICE

serves 8 to 10

Even using the hands-off oven method, brown rice still takes longer to cook than white rice. We also needed to experiment with the water-to-rice ratio to achieve the results we wanted—brown rice that was tender yet chewy and was neither scorched nor waterlogged. For an accurate measurement of boiling water, bring a full kettle of water to a boil, then measure out the desired amount. To halve this recipe, use an 8-inch baking dish; the baking time remains the same.

3 cups long-grain, medium-grain, or short-grain brown rice

4⅔ cups boiling water

4 teaspoons unsalted butter or oil

1 teaspoon table salt

1. Adjust oven rack to middle position and heat oven to 375 degrees. Spread rice in 13 by 9-inch baking dish.

2. Stir butter and salt into boiling water and pour water over rice in baking dish. Cover baking dish tightly with double layer of aluminum foil. Transfer baking dish to oven and bake rice until tender and no water remains, about 1 hour.

3. Remove dish from oven and uncover. Fluff rice with fork, scraping up any rice that has stuck to bottom. Cover dish with clean dish towel and let stand for 5 minutes. Uncover and let rice stand 5 minutes longer. Serve.

MEAL PLAN 01

MEAL 1 Skillet Turkey Burgers with Tomato and Arugula Salad

MEAL 2 Roasted Chicken Breasts with Green Pearl Couscous

MEAL 3 Pork Milanese with Arugula and Parmesan Salad

MEAL 4 Bucatini with Eggplant and Tomatoes

MEAL 5 Choose a Pantry Recipe *(we suggest Bulgur Salad with Spinach, Chickpeas, and Apples)*

WHY THIS MEAL PLAN WORKS

This crowd-pleasing "meat-and-a-side" meal plan offers three meals that are just that, but with a lighter, fresher take on what can otherwise be a tired-old-standby approach to dinner. We also add some variety with a comforting pasta dinner and a hearty bulgur salad. This plan is a great choice for a particularly hectic week when you have neither the time to shop nor much time to cook. While all our grocery lists are short, this one gets you in and out of the market exceptionally fast, with just seven fresh items. Most of the cooking for this plan is on the stovetop, so you barely have to turn on the oven except for our sheet-pan chicken, and the longest active cooking time is a mere 35 minutes. Ready, set, go!

GROCERY LIST

PROTEIN		Substitutions
☐ Bone-in split chicken breasts	4 (10 to 12 ounces each)	
☐ Ground turkey (not 99 percent lean)	1 pound	*Ground chicken (not 99 percent lean)*
☐ Pork cutlets	8 (3 ounces each), ½ inch thick	*Pork tenderloin or chicken cutlets*

PRODUCE		
☐ Eggplant	1 pound	
☐ Tomatoes	4	*1½ pounds cherry or grape tomatoes*
☐ Baby arugula	9 ounces	*Mixed baby greens*
☐ Parsley	1 large bunch (enough for 2½ cups leaves)	*Chives or basil (for chicken) or basil (for bucatini)*

PREP AHEAD

Chop eggplant

Core and cut tomatoes

Chop onion

Wash and pick parsley

Grate lemon zest (4¼ teaspoons)

Juice lemons (3 tablespoons plus 2 teaspoons)

Shave 1 ounce Parmesan (1 cup)

Grate ½ ounce Parmesan (¼ cup)

MAKE AHEAD

UP TO 2 DAYS	Whisk together lemon mayo for turkey burgers
UP TO 1 DAY	Mix and shape turkey burgers
	Bread pork cutlets
	Make eggplant-tomato sauce for bucatini

PANTRY ITEMS

CUPBOARD & COUNTER

			Substitutions
☐ Bucatini	1 pound		*Any strand pasta*
☐ Panko bread crumbs	2½ cups		
☐ Israeli couscous	1½ cups		
☐ All-purpose flour	1 cup		
☐ Oil	1½ cups		
☐ Sugar	1 teaspoon		
☐ Red pepper flakes	¼ teaspoon		
☐ Garlic cloves	7		
☐ Onion	1		*4 large shallots*

REFRIGERATOR

☐ Unsalted butter	4 tablespoons		*Oil*
☐ Feta cheese	4 ounces		*Goat cheese*
☐ Parmesan cheese	1½ ounces		*Pecorino Romano*
☐ Large eggs	2		
☐ Broth	4 cups		
☐ Mayonnaise	7 tablespoons		
☐ Lemons	2		

FREEZER

☐ Hamburger buns	4		

SKILLET TURKEY BURGERS *with* TOMATO *and* ARUGULA SALAD

SERVES 4 | ACTIVE TIME 30 MINUTES

7 tablespoons mayonnaise, divided

¾ teaspoon grated lemon zest plus
   2 tablespoons juice, divided

1 teaspoon pepper, divided

1 pound ground turkey

1 cup panko bread crumbs

4 ounces feta cheese, crumbled
   (1 cup), divided

¾ teaspoon table salt, divided

¼ cup oil, divided

1 garlic clove, minced

2 tomatoes, cored, cut into
   1-inch- thick wedges, and
   halved crosswise

5 ounces (5 cups) baby arugula,
   divided

4 hamburger buns

1. FOR THE LEMON MAYO Whisk 3 tablespoons mayonnaise, ¼ teaspoon lemon zest, 1 tablespoon lemon juice, and ¼ teaspoon pepper together in small bowl; set aside until ready to serve.

2. FOR THE BURGER PATTIES Using your hands, gently knead turkey, panko, ½ cup feta, ½ teaspoon salt, remaining ¼ cup mayonnaise, and ½ teaspoon pepper in bowl. Divide burger mixture into 4 lightly packed balls, then flatten gently into ¾-inch-thick patties.

3. FOR THE BURGERS AND SALAD Heat 2 tablespoons oil in 12-inch nonstick skillet over medium heat until shimmering. Add patties and cook until well browned and meat registers 160 degrees, 5 to 7 minutes per side.

4. Whisk remaining 2 tablespoons oil, garlic, remaining ½ teaspoon lemon zest, remaining 1 tablespoon lemon juice, remaining ¼ teaspoon pepper, and remaining ¼ teaspoon salt together in large bowl. Add tomatoes, 4 cups arugula, and remaining ½ cup feta and toss gently to combine. Season with salt and pepper to taste. Spread mayonnaise mixture on bun tops. Place burgers on buns and top with remaining 1 cup arugula. Serve with tomato and arugula salad.

PREP AHEAD

• Grate lemon zest and juice lemon

• Core and cut tomatoes

MAKE AHEAD

• Refrigerate lemon mayo for up to 2 days

• Refrigerate shaped burger patties for up to 1 day

NOTES FROM THE TEST KITCHEN

• The burger patties are easily doubled, and they freeze well

• Sub 12 ounces cherry or grape tomatoes for tomatoes

• Sub ground chicken for ground turkey

• Sub goat cheese for feta

• Sub mixed baby greens for baby arugula

ROASTED CHICKEN BREASTS
with GREEN PEARL COUSCOUS

SERVES 4 | ACTIVE TIME 35 MINUTES

4 cups broth, divided

2 cups fresh parsley leaves plus
 ¼ cup chopped

1 tablespoon grated lemon zest
 plus 1 tablespoon juice

1¼ teaspoons table salt, divided

¾ teaspoon pepper, divided

4 (10- to 12-ounce) bone-in split
 chicken breasts, trimmed

4 tablespoons unsalted butter, divided

1½ cups Israeli couscous

1 onion, chopped fine

3 garlic cloves, minced

1. Adjust oven rack to middle position and heat oven to 425 degrees. Process 1 cup broth, parsley leaves, lemon zest, ¾ teaspoon salt, and ½ teaspoon pepper in blender until smooth, about 30 seconds. Set aside.

2. Pat chicken dry with paper towels and sprinkle with remaining ½ teaspoon salt and remaining ¼ teaspoon pepper. Melt 1 tablespoon butter in Dutch oven over medium-high heat. Add chicken and cook until golden brown on both sides, about 6 minutes. Transfer chicken to rimmed baking sheet, transfer to oven, and roast until chicken registers 160 degrees, 18 to 20 minutes. Transfer chicken to plate, tent with aluminum foil, and let rest for 5 minutes.

3. Meanwhile, melt 1 tablespoon butter in now-empty pot over medium heat. Add couscous, onion, and garlic and cook until onion is softened and couscous is lightly toasted, about 5 minutes. Stir in parsley mixture and remaining 3 cups broth and bring to simmer. Cook, uncovered, stirring often, until nearly all liquid has been absorbed, about 14 minutes. Off heat, stir in chopped parsley, lemon juice, and remaining 2 tablespoons butter. Serve chicken with couscous.

PREP AHEAD

- Wash and pick parsley
- Grate lemon zest and juice lemon
- Chop onion

NOTES FROM THE TEST KITCHEN

- Sub chives or basil for parsley
- Sub 4 large shallots for onion

PORK MILANESE *with* ARUGULA *and* PARMESAN SALAD

SERVES 4 | ACTIVE TIME 25 MINUTES

1 cup all-purpose flour

2 large eggs

1½ cups panko bread crumbs

½ teaspoon grated lemon zest plus 2 teaspoons juice, plus lemon wedges for serving

1½ ounces Parmesan cheese (¼ cup grated, 1 cup shaved), divided

¾ teaspoon table salt, divided

¾ teaspoon pepper, divided

8 (3-ounce) boneless pork cutlets, ½ inch thick, trimmed

1 cup oil for frying

1 tablespoon oil

4 ounces (4 cups) baby arugula

1. FOR THE BREADED CUTLETS Spread flour in shallow dish. Beat eggs in second shallow dish. Combine panko, lemon zest, grated Parmesan, ½ teaspoon salt, and ½ teaspoon pepper in third shallow dish. Pat pork cutlets dry with paper towels. Working with 1 cutlet at a time, dredge cutlets in flour, shaking off excess; dip in eggs, allowing excess to drip off; and coat with panko mixture, pressing gently to adhere. Transfer to large plate.

2. FOR THE CUTLETS AND SALAD Line separate large plate with triple layer of paper towels. Heat 1 cup oil in 12-inch nonstick skillet over medium heat until shimmering. Place 4 cutlets in skillet and cook until golden brown and pork is cooked through, 3 to 5 minutes per side. Transfer cutlets to prepared plate to drain. Repeat with remaining 4 cutlets, adjusting heat as needed.

3. Whisk remaining 1 tablespoon oil, lemon juice, remaining ¼ teaspoon salt, and remaining ¼ teaspoon pepper together in large bowl. Add arugula and shaved Parmesan and toss gently to combine. Serve pork with salad, passing lemon wedges separately.

PREP AHEAD

- Grate lemon zest and juice lemon
- Grate and shave Parmesan

MAKE AHEAD

- Refrigerate breaded cutlets for up to 1 day

NOTES FROM THE TEST KITCHEN

- If you can't find pork cutlets, cut 2 pork tenderloins crosswise into 4 pieces each, then pound to ½-inch thickness
- Sub chicken cutlets for pork cutlets
- Sub Pecorino Romano for Parmesan
- Sub mixed baby greens for baby arugula

BUCATINI *with* EGGPLANT *and* TOMATOES

SERVES 4 | ACTIVE TIME 35 MINUTES

- 1 pound eggplant, cut into
  ½-inch pieces
- 1 teaspoon sugar
- 1 teaspoon table salt, plus
  salt for cooking pasta
- 3 tablespoons extra-virgin olive oil,
  plus extra for drizzling
- 3 garlic cloves, minced
- ¼ teaspoon red pepper flakes
- 2 tomatoes, cored and chopped
- 1 pound bucatini
- 2 tablespoons chopped fresh parsley

1. FOR THE EGGPLANT-TOMATO SAUCE Combine eggplant, sugar, and salt together in large bowl, then microwave, covered, until softened, about 6 minutes. Transfer eggplant to large plate lined with triple layer of paper towels to drain; set aside.

2. Heat oil in 12-inch skillet over medium-high heat until shimmering. Add eggplant and cook until eggplant begins to break down, about 4 minutes. Stir in garlic and pepper flakes and cook until fragrant, about 1 minute. Add tomatoes and ½ cup water and cook until tomatoes begin to break down, 2 to 5 minutes.

3. TO FINISH Meanwhile, bring 4 quarts water to boil in large pot. Add pasta and 1 tablespoon salt and cook, stirring often, until al dente. Reserve ½ cup cooking water, then drain pasta and return it to pot. Add sauce to pasta and toss to combine. Adjust consistency with reserved cooking water as needed. Sprinkle with parsley and season with salt and pepper to taste. Serve, drizzling individual portions with extra oil.

PREP AHEAD

- Chop eggplant
- Core and chop tomatoes
- Wash and pick parsley

MAKE AHEAD

- Refrigerate eggplant-tomato sauce for up to 1 day

NOTES FROM THE TEST KITCHEN

- Parcooking the eggplant in the microwave dries it out slightly and ensures it doesn't turn greasy or mushy in the sauce
- Sub any strand pasta for bucatini
- Sub 12 ounces cherry or grape tomatoes for tomatoes
- Sub basil for parsley

MEAL PLAN 02

MEAL 1 Pan-Seared Chicken Breasts with Artichokes and Spinach

MEAL 2 Quick White Wine–Braised Chicken and Potatoes

MEAL 3 Flank Steak with Farro and Mango Salsa

MEAL 4 Shrimp and White Bean Salad with Garlic Toasts

MEAL 5 Choose a Pantry Recipe
(we suggest Garlicky Spaghetti with Artichokes and Hazelnuts)

WHY THIS MEAL PLAN WORKS

This plan offers creative ways to cross-utilize ingredients in quite varied recipes, ensuring you use them up before you forget they're in your refrigerator. For example, we love fresh baby spinach but often run out of ideas for getting through the container or bunch before the delicate greens turn slimy. This meal plan deploys 12 ounces between the pan-seared chicken and the shrimp and bean salad. And while crème fraîche may not be a typical item on your grocery list, it brings a deliciously creamy element to two chicken recipes with different flavor profiles—and it all gets used up.

GROCERY LIST

PROTEIN		Substitutions
☐ Boneless, skinless chicken breasts	4 (6 to 8 ounces each)	
☐ Bone-in chicken thighs	8 (5 to 7 ounces each)	
☐ Flank steak	2 pounds	
PRODUCE		
☐ Leeks	1 pound	*Onions*
☐ Baby spinach	12 ounces	*Frozen spinach (for chicken); baby arugula (for shrimp and bean salad)*
☐ Red bell pepper	2	*Cherry or grape tomatoes*
☐ Mango	1	*1 large peach*
☐ Cilantro	1 small bunch (enough for ½ cup chopped)	*Parsley*
DAIRY		
☐ Crème fraîche	1 cup	*Sour cream*

PREP AHEAD

Halve potatoes

Trim leeks of dark green parts; wash and chop white and light green parts

Peel and slice carrots

Stem, seed, and finely chop bell peppers

Peel, pit, and chop mango

Finely chop red onion

Wash and pick cilantro

Thinly slice 3 garlic cloves

Grate lemon zest (1 tablespoon)

Juice lemons (5 tablespoons)

Thaw, peel, and devein shrimp

Trim and cut flank steak into 4 pieces

MAKE AHEAD

UP TO 3 DAYS	Boil farro for steak
UP TO 2 DAYS	Cook and assemble bean mixture for white bean salad
UP TO 1 DAY	Assemble mango salsa for steak
	Sear shrimp for white bean salad

PANTRY ITEMS

CUPBOARD & COUNTER		Substitutions
☐ Farro	2 cups	Brown rice or pearl barley
☐ Cannellini beans	2 (15-ounce) cans	Small white beans or chickpeas
☐ Extra-virgin olive oil	½ cup	
☐ Ground cumin	1 tablespoon	
☐ Dried thyme	¾ teaspoon	2¼ teaspoons fresh thyme leaves
☐ Red pepper flakes	¼ teaspoon	
☐ Extra-small red potatoes	1½ pounds	Extra-small white potatoes
☐ Garlic cloves	6	
☐ Red onion	1	4 large shallots
REFRIGERATOR		
☐ Unsalted butter	6 tablespoons	Oil
☐ Jarred baby artichoke hearts packed in water	2 cups (from two 10-ounce jars)	Frozen artichoke hearts
☐ Dry white wine	1 ¼ cups	Dry vermouth
☐ Carrots	4	
☐ Lemon	2	3 tablespoons white wine vinegar (for braised chicken and shrimp salad); 1 lime (for steak)
FREEZER		
☐ Extra-large shrimp (21 to 25 per pound)	1 pound	
☐ Rustic bread	4 slices	

PAN-SEARED CHICKEN BREASTS
with ARTICHOKES *and* SPINACH

SERVES 4 | ACTIVE TIME 25 MINUTES

4 (6- to 8-ounce) boneless, skinless
   chicken breasts, trimmed

¾ teaspoon dried thyme

1 teaspoon table salt, divided

¾ teaspoon pepper, divided

3 tablespoons unsalted butter, divided

2 cups jarred baby artichoke hearts
   packed in water, patted dry

3 garlic cloves, sliced thin

¼ cup dry white wine

1 tablespoon grated lemon zest

10 ounces (10 cups) baby spinach

½ cup crème fraîche

1. Pat chicken dry with paper towels and sprinkle with thyme, ½ teaspoon salt, and ½ teaspoon pepper. Melt 2 tablespoons butter in 12-inch nonstick skillet over medium-high heat. Add chicken and cook until golden brown and chicken registers 160 degrees, about 6 minutes per side. Transfer chicken to plate, tent with aluminum foil, and let rest while cooking vegetables.

2. Melt remaining 1 tablespoon butter in now-empty skillet over medium-high heat. Add artichokes and garlic and cook until lightly browned, about 2 minutes. Stir in wine and lemon zest and cook until fragrant, about 30 seconds. Stir in spinach, 1 handful at a time, until wilted, about 3 minutes.

3. Stir in crème fraîche, remaining ½ teaspoon salt, and remaining ¼ teaspoon pepper and cook until sauce is slightly thickened and vegetables are well coated with sauce, about 1 minute. Serve chicken with vegetables.

PREP AHEAD

- Slice garlic
- Grate lemon zest

NOTES FROM THE TEST KITCHEN

- Patting the artichokes dry before cooking helps them brown better and develop more flavor in the skillet
- Sub 2¼ teaspoons fresh thyme leaves for dried
- Sub thawed frozen artichoke hearts for jarred artichoke hearts
- Sub dry vermouth for white wine
- Sub thawed, squeezed dry frozen spinach for baby spinach
- Sub sour cream for crème fraîche

QUICK WHITE WINE–BRAISED CHICKEN *and* POTATOES

SERVES 4 | ACTIVE TIME 35 MINUTES

1½ pounds extra-small red potatoes, halved

3 tablespoons unsalted butter (2 tablespoons melted, 1 tablespoon softened)

½ teaspoon table salt, divided

¼ teaspoon pepper, divided

8 (5- to 7-ounce) bone-in chicken thighs, trimmed and halved

1 pound leeks, white and light green parts only, halved lengthwise, sliced ½ inch thick, and washed thoroughly

4 carrots, peeled and sliced ½ inch thick

1 cup dry white wine

½ cup crème fraîche

1 tablespoon lemon juice

1. Microwave potatoes, melted butter, ½ teaspoon salt, and ⅛ teaspoon pepper in covered bowl until tender, 8 to 10 minutes, stirring potatoes halfway through cooking.

2. Meanwhile, pat chicken dry with paper towels and sprinkle with remaining ¼ teaspoon salt and remaining ⅛ teaspoon pepper. Melt softened butter in 12-inch skillet over medium-high heat. Add chicken skin side down and cook until skin is crisped and golden, 7 to 9 minutes. Transfer chicken to plate and discard skin if desired.

3. Pour off all but 1 tablespoon fat from skillet. Add leeks and carrots and cook over medium heat until vegetables are softened and beginning to brown, about 5 minutes. Stir in wine, scraping up any browned bits, and bring to simmer. Nestle chicken into skillet, skin side up, along with any accumulated juices. Cover and cook over medium-low heat until chicken is tender and registers 175 degrees, 15 to 20 minutes.

4. Transfer chicken to large plate, tent loosely with aluminum foil, and let rest while finishing sauce. Increase heat to medium and reduce liquid in skillet until slightly thickened, 4 to 6 minutes. Off heat, stir in crème fraiche and lemon juice and season with salt and pepper to taste. Serve chicken and potatoes with sauce.

PREP AHEAD

- Halve potatoes
- Trim leeks of dark green parts; wash and chop white and light green parts
- Peel and slice carrots
- Juice lemon
- Trim and halve chicken

NOTES FROM THE TEST KITCHEN

- Cooking the potatoes in the microwave tenderizes them more quickly than braising them on the stovetop
- Sub onions for leeks
- Sub dry vermouth for white wine
- Sub sour cream for crème fraîche
- Sub white wine vinegar for lemon juice

FLANK STEAK *with* FARRO *and* MANGO SALSA

SERVES 4 | ACTIVE TIME 40 MINUTES

2 cups whole farro

1½ teaspoons table salt, divided, plus salt for cooking farro

1 mango, peeled, pitted, and chopped fine

1 red bell pepper, stemmed, seeded, and chopped fine

½ red onion, chopped fine

½ cup chopped fresh cilantro

3 tablespoons extra-virgin olive oil, divided, plus extra for drizzling

2 tablespoons lemon juice

1 teaspoon pepper, divided

1 (2-pound) flank steak, trimmed and cut into 4 equal steaks

1 tablespoon ground cumin

1. FOR THE FARRO Bring 2 quarts water to boil in large saucepan. Add farro and 1 tablespoon salt. Return to boil and cook until grains are tender with slight chew, 15 to 30 minutes. Drain farro well.

2. FOR THE MANGO SALSA Combine mango, bell pepper, onion, cilantro, 1 tablespoon oil, lemon juice, ¾ teaspoon salt, and ½ teaspoon pepper in bowl; set aside until ready to serve.

3. TO FINISH Meanwhile, pat steaks dry with paper towels and sprinkle with cumin, remaining ¾ teaspoon salt, and remaining ½ teaspoon pepper. Heat remaining 2 tablespoons oil in 12-inch nonstick skillet over medium-high heat until just smoking. Cook steaks until well browned and meat registers 120 to 125 degrees (for medium-rare), 5 to 7 minutes per side. Transfer to carving board, tent with aluminum foil, and let rest for 5 minutes.

4. Toss all but ½ cup reserved salsa with farro in bowl. Slice steaks against grain on bias. Serve steaks with farro and remaining salsa, drizzled with extra oil.

PREP AHEAD

- Peel, pit, and chop mango
- Stem, seed, and chop bell pepper
- Chop red onion
- Wash and pick cilantro
- Juice lemon
- Trim and cut steak

MAKE AHEAD

- Refrigerate farro for up to 3 days
- Refrigerate mango salsa for up to 1 day

NOTES FROM THE TEST KITCHEN

- To make 4 equal-size steaks, cut the steak in half lengthwise with the grain, then cut each piece in half crosswise against the grain
- Sub brown rice or pearl barley for farro
- Sub 1 large peach for mango
- Sub 8 ounces halved cherry or grape tomatoes for bell pepper
- Sub 2 large shallots for red onion
- Sub parsley for cilantro
- Sub lime juice for lemon juice

SHRIMP *and* WHITE BEAN SALAD *with* GARLIC TOASTS

SERVES 4 | ACTIVE TIME 30 MINUTES

1 pound extra-large shrimp (21 to 25 per pound), thawed, peeled, and deveined

½ teaspoon table salt, divided

⅛ teaspoon pepper

5 tablespoons extra-virgin olive oil, divided, plus extra for drizzling

1 red bell pepper, stemmed, seeded, and chopped fine

½ red onion, chopped fine

¼ teaspoon red pepper flakes

3 garlic cloves (2 cloves minced, 1 clove peeled)

2 (15-ounce) cans cannellini beans, rinsed

¼ cup water

4 (¾-inch-thick) slices rustic bread

2 ounces (2 cups) baby spinach

2 tablespoons lemon juice

1. FOR THE SEARED SHRIMP Adjust oven rack 6 inches from broiler element and heat broiler. Pat shrimp dry with paper towels and sprinkle with ¼ teaspoon salt and pepper. Heat 1 tablespoon oil in 12-inch nonstick skillet over high heat until just smoking. Add shrimp in single layer and cook, without stirring, until spotty brown and edges turn pink on first side, about 1 minute. Off heat, flip shrimp and let sit until opaque throughout, about 30 seconds. Transfer to serving bowl and cover.

2. FOR THE WHITE BEANS Heat 3 tablespoons oil in now-empty skillet over medium heat until shimmering. Add bell pepper, onion, and remaining ¼ teaspoon salt and cook until softened, about 5 minutes. Stir in pepper flakes and minced garlic and cook until fragrant, about 30 seconds. Add beans and water and cook until heated through, about 5 minutes; set aside off heat and cover.

3. TO FINISH Meanwhile, arrange bread in single layer on rimmed baking sheet. Broil, flipping as needed, until well toasted on both sides, about 4 minutes. Rub 1 side of each toast with peeled garlic, then drizzle with remaining 1 tablespoon oil and season with salt and pepper to taste.

4. Add shrimp, spinach, and lemon juice to reserved bean mixture and toss gently to combine. Season with salt and pepper to taste, and drizzle with extra oil. Serve salad with garlic toasts.

PREP AHEAD

• Stem, seed, and chop bell pepper

• Chop red onion

• Juice lemon

• Thaw, peel, and devein shrimp

MAKE AHEAD

• Refrigerate seared shrimp for up to 1 day

• Refrigerate white bean mixture for up to 2 days

NOTES FROM THE TEST KITCHEN

• Sub 8 ounces halved cherry or grape tomatoes for bell pepper

• Sub 2 large shallots for red onion

• Sub small white beans or chickpeas for cannellini beans

• Sub baby arugula for baby spinach

• Sub white wine vinegar for lemon juice

MEAL PLAN 03

WHY THIS MEAL PLAN WORKS

You might not associate meal prep with French cooking, but cooking foods en papillote, or in packets, is a classic French technique that can be a meal prepper's secret weapon. You can assemble these meals-in-a-packet entirely ahead of time and then bake them when you're ready. To mix things up, we also include a superfast and satisfying Southwestern steak with bean salad. And for our meal featuring pork tenderloin, just browning the lean pork in advance rather than cooking it entirely ahead ensures it stays juicy for serving. This recipe makes a generous amount of pork, so use any leftovers for lunchtime sandwiches. The grocery list comes in at a mere five items—perfect for weeks when you barely have time to sprint down the aisles. We recommend making the cod (or other fish, if you use one of the many substitutions) within 2 days of purchasing it (or see page 14 for short-term freezing).

GROCERY LIST

PROTEIN			Substitutions
☐ Skinless cod fillets	4 (6 to 8 ounces each), 1 inch thick		*Black sea bass, haddock, hake, or pollack*
☐ Skirt steak	1½ pounds		*Flank steak*
☐ Pork tenderloins	2 (12 to 16 ounces each)		
PRODUCE			
☐ Leeks	1 pound		*Onions*
☐ Parsley	1 bunch (enough for 10 tablespoons chopped)		*Cilantro (for steak); basil or chives (for shrimp)*

PREP AHEAD

Trim leeks of dark green parts; halve, wash thoroughly, and cut white and light green parts into matchsticks

Slice 6 shallots

Mince 5 shallots

Peel, core, and cut 2 apples into ½-inch-thick wedges

Peel and cut carrots into matchsticks

Grate lemon zest (1 teaspoon)

Juice 1 lemon (1 tablespoon)

Juice 1 lime (2 tablespoons)

Wash and pick parsley

Thaw, peel, and devein shrimp

Trim and cut skirt steak

MAKE AHEAD

UP TO 3 DAYS	Make pinto bean salad
UP TO 2 DAYS	Rub pork tenderloins with herbes de Provence
	Cook orzo risotto base
UP TO 1 DAY	Assemble cod foil packets
	Rub skirt steak with spice rub

PANTRY ITEMS

CUPBOARD & COUNTER		Substitutions
☐ Orzo	1½ cups	
☐ Pinto beans	2 (15-ounce) cans	*Kidney beans, black-eyed peas, or black beans*
☐ Oil	7 tablespoons	
☐ Herbes de Provence	3½ teaspoons	*Dried thyme (for cod); 1 teaspoon each dried thyme, dried rosemary, and dried marjoram (for pork)*
☐ Paprika	1½ teaspoons	
☐ Sugar	½ teaspoon	*Brown sugar*
☐ Shallots	11	*Red onion (for steak); yellow onion (for shrimp)*
☐ Garlic cloves	4	
☐ Golden Delicious apples	3	*Gala apples*
REFRIGERATOR		
☐ Unsalted butter	9 tablespoons	
☐ Broth	4 cups	
☐ Canned chipotle chile in adobo sauce	2 teaspoons	
☐ Lemons	2	
☐ Limes	2	*Red wine vinegar*
☐ Carrots	2	
FREEZER		
☐ Extra-large shrimp (21 to 25 per pound)	1½ pounds	

COD BAKED IN FOIL *with* LEEKS *and* CARROTS

SERVES 4 | ACTIVE TIME 25 MINUTES

6 tablespoons unsalted butter, softened

½ teaspoon dried herbes de Provence

2 garlic cloves, minced

½ teaspoon lemon zest, plus lemon wedges for serving

¾ teaspoon table salt, divided

½ teaspoon pepper, divided

2 carrots, peeled and cut into 2-inch-long matchsticks

1 pound leeks, white and light green parts only, halved lengthwise, washed thoroughly, and cut into 2-inch-long matchsticks

4 (6- to 8-ounce) skinless cod fillets, 1 inch thick

2 tablespoons minced fresh parsley

1. FOR THE COD PACKETS Adjust oven rack to lower-middle position and heat oven to 450 degrees. Mash butter, herbes de Provence, garlic, lemon zest, ¼ teaspoon salt, and ¼ teaspoon pepper in bowl. Arrange four 12-inch sheets aluminum foil flat on counter.

2. Divide carrots and leeks among foil sheets, arranging in center of each sheet, then top each with 2 teaspoons butter mixture. Pat cod dry with paper towels, sprinkle with remaining ½ teaspoon salt and remaining ¼ teaspoon pepper, and place on top of vegetables. Spread remaining butter mixture over fillets. Top each with 12-inch sheet foil and tightly crimp edges of foil together until packet is well sealed into rough 9-inch circles, leaving as much headroom as possible so steam can circulate. Place packets on rimmed baking sheet, overlapping as needed.

3. TO FINISH Bake packets until cod registers 135 degrees, 15 to 20 minutes (insert thermometer through packet into thick part of fish). Carefully open packets, allowing steam to escape away from you. Using thin metal spatula, gently slide cod and vegetables, and any accumulated juices, onto individual plates. Sprinkle with parsley and serve with lemon wedges.

PREP AHEAD

- Grate lemon zest
- Peel and cut carrots
- Trim leeks of dark green parts; halve, wash, and cut white and light green parts
- Wash and pick parsley

MAKE AHEAD

- Refrigerate cod packets for up to 1 day

NOTES FROM THE TEST KITCHEN

- Sub dried thyme for herbes de Provence
- Sub onions for leeks
- Sub black sea bass, haddock, hake, or pollack for cod

SKIRT STEAK *with* PINTO BEAN SALAD

SERVES 4 | ACTIVE TIME 20 MINUTES

1½ pounds skirt steak, trimmed and cut into thirds with grain

1½ teaspoons paprika

1 teaspoon table salt, divided

¾ teaspoon pepper, divided

3 tablespoons oil, divided

2 (15-ounce) cans pinto beans, rinsed

¼ cup chopped fresh parsley

2 shallots, minced

1 tablespoon lime juice, plus lime wedges for serving

2 teaspoons minced canned chipotle chile in adobo sauce

1. FOR THE STEAK Pat steak dry with paper towels and rub with paprika, ½ teaspoon salt, and ¼ teaspoon pepper.

2. Heat 1 tablespoon oil in 12-inch skillet over medium-high heat until just smoking. Cook steak until well browned and meat registers 120 to 125 degrees (for medium-rare), about 2 minutes per side. Transfer steak to cutting board, tent with aluminum foil, and let rest for 5 minutes.

3. FOR THE BEAN SALAD Meanwhile, combine beans, parsley, shallots, lime juice, chipotle, remaining 2 tablespoons oil, remaining ½ teaspoon salt, and remaining ½ teaspoon pepper in bowl.

4. TO FINISH Slice steak thin against grain and serve with bean salad.

PREP AHEAD

- Wash and pick parsley
- Mince shallots
- Juice 1 lime
- Trim and cut steak

MAKE AHEAD

- Refrigerate bean salad for up to 3 days
- Refrigerate rubbed steak for up to 1 day

NOTES FROM THE TEST KITCHEN

- Sub kidney beans, black-eyed peas, or black beans for pinto beans
- Sub cilantro for parsley
- Sub ½ red onion for shallots
- Sub red wine vinegar for lime juice
- Sub flank steak for skirt steak

ROASTED PORK TENDERLOIN
with APPLES *and* SHALLOTS

SERVES 4 I ACTIVE TIME 35 MINUTES

2 (12- to 16-ounce) pork tenderloins, trimmed

1 tablespoon herbes de Provence, crumbled

½ teaspoon table salt

¼ teaspoon pepper

¼ cup oil, divided

6 shallots, sliced ½ inch thick

3 Golden Delicious apples, peeled, cored, and cut into ½-inch- thick wedges

½ teaspoon sugar

1 tablespoon unsalted butter

1. FOR THE HERB-RUBBED PORK Adjust oven rack to lowest position and heat oven to 350 degrees. Pat pork dry with paper towels and sprinkle with herbes de Provence, salt, and pepper.

2. FOR THE PORK, APPLES, AND SHALLOTS Heat 2 tablespoons oil in 12-inch ovensafe skillet over medium-high heat until just smoking. Add pork to skillet and brown well on all sides, 8 to 10 minutes; transfer to plate. Add shallots, apples, sugar, and remaining 2 tablespoons oil to now-empty skillet. Cook over medium heat until shallots and apples begin to soften and brown lightly, 10 to 12 minutes.

3. Off heat, nestle tenderloins and any accumulated juices into apple mixture, then transfer skillet to oven and roast until pork registers 135 to 140 degrees, 15 to 20 minutes.

4. Carefully remove skillet from oven (skillet handle will be hot). Transfer pork to cutting board, tent with aluminum foil, and let rest for 5 minutes. Stir butter into apple mixture, then season with salt and pepper to taste. Slice pork into ½-inch-thick slices and serve with apple mixture.

PREP AHEAD

- Slice shallots
- Peel, core, and cut apples

MAKE AHEAD

- Refrigerate herb-rubbed pork for up to 2 days

NOTES FROM THE TEST KITCHEN

- Sub 1 teaspoon each of dried thyme, dried rosemary, and dried marjoram for herbes de Provence
- Sub Gala apples for Golden Delicious
- Sub brown sugar for granulated sugar

SHRIMP *and* ORZO RISOTTO

SERVES 4 | ACTIVE TIME 35 MINUTES

2 tablespoons unsalted butter

3 shallots, minced

2 garlic cloves, minced

1½ cups orzo

4 cups broth

¾ teaspoon table salt

¼ teaspoon pepper, divided

1½ pounds extra-large shrimp
(21 to 25 per pound), thawed,
peeled, and deveined

¼ cup chopped fresh parsley

½ teaspoon grated lemon zest plus
1 tablespoon juice

1. FOR THE ORZO Melt butter in Dutch oven over medium heat. Add shallots and garlic and cook until softened, about 4 minutes. Stir in orzo and cook until lightly toasted, about 3 minutes. Stir in broth, salt, and pepper and bring to boil. Reduce heat to medium-low, cover, and simmer, stirring occasionally, until orzo is nearly tender, about 12 minutes.

2. TO FINISH Pat shrimp dry with paper towels, then stir into risotto and cook, covered, until shrimp are opaque throughout and orzo is tender, about 5 minutes. Off heat, stir in parsley and lemon zest and juice, and season with salt and pepper to taste. Serve.

PREP AHEAD

- Mince shallots
- Wash and pick parsley
- Grate lemon zest and juice lemon
- Thaw, peel, and devein shrimp

MAKE AHEAD

- Refrigerate nearly tender orzo for up to 2 days

NOTES FROM THE TEST KITCHEN

- Sub 1 small onion for shallots
- Sub basil or chives for parsley

MEAL PLAN 04

Salmon, Grapefruit, and Avocado Salad
(page 64)

Pan-Roasted Chicken Thighs with Fennel-Apple Slaw
(page 65)

Balsamic Steak Tips with Tomato Salad
(page 66)

Grilled and Glazed Pork Chops with Radicchio Salad
(page 67)

Choose a Pantry Recipe
(we suggest Spicy Peanut Rice Noodles with Shrimp, page 272)

WHY THIS MEAL PLAN WORKS Fruit-and-vegetable salads feature prominently in this summery meal plan. Substitutions for nearly everything on the grocery list let you customize to suit your taste or purchase whatever looks best at the market. You'll only need asmall container of sour cream for the roasted chicken thighs and the grilled pork chops; if you don't think you can use up leftovers, you can substitute Greek yogurt. We also use a big bunch of bright, peppery watercress between the salmon salad and the steak tips. We recommend cooking the salmon within 2 days of buying it (or see page 14 for short-term freezing).Note that apple jelly is on this week's pantry list.

GROCERY LIST

PROTEIN		Substitutions
☐ Skin-on salmon fillets	4 (6 to 8 ounces each), 1 inch thick	*Wild salmon or Arctic char*
☐ Bone-in chicken thighs	8 (5 to 7 ounces each)	
☐ Sirloin steak tips	1½ pounds	
☐ Bone-in pork rib chops	4 (8 to 10 ounces each), ¾ to 1 inch thick	
PRODUCE		
☐ Heirloom tomatoes	1½ pounds	*Vine-ripened, cherry, or grape tomatoes*
☐ Radicchio	10 ounces	*Endive or frisée*
☐ Watercress	6 ounces	*Baby arugula*
☐ Red grapefruits	2	*2 large oranges*
☐ Avocado	1	
☐ Fennel	1 large bulb with fronds	*4 celery ribs*
☐ Mint	1 bunch (enough for ½ cup torn leaves)	*Cilantro (for salmon); basil (for chicken)*
DAIRY		
☐ Sour cream	½ cup (4 ounces)	*Greek yogurt*
☐ Blue cheese	5 ounces	*Goat cheese*

PREP AHEAD

Core and cut tomatoes into
1-inch wedges

Core and tear radicchio into
bite-size pieces

Core and thinly slice fennel;
reserve fronds

Core apples; thinly slice 1 apple,
cut 1 apple into 2-inch matchsticks

Cut peel and pith from grapefruits
and segment grapefruits; reserve juice

Thinly slice red onion

Juice lemon (5½ teaspoons)

Wash and pick mint

Toast and chop hazelnuts

Trim pork chops, then cut slits about
2 inches apart into fat and underlying
silverskin, opposite bone

Trim and cut steak tips into
2-inch pieces

Chop bacon

MAKE AHEAD

UP TO 2 DAYS	Roast salmon and flake into 2-inch pieces
	Make dressing for fennel-apple slaw
	Make balsamic reduction for steak tips
	Crisp bacon for steak tips

PANTRY ITEMS

CUPBOARD & COUNTER		Substitutions
☐ Oil	13 tablespoons plus 1 teaspoon	
☐ Balsamic vinegar	7 tablespoons	*Sherry vinegar (for pork)*
☐ Cayenne pepper	½ teaspoon	
☐ Blanched hazelnuts	¾ cup	*Almonds, pecans, or pistachios*
☐ Apples	2	*6 ounces jicama (for chicken); 1 large pear or 1¼ cups halved grapes (for pork)*
☐ Red onion	1 small	*3 shallots*
REFRIGERATOR		
☐ Apple jelly	6 tablespoons	*Apricot jam*
☐ Maple syrup	2 tablespoons	
☐ Dijon mustard	1 teaspoon	
☐ Lemon	1	*White wine vinegar*
FREEZER		
☐ Bacon	4 slices	*4 ounces pancetta*

SALMON, GRAPEFRUIT, *and* AVOCADO SALAD

SERVES 4 | ACTIVE TIME 25 MINUTES

- 4 (6- to 8-ounce) skin-on salmon fillets, 1 inch thick
- 3 tablespoons plus 1 teaspoon extra-virgin olive oil, divided
- 1 teaspoon table salt, divided
- ¼ teaspoon pepper
- 2 red grapefruits
- 1 teaspoon lemon juice
- 1 teaspoon Dijon mustard
- 4 ounces (4 cups) watercress, torn into bite-size pieces
- 1 ripe avocado, halved, pitted, and sliced ¼ inch thick
- ¼ cup fresh mint leaves, torn
- ¼ cup blanched hazelnuts, toasted and chopped

1. FOR THE SALMON Adjust oven rack to lowest position, place aluminum foil–lined rimmed baking sheet on rack, and heat oven to 500 degrees. Pat salmon dry with paper towels, rub with 1 teaspoon oil, and sprinkle with ½ teaspoon salt and pepper. Reduce oven temperature to 275 degrees. Carefully place salmon skin side down on hot sheet. Roast until center is still translucent when checked with tip of paring knife and registers 125 degrees (for medium-rare), 8 to 12 minutes. Let salmon cool to room temperature, about 20 minutes. Flake salmon into 2-inch pieces, discarding skin.

2. FOR THE SALAD While salmon cools, cut away peel and pith from grapefruits. Holding fruit over bowl, use paring knife to slice between membranes to release segments. Measure out 2 tablespoons grapefruit juice and transfer to small bowl.

3. Whisk lemon juice, mustard, and remaining ½ teaspoon salt into grapefruit juice in bowl. While whisking constantly, slowly drizzle in remaining 3 tablespoons oil until combined. Arrange watercress in even layer on serving platter. Arrange salmon pieces, grapefruit segments, and avocado on top of watercress. Drizzle dressing over top, then sprinkle with mint and hazelnuts. Serve.

PREP AHEAD

- Cut peel and pith from grapefruits and cut into segments; reserve 2 tablespoons juice
- Juice lemon
- Wash and pick mint
- Toast and chop hazelnuts

MAKE AHEAD

- Refrigerate roasted and flaked salmon for up to 2 days

NOTES FROM THE TEST KITCHEN

- Sub wild salmon or arctic char for farmed salmon (cook to 120 degrees)
- Sub 2 large oranges for grapefruits
- Sub white wine vinegar for lemon juice
- Sub baby arugula for watercress
- Sub cilantro for mint
- Sub almonds, pecans, or pistachios for hazelnuts

PAN-ROASTED CHICKEN THIGHS
with FENNEL-APPLE SLAW

SERVES 4 | ACTIVE TIME 30 MINUTES

¼ cup sour cream

2 tablespoons maple syrup

1½ tablespoons lemon juice

1¼ teaspoons table salt, divided

½ teaspoon pepper, divided

1 large fennel bulb, 2 tablespoons fronds chopped, stalks discarded, bulb halved, cored, and sliced thin

1 large apple, halved, cored, and sliced thin

8 (5- to 7-ounce) bone-in chicken thighs, trimmed

½ teaspoon cayenne pepper

1 tablespoon oil

¼ cup fresh mint leaves, torn

1. FOR THE DRESSING Adjust oven rack to middle position and heat oven to 450 degrees. Whisk sour cream, maple syrup, lemon juice, ¾ teaspoon salt, and ¼ teaspoon pepper together in large bowl.

2. FOR THE SLAW Add fennel bulb and apple to dressing and toss to combine; set aside.

3. FOR THE CHICKEN Pat chicken dry with paper towels and sprinkle with cayenne, remaining ½ teaspoon salt, and remaining ¼ teaspoon pepper. Heat oil in 12-inch nonstick skillet over medium-high heat until shimmering. Add chicken skin side down and cook until browned on both sides, about 5 minutes per side. Transfer chicken skin side up to rimmed baking sheet and roast until chicken registers 175 degrees, about 15 minutes. Transfer chicken to large plate, tent with aluminum foil, and let rest for 5 minutes.

4. TO FINISH Transfer salad to serving platter and sprinkle with mint and fennel fronds. Serve salad with chicken.

PREP AHEAD

- Juice lemon
- Core and slice fennel; reserve fronds
- Core and slice apple
- Wash and pick mint

MAKE AHEAD

- Refrigerate dressing for up to 2 days

NOTES FROM THE TEST KITCHEN

- Sub Greek yogurt for sour cream
- Sub 4 celery ribs for fennel
- Sub 6 ounces jicama, thinly sliced, for apple
- Sub basil for mint

BALSAMIC STEAK TIPS
with TOMATO SALAD

SERVES 4 I ACTIVE TIME 40 MINUTES

4 slices bacon, chopped

5 tablespoons balsamic vinegar, divided

1½ pounds sirloin steak tips, trimmed and cut into 2-inch pieces

½ teaspoon table salt

¼ teaspoon pepper

3 tablespoons oil, divided

1½ pounds heirloom tomatoes, cored and cut into 1-inch-thick wedges

1 small red onion, sliced thin

2 ounces (2 cups) watercress

3 ounces blue cheese, crumbled (¾ cup)

1. FOR THE BACON Cook bacon in 12-inch skillet over medium heat until crispy, 5 to 7 minutes. Using slotted spoon, transfer bacon to paper towel–lined plate.

2. FOR THE BALSAMIC REDUCTION Pour off fat and wipe out skillet with paper towels. Add ¼ cup vinegar and simmer over medium-high heat until syrupy and reduced to 2 tablespoons, about 4 minutes; transfer reduction to bowl.

3. FOR THE STEAK AND SALAD Rinse skillet and wipe dry. Pat steak tips dry with paper towels and sprinkle with salt and pepper. Heat 1 tablespoon oil in now-empty skillet over medium-high heat until just smoking. Add steak tips and cook until well browned all over and meat registers 120 to 125 degrees (for medium-rare), 6 to 8 minutes. Transfer to serving platter, tent with aluminum foil, and let rest for 5 minutes.

4. Combine tomatoes, onion, watercress, remaining 2 tablespoons oil, and remaining 1 tablespoon vinegar in large bowl and toss to combine. Season with salt and pepper to taste. Sprinkle with blue cheese and bacon. Drizzle balsamic glaze over steak tips and serve with salad.

PREP AHEAD

- Core and cut tomatoes
- Slice red onion
- Chop bacon
- Trim and cut steak tips

MAKE AHEAD

- Refrigerate crisped bacon for up to 2 days
- Refrigerate balsamic reduction for up to 2 days

NOTES FROM THE TEST KITCHEN

- Sub 4 ounces pancetta for bacon
- Sub vine-ripened, cherry, or grape tomatoes for heirloom tomatoes
- Sub 3 shallots for red onion
- Sub baby arugula for watercress
- Sub goat cheese for blue cheese

GRILLED *and* GLAZED PORK CHOPS *with* RADICCHIO SALAD

SERVES 4 | ACTIVE TIME 25 MINUTES

6 tablespoons apple jelly

6 tablespoons oil

1 head radicchio (10 ounces), halved, cored, and torn into bite-size pieces

1 apple, cored and cut into 2-inch-long matchsticks

2 ounces blue cheese, crumbled (½ cup)

½ cup blanched hazelnuts, toasted and chopped

¼ cup sour cream

2 tablespoons balsamic vinegar

1 teaspoon table salt, divided

¾ teaspoon pepper, divided

4 (8- to 10-ounce) bone-in pork rib chops, ¾ to 1 inch thick, trimmed

1. Whisk jelly and oil in large bowl until combined; measure out and reserve ½ cup jelly mixture. Add radicchio, apple, blue cheese, hazelnuts, sour cream, vinegar, ½ teaspoon salt, and ½ teaspoon pepper to remaining jelly mixture and toss to combine. Cover and refrigerate until ready to serve.

2. Cut slits about 2 inches apart into fat and underlying silverskin of chops, opposite bone of chop. Pat chops dry with paper towels and sprinkle with remaining ½ teaspoon salt and remaining ¼ teaspoon pepper. Measure out and reserve ¼ cup jelly mixture for serving. Brush each chop all over with 1 tablespoon remaining jelly mixture. Grill chops, covered, over hot fire until browned and meat registers 140 to 145 degrees, about 3 minutes per side.

3. Transfer chops to large plate and, using clean brush, brush with reserved ¼ cup jelly mixture. Tent with aluminum foil and let rest for 5 minutes. Serve chops with radicchio salad.

PREP AHEAD

- Core and tear radicchio
- Core and cut apple
- Toast and chop hazelnuts
- Trim pork chops, then cut slits about 2 inches apart into fat and underlying silverskin, opposite bone

NOTES FROM THE TEST KITCHEN

- We prefer a half-grill fire (page 25)
- Sub apricot jam for apple jelly
- Sub endive or frisée for radicchio
- Sub 1 large pear or 1¼ cups halved grapes for apple
- Sub goat cheese for blue cheese
- Sub almonds, pecans, or pistachios for hazelnuts
- Sub Greek yogurt for sour cream
- Sub sherry vinegar for balsamic vinegar

MEAL PLAN 05

MEAL 1 — Chicken and Leek Soup with Parmesan Dumplings

MEAL 2 — Garlicky Strip Steaks with Cauliflower

MEAL 3 — Pork Chops with Chorizo Rice

MEAL 4 — Orzo Primavera with Feta

MEAL 5 — Choose a Pantry Recipe
(we suggest Shrimp Scampi)

MEAL PLAN 05

WHY THIS MEAL PLAN WORKS

Though these five meals may look diverse, they all have something in common: They are simple dishes made infinitely more interesting—but not more complicated—by the addition of a bold flavor booster. Our chicken and leek soup uses a generous amount of Parmesan to flavor rich drop dumplings that cook right in the soup. The strip steaks with cauliflower are topped with a versatile roasted garlic butter that could also be used on anything from grilled bread to roasted potatoes to shrimp. Pork chops gain a deep smokiness with the addition of Spanish chorizo and smoked paprika. The orzo primavera uses tangy, zesty, creamy marinated feta as well as its seasoned oil. And our pantry recipe uses plenty of garlic. Even if all you do ahead this week is prep the leeks, chicken, and cauliflower, you've still made great progress toward several dinners.

GROCERY LIST

PROTEIN		Substitutions
☐ Rotisserie chicken	1 (2 ½ pounds)	
☐ Strip steaks	2 (1 pound each)	Rib-eye steaks
☐ Bone-in pork rib chops	4 (8 ounces each), ¾ inch thick	Center-cut pork chops or country-style ribs
☐ Spanish chorizo sausage	8 ounces	Mexican chorizo or Italian sausage
PRODUCE		
☐ Cauliflower	1 large head (3 pounds)	Broccoli
☐ Leeks	2 pounds	
☐ Asparagus	1 pound	
☐ Red bell pepper	1	Green, yellow, or orange bell pepper
DAIRY		
☐ Marinated feta cheese	6 ounces	Feta cheese and extra-virgin olive oil

PREP AHEAD

Core cauliflower and cut into 1½-inch florets

Trim off dark green parts from 1 pound leeks; slice white and light green parts ½ inch thick; wash thoroughly

For second 1 pound leeks, coarsely chop dark green parts; halve white and light green parts lengthwise and thinly slice; wash thoroughly

Trim and reserve ends of asparagus; cut asparagus stalks on bias into ½-inch lengths

Quarter 3 shallots through root end

Mince 2 shallots

Stem, seed, and chop bell pepper

Juice lemon (2 teaspoons)

Grate Parmesan (½ cup)

Pick meat from rotisserie chicken, discarding skin and bones, then shred into bite-size pieces

Trim pork chops, then cut slits about 2 inches apart through fat and underlying silverskin, opposite bone

Halve chorizo lengthwise, then slice crosswise ¼ inch thick

MAKE AHEAD

UP TO 5 DAYS	Make leek broth for orzo
UP TO 3 DAYS	Make base for chicken and leek soup
UP TO 1 DAY	Parcook rice for pork chops

PANTRY ITEMS

CUPBOARD & COUNTER		Substitutions
☐ Orzo	1½ cups	
☐ Long-grain white rice	1 cup	
☐ Oil	5 tablespoons plus 1 teaspoon	
☐ All-purpose flour	1 cup	
☐ Baking powder	½ teaspoon	
☐ Smoked paprika	1 teaspoon	
☐ Garlic cloves	8	
☐ Shallots	5 large	*Red onion (for steaks); yellow onion (for pork)*

REFRIGERATOR		
☐ Unsalted butter	10 tablespoons	
☐ Parmesan cheese	1 ounce	*Pecorino Romano*
☐ Egg	1 large	
☐ Broth	8 cups	
☐ Lemon	1	

FREEZER		
☐ Frozen peas	1 cup	*Frozen corn (for pork)*

CHICKEN *and* LEEK SOUP *with* PARMESAN DUMPLINGS

SERVES 4 | ACTIVE TIME 30 MINUTES

4 tablespoons unsalted butter

1 pound leeks, white and light green parts only, halved lengthwise, sliced ½ inch thick, and washed thoroughly

1 teaspoon table salt, divided

2 garlic cloves, minced

6 cups broth

1 cup all-purpose flour

1 ounce Parmesan cheese, grated (½ cup)

⅓ cup water

1 large egg, lightly beaten

½ teaspoon baking powder

¼ teaspoon pepper

1 (2½-pound) rotisserie chicken, skin and bones discarded, meat shredded into bite-size pieces (3 cups)

1. FOR THE SOUP BASE Melt butter in Dutch oven over medium-high heat. Add leeks and ½ teaspoon salt and cook until softened and beginning to brown, 8 to 10 minutes. Add garlic and cook until fragrant, about 1 minute. Stir in broth and bring base to simmer. Reduce heat to medium.

2. TO FINISH Combine flour, Parmesan, water, egg, remaining ½ teaspoon salt, baking powder, and pepper in bowl. Using 2 spoons, scrape rough tablespoon-size dumplings into soup and cook, without stirring, for 2 minutes. Stir gently to break up dumplings and continue to cook for 2 minutes longer. Carefully stir in chicken and cook until heated through, about 1 minute. Serve.

PREP AHEAD

• Trim, halve, slice, and wash leeks

• Grate Parmesan

• Shred rotisserie chicken

MAKE AHEAD

• Refrigerate soup base for up to 3 days

NOTES FROM THE TEST KITCHEN

• Sprinkle with chopped parsley, if you have it

• Sub Pecorino Romano for Parmesan

GARLICKY STRIP STEAKS
with CAULIFLOWER

SERVES 4 | ACTIVE TIME 25 MINUTES

1 large head cauliflower (3 pounds), cored and cut into 1½-inch florets

3 large shallots, quartered through root end

3 tablespoons oil, divided

6 garlic cloves, peeled

1¼ teaspoons table salt, divided

¾ plus ⅛ teaspoon pepper, divided

2 (1-pound) strip steaks, trimmed and halved crosswise

6 tablespoons unsalted butter, softened

1. Adjust oven rack to lowest position and heat oven to 425 degrees. Toss cauliflower, shallots, 2 tablespoons oil, garlic, ½ teaspoon salt, and ½ teaspoon pepper together on rimmed baking sheet. Roast until vegetables are tender and lightly browned, about 25 minutes, stirring halfway through roasting.

2. Meanwhile, pat steaks dry with paper towels and sprinkle with ½ teaspoon salt and ¼ teaspoon pepper. Heat remaining 1 tablespoon oil in 12-inch nonstick skillet over medium-high heat until just smoking. Add steaks and cook, flipping every 2 minutes, until well browned and meat registers 120 to 125 degrees (for medium-rare), 10 to 12 minutes. Transfer to serving platter and tent with aluminum foil.

3. Combine butter, roasted garlic, remaining ¼ teaspoon salt, and remaining ⅛ teaspoon pepper in bowl and mash with fork. Serve steaks with vegetables and garlic butter.

PREP AHEAD

- Core and cut cauliflower
- Quarter shallots

NOTES FROM THE TEST KITCHEN

- Flipping the steaks every 2 minutes increases their temperature gradually, allowing a crust to build up on the outside without overcooking the interior
- Double the garlic butter and store the extra in the freezer for next time
- Sub broccoli for cauliflower (roasting time will be shorter)
- Sub 1 red onion for shallots
- Sub rib-eye for strip steaks

PORK CHOPS
with CHORIZO RICE

SERVES 4 | ACTIVE TIME 40 MINUTES

2 cups broth, divided

1 cup long-grain white rice, rinsed

1 teaspoon plus 2 tablespoons oil, divided

8 ounces Spanish chorizo sausage, halved lengthwise and sliced crosswise ¼ inch thick

2 large shallots, minced

1 red bell pepper, stemmed, seeded, and chopped

4 (8-ounce) bone-in pork rib chops, ¾ inch thick, trimmed

1 teaspoon smoked paprika

½ teaspoon table salt

¼ teaspoon pepper

½ cup frozen peas

1. FOR THE RICE Combine 1½ cups broth and rice in large bowl, cover, and microwave until rice is softened and most of liquid has been absorbed, 10 to 12 minutes.

2. FOR THE SPANISH RICE AND PORK Meanwhile, heat 1 teaspoon oil in medium saucepan over medium heat until shimmering. Add chorizo and cook until browned, about 4 minutes. Using slotted spoon, transfer chorizo to small bowl; set aside. Add shallots and bell pepper to fat left in saucepan and cook until softened, about 5 minutes.

3. Stir in parcooked rice and remaining ½ cup broth and bring to boil. Reduce heat to medium-low, cover, and cook until rice is tender and liquid is absorbed, about 5 minutes.

4. Meanwhile, cut slits about 2 inches apart through fat on edge of each pork chop, opposite bone. Pat chops dry with paper towels and sprinkle with paprika, salt, and pepper. Heat remaining 2 tablespoons oil in 12-inch nonstick skillet over medium heat until just smoking. Add pork chops and cook until well browned on both sides and meat registers 140 to 145 degrees, 8 to 10 minutes. Transfer to plate, tent with aluminum foil, and let rest for 5 minutes.

5. Add chorizo and peas to rice and cook, stirring frequently, until hot, about 2 minutes. Season with salt and pepper to taste and serve with chops.

PREP AHEAD

- Halve and slice chorizo
- Mince shallot
- Stem, seed, and chop bell pepper
- Trim pork chops, then cut slits about 2 inches apart through fat and underlying silverskin, opposite bone

MAKE AHEAD

- Refrigerate parcooked rice for up to 1 day

NOTES FROM THE TEST KITCHEN

- Sub crumbled Mexican chorizo or Italian sausage for Spanish chorizo (cooking time may be longer)
- Sub ½ onion for shallots
- Sub green, yellow, or orange bell pepper for red bell pepper
- Sub center-cut pork chops or country-style ribs for rib chops
- Sub frozen corn for peas

ORZO PRIMAVERA *with* FETA

SERVES 4 | ACTIVE TIME 30 MINUTES

1 pound leeks, white and light green parts halved lengthwise, sliced thin, and washed thoroughly; dark green parts chopped coarse and washed thoroughly

1 pound asparagus, trimmed and cut on bias into ½-inch lengths; ends reserved

4 cups water, plus extra as needed

¾ teaspoon table salt, divided

1½ cups orzo

6 ounces marinated feta cheese, crumbled (1½ cups), plus 2 tablespoons marinade

½ cup frozen peas

2 teaspoons lemon juice

1. FOR THE LEEK BROTH Bring dark green parts of leeks, asparagus ends, water, and ¼ teaspoon salt to simmer in medium saucepan over medium-high heat, then lower heat to medium-low and simmer gently for 10 minutes. Strain through fine-mesh strainer into 4-cup liquid measuring cup, pressing on solids to extract as much liquid as possible. Add water as needed until liquid measures 3½ cups.

2. FOR THE ORZO Toast orzo in 12-inch nonstick skillet over medium-high heat until golden, 3 to 5 minutes; transfer to bowl. Add feta marinade, white and light green parts of leeks, and remaining ½ teaspoon salt to now-empty skillet and cook over medium heat until leeks are softened, about 5 minutes.

3. Stir in toasted orzo and 3 cups strained broth, cover, and simmer gently for 5 minutes. Stir in asparagus spears, cover, and continue to cook, stirring often, until asparagus is nearly tender, about 7 minutes. Stir in peas, cover, and cook until heated through, about 1 minute.

4. Off heat, stir in lemon juice and season with salt and pepper to taste. Loosen consistency of orzo with remaining ½ cup broth as needed. Sprinkle with feta and serve.

PREP AHEAD

- Slice and wash leeks (store white and light green parts separately from dark green parts)
- Trim and cut asparagus (store ends separately from spears)
- Juice lemon

MAKE AHEAD

- Refrigerate leek broth for up to 5 days

NOTES FROM THE TEST KITCHEN

- Sub unmarinated feta and extra-virgin olive oil for marinated feta and marinade

MEAL PLAN 06

WHY THIS MEAL PLAN WORKS

No one around the table will get bored with the widely varied flavor profiles in this week's meal plan. Drawing inspiration from all over the world, our menu carefully cross-utilizes ingredients to keep the grocery list short and make sure nothing goes to waste. Fresh tomatoes brighten a curry that's infused with cardamom, ginger, and garlic, and we also incorporate tomatoes into a zesty taco filling. This is a menu where it pays to have a well-stocked spice cabinet, as we use cumin in two recipes, as well as curry powder, cardamom, and ginger. Four of these five recipes (including the pantry recipe) can be made almost entirely ahead of time if desired, giving you plenty of flexibility for when you know you have especially busy weeknights ahead.

GROCERY LIST

PROTEIN		Substitutions
☐ Boneless, skinless chicken thighs	1½ pounds	
☐ 90 percent lean ground beef	1 pound	
☐ Pork tenderloins	2 (14 to 16 ounces each)	
☐ Mexican-style chorizo sausage	4 ounces	*Ground pork*
PRODUCE		
☐ Tomatoes	7	*2 pounds plus 10 ounces cherry or grape tomatoes*
☐ Poblano chile	1	*Green bell, Anaheim, or cubanelle pepper*
☐ Cilantro	1 bunch (enough for 6 tablespoons chopped)	*Parsley (for chicken curry); scallion (for tacos)*
DAIRY		
☐ Cotija cheese	2 ounces	*Queso fresco or feta cheese*

PREP AHEAD

Core tomatoes; coarsely chop 3 tomatoes; cut 4 tomatoes into ¼-inch pieces

Finely chop 3 onions

Stem, seed, and finely chop poblano chile

Grate lemon zest (1 teaspoon)

Juice lemon (1 tablespoon)

Wash and pick cilantro

Drain and chop canned tomatoes, reserving juice

Trim and cut chicken thighs into 1-inch pieces

Remove casing from chorizo

MAKE AHEAD

UP TO 3 DAYS	Make corn and tomato soup
UP TO 2 DAYS	Make chicken curry
UP TO 1 DAY	Make filling for beef tacos

PANTRY ITEMS

CUPBOARD & COUNTER		Substitutions
☐ Egg noodles	12 ounces	
☐ Whole peeled tomatoes	1 (28-ounce) can	*Crushed tomatoes*
☐ Oil	2 tablespoons	
☐ Yellow curry powder	1 tablespoon	
☐ Ground cumin	1 tablespoon	
☐ Ground cardamom	1 teaspoon	
☐ Ground ginger	¾ teaspoon	*3 tablespoons chopped fresh ginger*
☐ Honey	2 tablespoons	
☐ Garlic cloves	10	
☐ Onions	4	*12 large shallots*
REFRIGERATOR		
☐ Broth	5¼ cups	
☐ Unsalted butter	5 tablespoons	
☐ Plain yogurt	½ cup	
☐ Whole-grain mustard	¼ cup	
☐ Canned chipotle chile in adobo sauce	3–4 teaspoons	
☐ Lemon	1	
FREEZER		
☐ Corn or flour tortillas	12–18 (6-inch)	*Taco shells*
☐ Frozen corn	2½ cups	*Fresh corn*

CHICKEN CURRY *with* TOMATOES *and* GINGER

SERVES 4 | ACTIVE TIME 30 MINUTES

2 tablespoons oil

1 onion, chopped fine

1 teaspoon table salt

1 tablespoon yellow curry powder

4 garlic cloves, minced

1 teaspoon ground cardamom

¾ teaspoon ground ginger

1½ pounds boneless, skinless chicken thighs, trimmed and cut into 1-inch pieces

¾ cup broth

3 tomatoes, cored and chopped coarse, divided

½ cup plain yogurt

2 tablespoons chopped fresh cilantro

1. FOR THE CHICKEN CURRY Heat oil in 12-inch skillet over medium heat until shimmering. Add onion and salt and cook until softened, about 5 minutes. Add curry powder, garlic, cardamom, and ginger and cook until fragrant, about 30 seconds. Pat chicken dry with paper towels, then stir into spice mixture in skillet and cook until lightly browned, about 3 minutes.

2. Stir in broth and half of tomatoes, scraping up any browned bits, and bring to boil. Reduce heat to medium-low and simmer until chicken is tender and sauce is slightly thickened and reduced by about half, 8 to 10 minutes; remove skillet from heat.

3. TO FINISH In small bowl, whisk yogurt until smooth. Whisking constantly, slowly ladle about 1 cup hot liquid from skillet into yogurt and whisk until combined, then stir yogurt mixture back into skillet until combined. Stir in cilantro and remaining tomatoes and season with salt and pepper to taste. Serve.

PREP AHEAD

- Chop onion
- Core and chop tomatoes
- Wash and pick cilantro
- Trim and cut chicken

MAKE AHEAD

- Refrigerate chicken curry for up to 2 days (or freeze for up to 1 month)

NOTES FROM THE TEST KITCHEN

- Serve over rice (pages 34–35), if you like
- Garnish with scallions and lime wedges, if you like
- Sub 4 large shallots for onion
- Sub 3 tablespoons chopped fresh ginger for ground ginger
- Sub 18 ounces cherry or grape tomatoes for tomatoes
- Sub parsley for cilantro

GROUND BEEF TACOS

SERVES 4 TO 6 | ACTIVE TIME 30 MINUTES

1 pound 90 percent lean ground beef

4 ounces Mexican-style chorizo sausage, casings removed

1 teaspoon pepper

¾ teaspoon table salt

1 onion, chopped fine

1 poblano chile, stemmed, seeded, and chopped fine

4 garlic cloves, minced

1 tablespoon ground cumin

1–2 teaspoons minced canned chipotle chile in adobo sauce

4 tomatoes, cored and cut into ¼-inch pieces

½ cup water

¼ cup chopped fresh cilantro

12–18 (6-inch) corn or flour tortillas, warmed

1. FOR THE TACO FILLING Cook beef, chorizo, pepper, and salt in 12-inch nonstick skillet over medium-high heat until beef is no longer pink, 6 to 8 minutes, breaking up meat with wooden spoon. Stir in onion and poblano and cook until softened, 6 to 8 minutes. Add garlic, cumin, and chipotle and cook until fragrant, about 30 seconds.

2. Stir in tomatoes and water and bring to simmer. Reduce heat to medium-low, cover, and continue to cook until tomatoes are beginning to break down, about 10 minutes.

3. TO FINISH Off heat, stir in cilantro. Serve with tortillas.

PREP AHEAD

- Chop onion
- Stem, seed, and chop poblano chile
- Mince chipotle chile in adobo
- Core and cut tomatoes
- Wash and pick cilantro
- Remove casing from chorizo

MAKE AHEAD

- Refrigerate taco filling for up to 1 day (or freeze for up to 1 month)

NOTES FROM THE TEST KITCHEN

- Serve with your favorite garnishes, such as shredded cheese, shredded lettuce, diced avocado, salsa, and/or sour cream
- Sub ground pork for Mexican chorizo
- Sub 4 large shallots for onion
- Sub bell pepper, Anaheim, or cubanelle for poblano
- Sub 1½ pounds cherry or grape tomatoes for tomatoes
- Sub scallion for cilantro
- Sub taco shells for tortillas

HONEY-MUSTARD PORK TENDERLOIN *with* EGG NOODLES

SERVES 4 | ACTIVE TIME 40 MINUTES

¼ cup whole-grain mustard

2 tablespoons honey

1 teaspoon grated lemon zest plus
1 tablespoon juice, divided

2 (14- to 16-ounce) pork tenderloins,
trimmed

1½ teaspoons table salt, plus salt
for cooking noodles

½ teaspoon pepper

3 tablespoons unsalted butter, divided

12 ounces (6 cups) egg noodles

½ cup broth

¼ cup grated onion

1. Adjust oven rack to middle position and heat oven to 375 degrees. Combine mustard, honey, and 1 teaspoon lemon juice in bowl; set aside. Pat pork dry with paper towels and sprinkle each tenderloin with ¾ teaspoon salt and ¼ teaspoon pepper. Melt 1 tablespoon butter in 12-inch skillet over medium-high heat. Cook pork until browned on all sides, 5 to 7 minutes. Off heat, brush mustard mixture evenly over top of pork. Transfer skillet to oven and roast until meat registers 135 to 140 degrees, 10 to 14 minutes. Transfer pork to carving board, tent with aluminum foil, and let rest for 5 minutes. Do not wash skillet.

2. Meanwhile, bring 4 quarts water to boil in large pot. Add noodles and 1 tablespoon salt and cook, stirring occasionally, until tender. Drain noodles and return them to pot.

3. Add and onion to now-empty skillet. Bring to simmer over medium heat and cook until slightly thickened, about 2 minutes, scraping up any browned bits. Off heat, stir in lemon zest, remaining 2 tablespoons butter, and remaining 2 teaspoons lemon juice. Add sauce to noodles and toss to coat. Slice pork ½ inch thick and serve over noodles.

PREP AHEAD

• Grate lemon zest and juice lemon

NOTES FROM THE TEST KITCHEN

• Sprinkle with 2 tablespoons chopped fresh dill, if you have it

• Sub 2 shallots, minced, for onion

SPICY CORN *and* TOMATO SOUP

SERVES 4 | ACTIVE TIME 25 MINUTES

1 (28-ounce) can whole peeled tomatoes

2 tablespoons unsalted butter

1 onion, chopped fine

2 garlic cloves, minced

1½ teaspoons ground cumin

1 teaspoon table salt, divided

½ teaspoon pepper

4 cups broth

2½ cups frozen corn

2 teaspoons minced canned chipotle chile in adobo sauce

2 ounces cotija cheese, crumbled (½ cup)

1. FOR THE SOUP Drain tomatoes in fine-mesh strainer set over bowl; reserve juice. Chop tomatoes coarse. Melt butter in Dutch oven over medium heat. Add onion, garlic, cumin, ½ teaspoon salt, and pepper and cook until onion is softened, about 5 minutes.

2. Increase heat to medium-high. Stir in broth, corn, chipotle, tomatoes and reserved juice, and remaining ½ teaspoon salt and bring to boil, scraping up any browned bits. Reduce heat to medium-low, cover, and simmer until flavors have melded, about 20 minutes.

3. TO FINISH Season with salt and pepper to taste. Serve, sprinkled with cotija.

PREP AHEAD

- Drain and chop tomatoes, reserving juice
- Chop onion
- Mince chipotle chile in adobo

MAKE AHEAD

- Refrigerate soup for up to 3 days (or freeze for up to 1 month)

NOTES FROM THE TEST KITCHEN

- Top with thinly sliced radishes and diced avocado, if you have them
- Sub crushed tomatoes for whole peeled tomatoes
- Sub 4 large shallots for onion
- Sub fresh corn for frozen
- Sub queso fresco or feta for cotija

MEAL PLAN 07

MEAL 1 Skillet Chicken with Spicy Red Beans and Rice

MEAL 2 Lemon-Herb Pork Tenderloin with Green Beans

MEAL 3 Pork Chops with Cauliflower and Roasted Red Pepper Sauce

MEAL 4 Shiitake Mushroom Frittata with Pecorino Romano

MEAL 5 Choose a Pantry Recipe *(we suggest Cacio e Pepe)*

WHY THIS MEAL PLAN WORKS

This seasonless menu offers plenty of rich flavors thanks to a combination of fresh and pantry-friendly ingredients including roasted red peppers, andouille sausage, and shiitake mushrooms. Both the skillet chicken and the mushroom frittata come together entirely in a 12-inch nonstick skillet (and just one mixing bowl), and the frittata can be made ahead—ideal if your week includes a night when you'll have zero time to cook. The Lemon-Herb Pork Tenderloin with Green Beans is a sheet-pan dinner that roasts quickly in the high heat of the oven. And if you don't want to have pork two nights, the make-ahead roasted red pepper sauce for the chops would be just as delicious served on chicken or a thick white fish fillet.

GROCERY LIST

PROTEIN		Substitutions
☐ Boneless, skinless chicken breasts	4 (6 to 8 ounces each)	
☐ Pork tenderloin	2 (12 to 16 ounces each)	
☐ Bone-in pork rib or center-cut chops	4 (8 to 10 ounces each), ¾ to 1 inch thick	
☐ Andouille sausage	8 ounces	*Spanish chorizo*
PRODUCE		
☐ Cauliflower	1 head (2 pounds)	
☐ Green beans	1½ pounds	
☐ Shiitake mushrooms	1 pound	*Portobello or cremini mushrooms*
☐ Green bell pepper	1	*8 ounces poblano, Anaheim, or cubanelle peppers*
☐ Scallions	10	

PREP AHEAD

Trim green beans

Stem shiitake mushrooms and cut into ½-inch pieces

Mince scallion whites; thinly slice scallion greens

Stem, seed, and chop bell pepper

Core cauliflower and cut into 1-inch florets

Grate lemon zest (5 teaspoons)

Juice lemon (1 teaspoon)

Toast ½ cup sliced almonds

Shred Pecorino Romano (¾ cup)

Trim pork chops, then cut slits about 2 inches apart into fat and underlying silverskin, opposite bone

Halve andouille sausage, then cut crosswise ½ inch thick

MAKE AHEAD

UP TO 2 DAYS	Make roasted red pepper sauce for pork chops	
	Roast cauliflower for pork chops	
	Sauté mushrooms for frittata	
	Cook frittata	
UP TO 1 DAY	Parcook rice for skillet chicken	
	Season pork tenderloin	
	Season pork chops	

PANTRY ITEMS

CUPBOARD & COUNTER		Substitutions
☐ Long-grain white rice	1 cup	
☐ Red kidney beans	1 (15-ounce) can	*Black or pinto beans*
☐ Oil	14 tablespoons, plus 1 teaspoon	
☐ Sherry vinegar	1 tablespoon	
☐ Paprika	1 tablespoon	
☐ Dried thyme	1 tablespoon	*3 tablespoons chopped fresh thyme*
☐ Cayenne pepper	¼ teaspoon plus ⅛ teaspoon	
☐ Garlic cloves	7	
REFRIGERATOR		
☐ Pecorino Romano	2¼ ounces	*Parmesan*
☐ Whole milk	⅓ cup	
☐ Eggs	12 large	
☐ Broth	2 cups	
☐ Jarred roasted red peppers	1 cup (from 12-ounce jar)	
☐ Lemons	2	
FREEZER		
☐ Hearty white sandwich bread	1 slice	*Any bread*
☐ Sliced almonds	¾ cup	*Chopped walnuts, pistachios, or pine nuts*

SKILLET CHICKEN *with* SPICY RED BEANS *and* RICE

SERVES 4 | ACTIVE TIME 35 MINUTES

2 cups broth, divided

1 cup long-grain white rice, rinsed

1¼ teaspoons table salt, divided

4 (6- to 8-ounce) boneless, skinless chicken breasts, trimmed

½ teaspoon pepper, divided

3 tablespoons oil, divided

1 green bell pepper, stemmed, seeded, and chopped

8 scallions, white parts minced, green parts sliced thin

8 ounces andouille sausage, halved lengthwise and cut crosswise ½ inch thick

3 garlic cloves, minced

¾ teaspoon dried thyme

¼ teaspoon cayenne pepper

1 (15-ounce) can red kidney beans, rinsed

1. FOR THE RICE Combine 1 cup broth, rice, and ¾ teaspoon salt in bowl. Cover and microwave until liquid is absorbed, 10 to 12 minutes.

2. FOR THE CHICKEN AND BEANS Meanwhile, pat chicken dry with paper towels and sprinkle with remaining ½ teaspoon salt and ¼ teaspoon pepper. Heat 1 tablespoon oil in 12-inch nonstick skillet over medium-high heat until just smoking. Add chicken and cook until golden brown, about 2 minutes per side. Transfer to plate.

3. Heat remaining 2 tablespoons oil in now-empty skillet over medium-high heat until shimmering. Add bell pepper, scallion whites, and sausage and cook until pepper begins to soften and sausage is lightly browned, about 4 minutes. Add garlic, thyme, cayenne, and remaining ¼ teaspoon pepper and cook until fragrant, about 30 seconds.

4. Stir rice, beans, and remaining 1 cup broth into skillet and bring to boil. Reduce heat to medium-low, nestle chicken into rice, and cook, covered, until liquid is absorbed and chicken registers 160 degrees, about 10 minutes. Transfer chicken to cutting board, tent with aluminum foil, and let rest for 5 minutes. Slice chicken, sprinkle scallion greens over chicken and rice, and serve.

PREP AHEAD

- Stem, seed, and chop bell pepper
- Mince scallion whites
- Slice scallion greens
- Halve and cut andouille crosswise

MAKE AHEAD

- Refrigerate parcooked rice for up to 1 day

NOTES FROM THE TEST KITCHEN

- Sub 8 ounces poblano, Anaheim, or cubanelle pepper for green bell pepper
- Sub Spanish chorizo for andouille
- Sub 2¼ teaspoons fresh thyme for dried
- Sub black or pinto beans for kidney beans

LEMON-HERB PORK TENDERLOIN *with* GREEN BEANS

SERVES 4 | ACTIVE TIME 30 MINUTES

2 (12- to 16-ounce) pork tenderloins, trimmed

1 teaspoon plus 3 tablespoons oil, divided

5 teaspoons grated lemon zest, divided, plus 1 teaspoon juice (2 lemons)

1¾ teaspoons dried thyme

1¼ teaspoons table salt, divided

¾ teaspoon pepper, divided

1½ pounds green beans, trimmed

½ cup sliced almonds, toasted

2 garlic cloves, minced

1. FOR THE SEASONED PORK Adjust oven rack to middle position and heat oven to 450 degrees. Pat pork dry with paper towels and rub with 1 teaspoon oil. Sprinkle with 1 tablespoon lemon zest, thyme, ¾ teaspoon salt, and ½ teaspoon pepper.

2. FOR THE BEANS AND PORK Toss green beans, 1 tablespoon oil, remaining ½ teaspoon salt, and remaining ¼ teaspoon pepper together on rimmed baking sheet. Push green beans to sides of sheet, leaving center of sheet clear.

3. Heat 1 tablespoon oil in 12-inch nonstick skillet over medium-high heat until just smoking. Add pork and cook until browned on all sides, 5 to 7 minutes. Transfer pork to center of prepared sheet. Roast until pork registers 135 to 140 degrees and green beans are tender, about 15 minutes.

4. Transfer pork to cutting board, tent with aluminum foil, and let rest while finishing green beans. Add almonds, garlic, remaining 2 teaspoons lemon zest, lemon juice, and remaining 1 tablespoon oil to green beans and toss to combine. Slice pork and serve with green beans.

PREP AHEAD

• Grate lemon zest and juice lemon

• Trim green beans

• Toast almonds

MAKE AHEAD

• Refrigerate seasoned pork tenderloin for up to 1 day

NOTES FROM THE TEST KITCHEN

• Sub 5¼ teaspoons fresh thyme for dried

• Sub chopped walnuts, pistachios, or pine nuts for almonds

PORK CHOPS *with* CAULIFLOWER *and* ROASTED RED PEPPER SAUCE

SERVES 4 | ACTIVE TIME 30 MINUTES

1 cup jarred roasted red peppers

¼ cup sliced almonds

1 slice hearty white sandwich bread, lightly toasted and torn into pieces

2 tablespoons water

2 garlic cloves, minced

⅛ teaspoon cayenne pepper

7 tablespoons oil, divided

1 head cauliflower (2 pounds), cored and cut into 1-inch florets

1 tablespoon paprika

1 teaspoon table salt, divided

½ teaspoon pepper, divided

4 (8- to 10-ounce) bone-in pork rib or center-cut chops, ¾ to 1 inch thick, trimmed

1. FOR THE ROASTED RED PEPPER SAUCE Adjust oven rack to middle position and heat oven to 425 degrees. Process red peppers, almonds, bread pieces, water, garlic, and cayenne in food processor until smooth, about 15 seconds. Scrape down sides of processor bowl. With processor running, slowly add ¼ cup oil until incorporated, about 30 seconds. Transfer to bowl, season with salt and pepper to taste, and set aside until ready to serve.

2. FOR THE CAULIFLOWER Toss cauliflower, paprika, ½ teaspoon salt, ¼ teaspoon pepper, and 2 tablespoons oil together on rimmed baking sheet. Roast until cauliflower is tender and lightly browned, about 20 minutes.

3. FOR THE PORK CHOPS Meanwhile, cut slits about 2 inches apart into fat and underlying silverskin, opposite bone of each chop. Pat chops dry with paper towels and sprinkle with remaining ½ teaspoon salt and remaining ¼ teaspoon pepper.

4. TO FINISH Heat remaining 1 tablespoon oil in 12-inch skillet over medium-high heat until just smoking. Add chops and cook until well browned and meat registers 140 to 145 degrees, 3 to 5 minutes per side. Transfer to large plate, tent loosely with aluminum foil, and let rest for 5 minutes. Serve with reserved red pepper sauce and cauliflower.

PREP AHEAD

- Core and cut cauliflower
- Trim pork chops, then cut slits about 2 inches apart into fat and underlying silverskin, opposite bone

MAKE AHEAD

- Refrigerate roasted red pepper sauce for up to 2 days
- Refrigerate roasted cauliflower for up to 2 days
- Refrigerate seasoned pork chops for up to 1 day

NOTES FROM THE TEST KITCHEN

- Sub chopped walnuts, pistachios, or pine nuts for almonds
- Sub any bread for white bread

SHIITAKE MUSHROOM FRITTATA
with PECORINO ROMANO

SERVES 4 | ACTIVE TIME 25 MINUTES

1 tablespoon oil

1 pound shiitake mushrooms, stemmed and cut into ½-inch pieces

¾ teaspoon table salt, divided

¼ teaspoon pepper

2 tablespoons water

2 scallions, white parts minced, green parts sliced thin

1 tablespoon sherry vinegar

½ teaspoon dried thyme

12 large eggs

2¼ ounces Pecorino Romano, shredded (¾ cup)

⅓ cup whole milk

1. FOR THE MUSHROOM MIXTURE Adjust oven rack to middle position and heat oven to 350 degrees. Heat oil in 12-inch ovensafe nonstick skillet over medium-high heat until shimmering. Add mushrooms, ¼ teaspoon salt, and pepper and cook, stirring frequently, until mushrooms are tender and spotty brown, 7 to 9 minutes. Add water, scallion whites, vinegar, and thyme and cook, stirring constantly, until no water remains in skillet, about 1 minute.

2. FOR THE FRITTATA Whisk eggs, Pecorino, milk, scallion greens, and remaining ½ teaspoon salt in bowl until well combined, then add to skillet and cook, using heat-resistant rubber spatula to stir and scrape bottom of skillet until large curds form and spatula leaves trail through eggs but eggs are still very wet, about 30 seconds. Smooth curds into even layer and cook, without stirring, for 30 seconds. Transfer skillet to oven and bake until frittata is slightly puffy and surface bounces back when lightly pressed, 6 to 9 minutes. Using rubber spatula, loosen frittata from skillet and transfer to cutting board. Let sit for 5 minutes, then slice and serve.

PREP AHEAD

- Stem and cut mushrooms
- Mince scallion whites
- Slice scallion greens
- Shred Pecorino Romano

MAKE AHEAD

- Refrigerate sautéed mushroom mixture for up to 2 days
- Refrigerate frittata for up to 2 days

NOTES FROM THE TEST KITCHEN

- You will need a 12-inch ovensafe nonstick skillet
- Serve with Simplest Salad (page 32), if you like
- Sub portobello or cremini mushrooms for shiitakes
- Sub 1½ teaspoons fresh thyme for dried
- Sub Parmesan for Pecorino Romano

MEAL PLAN 08

WHY THIS MEAL PLAN WORKS

Bring restaurant food home this week with elegant seared scallops, impressive stuffed portobello mushroom caps, big juicy steaks, a Thai-inspired entrée salad, and loads of fresh herbs. All of the proteins in this plan are cooked by quickly searing and browning them on the stovetop, which helps all of the meals clock in at less than half an hour of active cooking time. As for all of those fresh herbs, we use mint in both our chicken salad and the Spinach-Stuffed Portobello Caps, while a bunch of sage pulls double duty in a flavorful rub for the steaks and in the sweet-and-earthy pureed butternut squash. We recommend making the scallops within 2 days of purchasing them (or see page 14 for short-term freezing).

GROCERY LIST

PROTEIN		Substitutions
☐ Large sea scallops ("dry" rather than "wet" scallops)	1½ pounds	*Extra-large shrimp*
☐ Boneless, skinless chicken breasts	4 (6 to 8 ounces each)	
☐ Boneless rib-eye steaks	2 (1 pound each), 1½ inches thick	*Strip steaks*
PRODUCE		
☐ Butternut squash	2 pounds	
☐ Portobello mushroom caps	8 large	
☐ Bibb lettuce	2 heads	*Any soft lettuce*
☐ English cucumber	1	
☐ Baby spinach	11 ounces (11 cups)	*Frozen spinach*
☐ Mint	1 bunch (enough for ½ cup chopped)	*Basil (for chicken salad); scallions (for portobello caps)*
☐ Sage	1 small bunch (enough for 2 tablespoons minced)	

PREP AHEAD

Peel butternut squash, then seed and cut into 1-inch pieces

Halve red potatoes

Remove gills from portobello mushroom caps

Peel carrots and halve lengthwise

Halve 2 large shallots

Mince 1 medium shallot

Cut cucumber into 2-inch-long matchsticks

Separate and wash Bibb lettuce leaves

Slice jarred hot cherry peppers

Wash and pick mint

Wash and pick sage

Grate lemon zest (2 teaspoons)

Juice lemon (1 tablespoon)

MAKE AHEAD

UP TO 3 DAYS	Stuff and bake portobello caps
	Make squash puree for scallops
UP TO 2 DAYS	Sear chicken for chicken salad
	Make peanut dressing for chicken salad
	Make sage butter for steaks

PANTRY ITEMS

CUPBOARD & COUNTER

			Substitutions
☐ Panko bread crumbs	1½ cups		
☐ Creamy peanut butter	3 tablespoons		*Almond butter*
☐ Fish sauce	1½ tablespoons		
☐ Oil	10 tablespoons		
☐ Seasoned rice vinegar	¼ cup		
☐ Small red potatoes	12 ounces		*Small white potatoes*
☐ Garlic cloves	4		
☐ Shallots	2 large, 1 medium		*1 red onion for 2 large shallots (for steaks)*
☐ Cayenne pepper	⅛ teaspoon		

REFRIGERATOR

☐ Unsalted butter	13 tablespoons		*Vegetable oil or extra-virgin olive oil (for steaks)*
☐ Feta cheese	7 ounces		*Goat cheese*
☐ Jarred hot cherry peppers	¼ cup		
☐ Carrots	6		
☐ Lemon	1		

BIBB LETTUCE *and* CHICKEN SALAD *with* PEANUT DRESSING

SERVES 4 | ACTIVE TIME 25 MINUTES

4 (6- to 8-ounce) boneless, skinless chicken breasts, trimmed

½ teaspoon table salt

¼ teaspoon pepper

5 tablespoons oil, divided

¼ cup seasoned rice vinegar

3 tablespoons creamy peanut butter

1½ tablespoons fish sauce

2 heads Bibb lettuce (1 pound), leaves separated

1 English cucumber, cut into 2-inch-long matchsticks

¼ cup thinly sliced jarred hot cherry peppers

¼ cup fresh mint leaves, torn

1. FOR THE CHICKEN Pat chicken dry with paper towels and sprinkle with salt and pepper. Heat 1 tablespoon oil in 12-inch nonstick skillet over medium-high heat until just smoking. Add chicken and cook until golden brown and meat registers 160 degrees, about 6 minutes per side. Transfer chicken to cutting board, tent with aluminum foil, and let rest for 5 minutes.

2. FOR THE PEANUT DRESSING Microwave vinegar, peanut butter, and fish sauce in medium bowl until peanut butter has just softened, about 15 seconds. Whisk in remaining ¼ cup oil until combined.

3. TO FINISH Toss lettuce, cucumber, cherry peppers, and 3 tablespoons dressing together in large bowl. Divide salad among 4 plates. Slice chicken and divide among salads. Drizzle remaining dressing over top and sprinkle with mint. Serve.

PREP AHEAD

- Separate and wash lettuce leaves
- Cut cucumber
- Slice hot cherry peppers
- Wash and pick mint

MAKE AHEAD

- Refrigerate seared chicken for up to 2 days
- Refrigerate peanut dressing for up to 2 days

NOTES FROM THE TEST KITCHEN

- Sub almond butter for peanut butter
- Sub any soft lettuce for Bibb lettuce
- Sub basil for mint

RIB-EYE STEAKS *with* ROASTED VEGETABLES *and* SAGE BUTTER

SERVES 4 | ACTIVE TIME 25 MINUTES

1 tablespoon minced fresh sage

1 teaspoon grated lemon zest

6 tablespoons unsalted butter
(4 tablespoons softened, divided,
2 tablespoons melted)

6 carrots, peeled and halved
lengthwise

12 ounces small red potatoes,
unpeeled, halved

2 large shallots, halved

2½ teaspoons table salt, divided

1¼ teaspoons pepper, divided

2 (1-pound) boneless rib-eye steaks,
1½ inches thick, trimmed

1. FOR THE SAGE BUTTER Adjust oven rack to lowest position and heat oven to 450 degrees. Combine sage, lemon zest, and 2 tablespoons softened butter in bowl and mash with fork; set aside.

2. FOR THE VEGETABLES Toss carrots, potatoes, shallots, melted butter, ½ teaspoon salt, and ¼ teaspoon pepper together on rimmed baking sheet, then spread vegetables into even layer, cut sides down. Roast until tender and cut sides of vegetables are well browned, about 25 minutes.

3. FOR THE STEAKS Meanwhile, pat steaks dry with paper towels and sprinkle with remaining 2 teaspoons salt and remaining 1 teaspoon pepper.

4. Melt remaining 2 tablespoons softened butter in 12-inch skillet over medium heat. Add steaks and cook, flipping every 2 minutes, until well browned and meat registers 120 to 125 degrees (for medium-rare), 10 to 12 minutes. Transfer steaks to cutting board, dollop with sage butter, tent with aluminum foil, and let rest for 5 minutes. Slice steaks thin and serve with roasted vegetables.

PREP AHEAD

- Wash and pick sage

- Grate lemon zest

- Peel and halve carrots

- Halve potatoes

- Halve shallots

MAKE AHEAD

- Refrigerate sage butter for up to 2 days

NOTES FROM THE TEST KITCHEN

- Flipping the steaks frequently ensures they heat and therefore cook more evenly; it also prevents the herb crust from burning

- Sub 1 small red onion for shallots

- Sub vegetable oil or extra-virgin olive oil for butter

- Sub strip steaks for rib-eyes

SEARED SCALLOPS *with* SQUASH PUREE *and* SAGE BUTTER

SERVES 4 | ACTIVE TIME 25 MINUTES

1½ pounds large sea scallops, tendons removed

2 pounds butternut squash, peeled, seeded, and cut into 1-inch pieces (5 cups)

7 tablespoons unsalted butter, divided

1 teaspoon table salt, divided

⅛ teaspoon cayenne pepper

¼ teaspoon pepper

1 shallot, minced

1 tablespoon minced fresh sage

1 tablespoon lemon juice

1. Place scallops on large plate lined with triple layer of paper towels. Top with paper towels and press gently on scallops to dry. Let scallops sit at room temperature for 10 minutes.

2. FOR THE SQUASH PUREE Meanwhile, place squash in bowl, cover, and microwave until tender, 8 to 12 minutes, stirring halfway through. Drain if necessary, then transfer to food processor. Add 2 tablespoons butter, ½ teaspoon salt, and cayenne and process until smooth, about 20 seconds. Return to bowl, season with salt and pepper to taste, and set puree aside.

3. FOR THE SEARED SCALLOPS Sprinkle scallops with remaining ½ teaspoon salt and pepper. Melt 1 tablespoon butter in 12-inch nonstick skillet over high heat. Add half of scallops in single layer, flat side down, and cook until well browned, 1½ to 2 minutes. Flip scallops and cook until sides are firm and centers are opaque, 30 to 90 seconds (remove smaller scallops as they finish cooking). Transfer to plate and tent with aluminum foil. Wipe out skillet with paper towels and repeat with 1 tablespoon butter and remaining scallops.

4. TO FINISH Melt remaining 3 tablespoons butter in now-empty skillet over medium heat. Continue to cook, swirling skillet constantly, until butter is starting to brown and has nutty aroma, 1 to 2 minutes. Add shallot and sage and cook until fragrant, about 1 minute. Off heat, stir in lemon juice. Pour sauce over scallops and serve with squash puree.

PREP AHEAD

- Peel, seed, and cut butternut squash
- Mince shallot
- Wash and pick sage
- Juice lemon

MAKE AHEAD

- Refrigerate squash puree for up to 3 days

NOTES FROM THE TEST KITCHEN

- We prefer "dry" scallops because they don't have chemical additives, so they brown better than "wet" scallops
- Sub extra-large shrimp for scallops

SPINACH-STUFFED PORTOBELLO CAPS

SERVES 4 | ACTIVE TIME 25 MINUTES

8 large portobello mushroom caps, gills removed

5 tablespoons extra-virgin olive oil, divided, plus extra for drizzling

¾ teaspoon table salt, divided

½ teaspoon pepper, divided

1½ cups panko bread crumbs

4 garlic cloves, minced

11 ounces (11 cups) baby spinach

7 ounces feta cheese, crumbled (1¾ cups), divided

1 teaspoon grated lemon zest

¼ cup fresh mint leaves, torn

1. FOR THE STUFFED PORTOBELLO CAPS Adjust oven racks to upper-middle and lower-middle positions and heat oven to 475 degrees. Toss mushrooms with 3 tablespoons oil, ½ teaspoon salt, and ¼ teaspoon pepper, then arrange mushrooms gill side down on rimmed baking sheet and roast on lower rack until tender, about 15 minutes.

2. Meanwhile, combine panko, garlic, remaining ¼ teaspoon salt, remaining ¼ teaspoon pepper, and remaining 2 tablespoons oil in Dutch oven; cook over medium heat, stirring constantly, until panko is lightly browned, about 2 minutes. Stir in spinach, one handful at a time, and cook until wilted, about 5 minutes. Off heat, stir in 1 cup feta and lemon zest.

3. Flip mushrooms gill side up on sheet, then pack evenly with spinach mixture. Sprinkle remaining ¾ cup feta over top and bake on upper rack until feta starts to brown, about 8 minutes.

4. TO FINISH Drizzle with extra oil, sprinkle with mint, and serve.

PREP AHEAD

- Remove mushroom gills
- Grate lemon zest
- Wash and pick mint

MAKE AHEAD

- Refrigerate baked stuffed portobello caps for up to 3 days

NOTES FROM THE TEST KITCHEN

- Use a spoon to gently scrape the dark gills from the underside of each mushroom cap
- Sub frozen spinach for baby spinach
- Sub goat cheese for feta
- Sub scallions for mint

MEAL PLAN 09

WHY THIS MEAL PLAN WORKS

An Italian theme (with a bit of Spanish flair) pulls this meal plan together. This week's short grocery list focuses primarily on the proteins, along with a couple of fresh vegetables and a bunch of basil (which we use up between two recipes), while the pantry list relies on a well-stocked stash of filled pasta and rice as well as frozen, canned, and shelf-stable vegetables. This is a great plan for those weeks when you don't have a lot of time (or desire) to prep on Sunday. Although there are plenty of options for prepping ingredients and meal components ahead, we don't recommend fully cooking any of these recipes in advance. But that's just fine, because we've managed to keep the active weeknight cooking times for all these meals to 40 minutes or less.

GROCERY LIST

PROTEIN		Substitutions
☐ Boneless, skinless chicken breasts	4 (8 ounces each)	*Chicken cutlets (for Parmesan chicken)*
☐ Pork tenderloins	2 (12 to 16 ounces each)	
☐ Sweet or hot Italian sausage	1 pound	
☐ Spanish-style chorizo sausage	8 ounces	*Andouille*
☐ Prosciutto	8 thin slices	
PRODUCE		
☐ Cherry tomatoes	18 ounces	*Grape tomatoes*
☐ Broccolini	1 pound	*Broccoli rabe*
☐ Basil	1 small bunch (enough for ¼ cup chopped)	*Parsley or chives*

PREP AHEAD

Quarter 12 ounces cherry tomatoes

Halve 6 ounces cherry tomatoes

Trim broccolini and cut into
2-inch lengths

Drain and halve artichoke hearts

Chop onion

Wash and pick basil

Grate lemon zest (2 teaspoons)

Juice lemon (1 tablespoon)

Shred Parmesan (1 cup)

Trim and halve 2 chicken breasts
horizontally, then pound ½ inch thick

Trim and thinly slice 2 chicken breasts

Remove casings from Italian sausage

Slice chorizo ½ inch thick

MAKE AHEAD

UP TO 2 DAYS	Parcook rice for chicken and rice
UP TO 1 DAY	Bread chicken for Parmesan chicken
	Coat pork tenderloins with seasonings and wrap with prosciutto

PANTRY ITEMS

CUPBOARD & COUNTER

			Substitutions
☐ Dried cheese tortellini	12 ounces		
☐ Long-grain white rice	1 cup		
☐ Panko bread crumbs	1 cup		
☐ Diced tomatoes	1 (14.5-ounce) can		*Fresh tomatoes*
☐ All-purpose flour	½ cup		
☐ Oil	¾ cup		
☐ Fennel seeds	1 teaspoon		
☐ Dried rosemary	½ teaspoon		
☐ Garlic powder	½ teaspoon		
☐ Garlic cloves	5		
☐ Onion	1		*4 large shallots*

REFRIGERATOR

☐ Parmesan cheese	3 ounces, plus extra for serving		*Pecorino Romano*
☐ Eggs	2 large		
☐ Broth	4 cups		
☐ Jarred whole artichoke hearts packed in water	9 ounces		*Frozen artichoke hearts*
☐ Lemon	1		

FREEZER

☐ Frozen peas	½ cup	
☐ Crusty bread	1 (8- to 12-ounce) loaf	

PARMESAN CHICKEN *with* CHERRY TOMATO SALAD

SERVES 4 | ACTIVE TIME 25 MINUTES

½ cup all-purpose flour

2 large eggs

1 cup panko bread crumbs

3 ounces Parmesan cheese, shredded (1 cup)

2 (8-ounce) boneless, skinless chicken breasts, trimmed, halved horizontally, and pounded ½ inch thick

½ teaspoon table salt

¼ teaspoon pepper

7 tablespoons oil, divided

12 ounces cherry tomatoes, quartered

2 tablespoons chopped fresh basil

1 (8- to 12-ounce) loaf crusty bread

1. FOR THE BREADED CHICKEN Spread flour in shallow dish. Beat eggs in second shallow dish. Combine panko and Parmesan in third shallow dish. Pat chicken dry with paper towels and sprinkle with salt and pepper. Working with 1 cutlet at a time, dredge cutlets in flour, dip in egg, then coat with panko mixture, pressing gently to adhere.

2. FOR THE CUTLETS AND SALAD Heat 3 tablespoons oil in 12-inch nonstick skillet over medium heat until shimmering. Cook 2 cutlets until golden brown and crisp, about 2 minutes per side. Transfer to paper towel–lined plate. Repeat with 3 tablespoons oil and remaining cutlets.

3. Toss tomatoes, basil, and remaining 1 tablespoon oil together in bowl and season with salt and pepper to taste. Transfer cutlets to individual plates and top with cherry tomato mixture. Serve with bread.

PREP AHEAD

- Shred Parmesan
- Quarter cherry tomatoes
- Wash and pick basil
- Trim, halve, and pound chicken

MAKE AHEAD

- Refrigerate breaded chicken for up to 1 day

NOTES FROM THE TEST KITCHEN

- Sub Pecorino Romano for Parmesan
- Sub chicken cutlets for boneless, skinless chicken breasts
- Sub grape tomatoes for cherry tomatoes
- Sub parsley or chives for basil

CHICKEN *and* RICE *with* CHORIZO *and* ARTICHOKES

SERVES 4 | ACTIVE TIME 35 MINUTES

2 cups water, divided

1 cup long-grain white rice

1¼ teaspoons table salt, divided

2 tablespoons oil, divided

8 ounces Spanish-style chorizo sausage, sliced ½ inch thick

2 (8-ounce) boneless, skinless chicken breasts, trimmed and sliced thin crosswise

¼ teaspoon pepper

1 onion, chopped

3 garlic cloves, minced

1 (14.5-ounce) can diced tomatoes

1½ cups (9 ounces) jarred whole artichoke hearts packed in water, drained and halved

½ cup frozen peas

1. FOR THE RICE Combine 1½ cups water, rice, and ¾ teaspoon salt in bowl. Cover and microwave until rice is softened and most of liquid is absorbed, 10 to 12 minutes.

2. FOR THE CHICKEN Meanwhile, heat 1 tablespoon oil in 12-inch nonstick skillet over medium-high heat until just smoking. Add chorizo and cook until lightly browned, 2 to 4 minutes. Using slotted spoon, transfer to large plate. Pat chicken dry with paper towels and sprinkle with remaining ½ teaspoon salt and pepper. Add to fat left in skillet and cook until lightly browned and no longer pink, 2 to 4 minutes. Transfer to plate with chorizo.

3. TO FINISH Add onion and remaining 1 tablespoon oil to now-empty skillet and cook until softened, about 5 minutes. Stir in garlic and cook until fragrant, about 30 seconds. Stir in tomatoes and their juice, rice, and remaining ½ cup water and bring to boil, scraping up any browned bits. Reduce heat to medium and cook until rice is tender and liquid is absorbed, 10 to 12 minutes.

4. Stir in chorizo, chicken and any accumulated juices, artichoke hearts, and peas and cook, stirring frequently, until warmed through, 2 to 3 minutes. Season with salt and pepper to taste. Serve.

PREP AHEAD

- Chop onion
- Slice chorizo
- Trim and slice chicken

MAKE AHEAD

- Refrigerate parcooked rice for up to 2 days

NOTES FROM THE TEST KITCHEN

- Sub andouille for chorizo
- Sub 4 large shallots for onion
- Sub fresh tomatoes for canned
- Sub thawed frozen artichoke hearts for jarred

PROSCIUTTO-WRAPPED PORK
with LEMONY BROCCOLINI

2 (12- to 16-ounce) pork tenderloins, trimmed

1 teaspoon fennel seeds

1½ teaspoons table salt, divided

¾ teaspoon pepper, divided

½ teaspoon dried rosemary

½ teaspoon garlic powder

8 thin slices prosciutto

2 tablespoons oil

1 pound broccolini, trimmed and cut into 2-inch lengths

¼ cup water

2 teaspoons grated lemon zest plus 1 tablespoon juice

1. FOR THE PROSCIUTTO-WRAPPED PORK Adjust oven rack to middle position and heat oven to 375 degrees. Set wire rack in aluminum foil–lined rimmed baking sheet. Pat pork dry with paper towels, then sprinkle with fennel seeds, 1 teaspoon salt, ½ teaspoon pepper, rosemary, and garlic powder. For each tenderloin, shingle 4 slices of prosciutto on cutting board, overlapping edges slightly, and lay pork in center. (Tuck thinner tail ends of tenderloins under themselves as needed to create uniform thickness.) Fold prosciutto around pork, pressing on overlapping ends to secure.

2. FOR THE ROASTED PORK AND BROCCOLINI Heat oil in 12-inch nonstick skillet over medium-high heat until just smoking. Add pork and cook until browned on all sides, 5 to 7 minutes. Transfer pork to prepared rack. Roast until meat registers 135 to 140 degrees, 12 to 15 minutes. Transfer pork to clean cutting board, tent with foil, and let rest for 5 minutes.

3. Meanwhile, heat fat left in skillet over medium-high heat until just smoking. Add broccolini, water, remaining ½ teaspoon salt, and remaining ¼ teaspoon pepper; cover and cook until crisp-tender, 6 to 8 minutes. Off heat, stir in lemon zest and juice. Slice pork ½ inch thick and serve with broccolini.

PREP AHEAD

- Trim and cut broccolini
- Zest and juice lemon

MAKE AHEAD

- Refrigerate seasoned prosciutto-wrapped pork for up to 1 day

NOTES FROM THE TEST KITCHEN

- Sub broccoli rabe for broccolini

SKILLET TORTELLINI *with* SAUSAGE *and* TOMATOES

SERVES 4 | ACTIVE TIME 35 MINUTES

1 tablespoon oil

1 pound sweet or hot Italian sausage, casings removed

2 garlic cloves, sliced thin

4 cups broth

12 ounces dried cheese tortellini

6 ounces cherry tomatoes, halved

2 tablespoons chopped fresh basil

Grated Parmesan cheese

1. Heat oil in 12-inch nonstick skillet over medium heat until shimmering. Add sausage and cook, breaking meat into small pieces with spoon, until no longer pink, about 4 minutes.

2. Add garlic and cook until fragrant, about 30 seconds. Add broth and pasta and bring to boil. Cook, stirring occasionally, until pasta is tender, about 15 minutes.

3. Stir in tomatoes and cook until slightly softened, about 2 minutes. Sprinkle with basil and serve with Parmesan.

PREP AHEAD

- Halve cherry tomatoes
- Wash and pick basil
- Remove casings from sausage

NOTES FROM THE TEST KITCHEN

- Sub grape tomatoes for cherry tomatoes
- Sub parsley or chives for basil
- Sub Pecorino Romano for Parmesan

MEAL PLAN 10

WHY THIS MEAL PLAN WORKS

When you know your weeknights will be anything but leisurely yet you have some weekend time to get a head start on things, turn to this meal plan. The proteins and vegetables can all be prepped ahead, and if you want to go further, three meals—the chili, the chicken-and-vegetable foil packets, and the sesame noodles—have substantial make-ahead angles. We use sweet potatoes twice, with the chicken and the pork, but in such different ways that no one at the table will get bored; we pair them once with peppery radishes to bring out their earthiness and once with bacon to emphasize their sweetness. Oh, and this is a plan for garlic lovers as well—we make use of two whole heads.

GROCERY LIST

PROTEIN		Substitutions
☐ Boneless, skinless chicken breasts	4 (6 to 8 ounces each)	
☐ 85 percent lean ground beef	1½ pounds	
☐ Bone-in pork rib or center-cut chops	4 (12 ounces each), 1 to 1½ inches thick	
PRODUCE		
☐ Snow peas	6 ounces	
☐ Radishes	2 bunches (13 radishes)	
☐ Red bell pepper	1	Yellow or orange bell pepper
☐ Fresh ginger	1 knob (enough for 3 tablespoons grated)	
☐ Cilantro	1 bunch (enough for ⅔ cup chopped)	Scallions (for chicken and chili)
OTHER		
☐ Fresh Chinese noodles	12 ounces	1 pound dried lo mein noodles, spaghetti, or linguine

PREP AHEAD

Peel 1¼ pounds sweet potatoes and cut into ¾-inch pieces

Peel 12 ounces sweet potatoes and slice crosswise ¼ inch thick

Remove strings from snow peas and halve lengthwise

Trim and quarter 8 radishes

Trim, halve, and thinly slice 5 radishes

Stem, seed, and cut bell pepper into ¼-inch-wide strips

Slice small red onion ½ inch thick and separate layers

Finely chop medium red onion

Juice limes (6 tablespoons)

Wash and pick cilantro

Finely chop bacon

Trim pork chops, then cut slits about 2 inches apart into fat and underlying silverskin, opposite bone

MAKE AHEAD

UP TO 3 DAYS	Make chili (or make and freeze for up to 1 month)
UP TO 2 DAYS	Boil and rinse noodles for sesame noodles
	Make sauce for sesame noodles
UP TO 1 DAY	Assemble chicken foil packets
	Parcook sweet potatoes for sweet potato–bacon hash

PANTRY ITEMS

CUPBOARD & COUNTER		Substitutions
☐ Kidney beans	2 (15-ounce) cans	Pinto or black beans
☐ Diced tomatoes	2 (14.5-ounce) cans	28-ounce can crushed tomatoes
☐ Peanut butter	½ cup	Almond butter
☐ Oil	¼ cup	
☐ Cider vinegar	1 tablespoon	
☐ Chili powder	3 tablespoons	
☐ Ground cumin	2 teaspoons	
☐ Dried thyme	¾ teaspoon	
☐ Granulated sugar	2 teaspoons	
☐ Red pepper flakes	¼ teaspoon	
☐ Sweet potatoes	2 pounds	Butternut squash
☐ Garlic cloves	14 (2 heads)	
☐ Red onions	1 small, 1 medium	Onions
REFRIGERATOR		
☐ Maple syrup	10 tablespoons	
☐ Tahini	6 tablespoons	
☐ Soy sauce	2 tablespoons	
☐ Dijon mustard	2 teaspoons	
☐ Limes	5	
FREEZER		
☐ Bacon	6 slices	6 ounces pancetta

FOIL-BAKED CHICKEN *with* SWEET POTATOES *and* RADISHES

SERVES 4 | ACTIVE TIME 25 MINUTES

¼ cup oil

6 garlic cloves, sliced thin

1 tablespoon grated fresh ginger

¼ teaspoon red pepper flakes

12 ounces sweet potatoes, peeled and sliced crosswise ¼ inch thick

8 radishes, trimmed and quartered

1 small red onion, sliced ½ inch thick, layers separated

¾ teaspoon table salt, divided

4 (6- to 8-ounce) boneless, skinless chicken breasts, trimmed

½ teaspoon pepper

2 tablespoons minced fresh cilantro

Lime wedges

1. FOR THE CHICKEN PACKETS Adjust oven rack to lowest position and heat oven to 475 degrees. Microwave oil, garlic, ginger, and pepper flakes in large bowl until garlic begins to brown, about 1 minute. Add potatoes, radishes, onion, and ¼ teaspoon salt to oil mixture in bowl and toss to coat. Arrange four 12-inch sheets aluminum foil flat on counter and spray with vegetable oil spray.

2. Pat chicken dry with paper towels, then sprinkle with remaining ½ teaspoon salt and pepper. Divide potatoes evenly among foil, then arrange in 2 overlapping rows in center of each sheet foil. Top with chicken and remaining vegetables from bowl, drizzling with any remaining oil in bowl. Top each with 12-inch sheet foil and tightly crimp edges of foil together, until packet is well sealed, leaving as much headroom as possible so steam can circulate. Place packets on rimmed baking sheet, overlapping as needed.

3. TO FINISH Bake packets until chicken registers 160 degrees, 18 to 23 minutes (insert thermometer through packet into thick part of chicken). Carefully open packets, allowing steam to escape away from you, and let chicken rest for 5 minutes. Using thin metal spatula, gently slide chicken and vegetables, and any accumulated juices, onto individual plates. Sprinkle with cilantro and serve with lime wedges.

PREP AHEAD

- Peel and slice sweet potatoes
- Trim and quarter radishes
- Slice red onion
- Wash and pick cilantro

MAKE AHEAD

- Refrigerate fully assembled chicken packets for up to 1 day

NOTES FROM THE TEST KITCHEN

- Sub butternut squash for sweet potatoes
- Sub 1 small onion for red onion
- Sub scallions for cilantro

BEEF *and* BEAN CHILI

SERVES 4 TO 6 | ACTIVE TIME 35 MINUTES

2 (15-ounce) cans kidney beans, rinsed, divided

2 (14.5-ounce) cans diced tomatoes, divided

1½ pounds 85 percent lean ground beef

1 red onion, chopped fine

3 tablespoons chili powder

4 garlic cloves, minced

2 teaspoons ground cumin

2 teaspoons sugar

¼ cup chopped fresh cilantro

1. FOR THE CHILI Process half of beans and one can of tomatoes with their juice in food processor to coarse paste, about 30 seconds; set aside. Cook beef and onion in Dutch oven over medium heat, breaking up meat with wooden spoon, until meat is no longer pink, about 5 minutes. Stir in chili powder, garlic, cumin, and sugar and cook until fragrant, about 1 minute. Stir in reserved pureed bean-tomato mixture, remaining beans, and remaining can tomatoes with their juice, scraping up any browned bits.

2. Bring chili to vigorous simmer, then reduce heat to low and simmer, covered, stirring occasionally, until thickened slightly, about 15 minutes.

3. TO FINISH Off heat, season with salt and pepper to taste, and sprinkle with cilantro. Serve.

PREP AHEAD

- Chop onion
- Wash and pick cilantro

MAKE AHEAD

- Refrigerate chili for up to 3 days (or freeze for up to 1 month)

NOTES FROM THE TEST KITCHEN

- Serve with pickled jalapeños, shredded cheese, sour cream, diced avocado, or any of your favorite toppings
- This recipe can be easily doubled, and it freezes well
- Sub pinto or black beans for kidney beans
- Sub 1 (28-ounce) can crushed tomatoes for diced tomatoes
- Sub 1 onion for red onion
- Sub scallions for cilantro

MAPLE PORK CHOPS *with* SWEET POTATO–BACON HASH

SERVES 4 | ACTIVE TIME 40 MINUTES

1¼ pounds sweet potatoes, peeled and cut into ¾-inch pieces

6 slices bacon, chopped fine

4 (12-ounce) bone-in pork rib or center-cut chops, 1 to 1½ inches thick, trimmed

½ teaspoon table salt

¼ teaspoon pepper

¾ teaspoon dried thyme

½ cup maple syrup

1 tablespoon cider vinegar

2 teaspoons Dijon mustard

1. FOR THE SWEET POTATOES Microwave potatoes in covered bowl until tender, 4 to 7 minutes.

2. FOR THE BACON Meanwhile, cook bacon in 12-inch nonstick skillet over medium heat until crispy, 5 to 7 minutes. Using slotted spoon, transfer bacon to paper towel–lined bowl. Pour off fat, reserving 2 tablespoons.

3. FOR THE PORK CHOPS Cut slits about 2 inches apart into fat and underlying silverskin, opposite bone of chops. Pat chops dry with paper towels and sprinkle with salt and pepper. Heat 1 tablespoon reserved fat in now-empty skillet over medium-high heat until just smoking. Place chops in skillet in pinwheel formation and brown on both sides, 8 to 10 minutes; transfer to plate.

4. FOR THE HASH Add remaining 1 tablespoon reserved fat, potatoes, and thyme to again-empty skillet and cook, stirring occasionally, until well browned, 5 to 7 minutes. Stir in bacon and season with salt and pepper to taste. Transfer to serving bowl and cover to keep warm.

5. Add maple syrup, vinegar, and mustard to again-empty skillet and cook until thickened, about 2 minutes. Return pork chops to skillet along with any accumulated juices and simmer, turning often, until glaze coats chops and pork registers 140 to 145 degrees, about 2 minutes. Serve with hash.

PREP AHEAD

- Peel and cut sweet potatoes
- Chop bacon
- Trim pork chops, then cut slits about 2 inches apart into fat and underlying silverskin, opposite bone

MAKE AHEAD

- Refrigerate parcooked sweet potatoes for up to 1 day

NOTES FROM THE TEST KITCHEN

- Sub butternut squash for sweet potatoes
- Sub pancetta for bacon

SESAME NOODLES *with* SNOW PEAS, RADISHES, *and* BELL PEPPERS

SERVES 4 TO 6 | ACTIVE TIME 30 MINUTES

12 ounces fresh Chinese noodles

½ cup creamy or chunky peanut butter

6 tablespoons tahini

6 tablespoons lime juice, plus lime wedges for serving (4 limes)

2 tablespoons grated fresh ginger

2 tablespoons soy sauce

2 tablespoons maple syrup

4 garlic cloves, minced

½ teaspoon table salt

6 ounces snow peas, strings removed and halved lengthwise

1 red bell pepper, stemmed, seeded, and cut into ¼-inch-wide strips

5 radishes, trimmed, halved, and sliced thin

¼ cup chopped fresh cilantro

1. FOR THE NOODLES Bring 4 quarts water to boil in large pot. Add noodles and cook, stirring often, until almost tender. Drain noodles and rinse under cold running water until water runs clear. Drain well.

2. FOR THE SAUCE Meanwhile, whisk peanut butter, tahini, lime juice, ginger, soy sauce, maple syrup, garlic, and salt together in large bowl until well combined. Whisking constantly, add hot water, 1 tablespoon at a time (up to ¾ cup), until dressing has consistency of heavy cream.

3. TO FINISH Add drained noodles, snow peas, bell pepper, and radishes to sauce and toss well to combine. Season with salt and pepper to taste, and sprinkle with cilantro. Serve with lime wedges.

PREP AHEAD

- Juice limes
- Remove strings and halve snow peas
- Stem, seed, and cut bell pepper
- Trim, halve, and slice radishes
- Wash and pick cilantro

MAKE AHEAD

- Refrigerate cooked noodles for up to 2 days
- Refrigerate sauce for up to 2 days

NOTES FROM THE TEST KITCHEN

- Garnish with chopped peanuts, almonds, or sesame seeds, if you have any
- Sub 1 pound lo mein noodles, spaghetti, or linguine for fresh Chinese noodles
- Sub almond butter for peanut butter

MEAL PLAN 11

MEAL 1   Glazed Strip Steaks with Roasted Broccoli Rabe

MEAL 2   Italian Sausages with Balsamic Stewed Tomatoes

MEAL 3   Penne with Fresh Tomato Sauce

MEAL 4   Broccoli Rabe and Portobello Melts

MEAL 5   Choose a Pantry Recipe
(we suggest Fried Eggs with Potato and Parmesan Pancake)

WHY THIS MEAL PLAN WORKS

Simple Italian-inspired comfort foods make this plan a family favorite—and the short pantry list makes this a cook's favorite. True to Italian style, there are boldly flavored ingredients embedded in the comfort: broccoli rabe, balsamic vinegar, basil, and tomatoes. The chameleon-like sweet-sour quality of balsamic vinegar brightens the richness of glazed strip steaks, tempers the acidity of stewed tomatoes, and adds a mellowing element to sautéed broccoli rabe in the vegetarian melts. Assertive broccoli rabe is a favorite in Italian cuisine, and here we've shown you how to soften its natural bitterness while retaining all its flavor.

GROCERY LIST

PROTEIN		Substitutions
☐ Strip steaks	2 (1 pound each), 1 inch thick	*Flank steak*
☐ Sweet or hot Italian sausage	1½ pounds	
PRODUCE		
☐ Plum tomatoes	3½ pounds	*Cherry or grape tomatoes (for sausages); vine-ripened tomatoes (for penne)*
☐ Broccoli rabe	2¼ pounds	*Broccolini*
☐ Portobello mushroom caps	6	*18 ounces cremini mushrooms*
☐ Basil	1 bunch (enough for ½ cup chopped)	*Parsley*
DAIRY		
☐ Deli American cheese	8 slices (8 ounces)	*Provolone*
BREAD		
☐ Italian sub rolls	4 (8 inches long)	

PREP AHEAD

Core and chop tomatoes

Trim broccoli rabe; cut 12 ounces into ½-inch pieces

Thinly slice shallots

Remove gills from portobello mushroom caps; halve caps and thinly slice

Wash and pick basil

Trim steaks and halve crosswise

MAKE AHEAD

UP TO 3 DAYS	Make Italian Sausages with Balsamic Stewed Tomatoes
UP TO 1 DAY	Cook broccoli rabe and mushrooms for Broccoli Rabe and Portobello Melts

PANTRY ITEMS

CUPBOARD & COUNTER		Substitutions
☐ Penne	1 pound	*Ziti, farfalle, or campanelle*
☐ Oil	13 tablespoons	
☐ Balsamic vinegar	¼ cup plus ⅓ cup	
☐ Sugar	2½ teaspoons	
☐ Red pepper flakes	⅛ teaspoon	
☐ Shallots	11	*2 small onions (for sausages)*
☐ Garlic cloves	4	
REFRIGERATOR		
☐ Unsalted butter	2 tablespoons	
☐ Dry white wine	¼ cup	*Dry vermouth*
FREEZER		
☐ Crusty bread	1 (8- to 12-ounce) loaf	

GLAZED STRIP STEAKS *with* ROASTED BROCCOLI RABE

SERVES 4 | ACTIVE TIME 25 MINUTES

2 (1-pound) strip steaks, 1 inch thick, trimmed and halved crosswise

1½ plus ⅛ teaspoon table salt, divided

½ teaspoon pepper, divided

5 tablespoons oil, divided

1½ pounds broccoli rabe, trimmed

2 teaspoons sugar

3 shallots, sliced thin

⅓ cup balsamic vinegar

2 tablespoons unsalted butter

1. Adjust oven rack to lowest position and heat oven to 450 degrees. Pat steaks dry with paper towels and sprinkle with ½ teaspoon salt and ¼ teaspoon pepper. Heat 1 tablespoon oil in 12-inch skillet over medium-high heat until just smoking. Cook steaks until well browned and meat registers 120 to 125 degrees (for medium-rare), 3 to 5 minutes per side. Transfer to plate, tent with aluminum foil, and let rest while preparing broccoli rabe and sauce.

2. Meanwhile, toss broccoli rabe with sugar, 1 teaspoon salt, remaining ¼ teaspoon pepper, and 3 tablespoons oil on rimmed baking sheet. Roast until tender, about 10 minutes.

3. Add remaining 1 tablespoon oil to now-empty skillet and heat over medium-high heat until shimmering. Add shallots and remaining ⅛ teaspoon salt and cook until beginning to soften, about 1 minute. Add vinegar, scraping up any browned bits, and cook until slightly thickened, about 1 minute. Off heat, whisk in butter. Serve steaks with sauce and broccoli rabe.

PREP AHEAD

- Trim broccoli rabe
- Slice shallots
- Trim and halve steaks

NOTES FROM THE TEST KITCHEN

- Adding a little sugar to the broccoli rabe before roasting helps to tame its natural bitterness
- Sub flank steak for strip steaks
- Sub broccolini for broccoli rabe

ITALIAN SAUSAGES *with* BALSAMIC STEWED TOMATOES

SERVES 4 | ACTIVE TIME 25 MINUTES

1½ pounds sweet or hot Italian sausages

8 shallots, sliced thin

¼ cup dry white wine

2 tablespoons oil, divided

2 tablespoons balsamic vinegar, divided

1 tablespoon water

½ teaspoon table salt

¼ teaspoon pepper

1½ pounds plum tomatoes, cored and chopped

¼ cup chopped fresh basil

1 (8- to 12-ounce) loaf crusty bread

1. Combine sausages, shallots, wine, 1 tablespoon oil, 1 tablespoon vinegar, water, salt, and pepper in 12-inch nonstick skillet and bring to simmer over medium heat. Cover and cook until sausages are no longer pink and shallots are tender, about 8 minutes.

2. Uncover and increase heat to medium-high. Continue to cook until sausages are browned and register 160 degrees, about 3 minutes longer. Transfer sausages to platter.

3. Add tomatoes, remaining 1 tablespoon oil, and remaining 1 tablespoon vinegar to skillet. Cook until tomatoes begin to break down and sauce has thickened, 2 to 5 minutes. Stir in basil and season with salt and pepper to taste. Pour tomato mixture over sausages. Serve with bread.

PREP AHEAD

- Slice shallots
- Core and chop tomatoes
- Wash and pick basil

MAKE AHEAD

- Refrigerate sausages and stewed tomatoes for up to 3 days

NOTES FROM THE TEST KITCHEN

- You will need a 12-inch nonstick skillet with a tight-fitting lid
- Sub 2 small onions for shallots
- Sub dry vermouth for dry white wine
- Sub cherry or grape tomatoes for plum tomatoes
- Sub parsley for basil

PENNE *with* FRESH TOMATO SAUCE

SERVES 4 TO 6 | ACTIVE TIME 30 MINUTES

3 tablespoons oil

2 garlic cloves, minced

2 pounds plum tomatoes, cored and chopped

¾ teaspoon table salt

½ teaspoon pepper

½ teaspoon sugar

5 cups water, plus extra as needed

1 pound penne

2 tablespoons chopped fresh basil

1. Cook oil and garlic in Dutch oven over medium heat until fragrant, 1 to 2 minutes. Stir in tomatoes, salt, pepper, and sugar. Increase heat to medium-high and cook until tomatoes are broken down and sauce is slightly thickened, about 10 minutes.

2. Stir in water and pasta and bring to vigorous simmer. Reduce heat to medium, cover, and cook, stirring gently and often, until pasta is nearly tender, about 12 minutes; if sauce becomes too thick, add extra water as needed.

3. Uncover and continue to simmer, stirring often, until pasta is tender and sauce has thickened, 3 to 5 minutes. Off heat, stir in basil and season with salt and pepper to taste. Serve.

PREP AHEAD

- Core and chop tomatoes
- Wash and pick basil

NOTES FROM THE TEST KITCHEN

- Sub vine-ripened tomatoes for plum tomatoes
- Sub ziti, farfalle, or campanelle for penne
- Sub parsley for basil

BROCCOLI RABE *and* PORTOBELLO MELTS

SERVES 4 | ACTIVE TIME 35 MINUTES

3 tablespoons oil, divided

2 garlic cloves, sliced thin

⅛ teaspoon red pepper flakes

12 ounces broccoli rabe, trimmed and cut into ½-inch pieces

2 tablespoons water

½ teaspoon table salt

2 tablespoons balsamic vinegar

6 portobello mushroom caps, gills removed, halved, and sliced thin crosswise

8 slices (8 ounces) deli American cheese

4 (8-inch) Italian sub rolls, split lengthwise and toasted

1. FOR THE BROCCOLI RABE AND MUSHROOMS Heat 1 tablespoon oil in 12-inch nonstick skillet over medium heat until shimmering. Add garlic and pepper flakes and cook until fragrant, about 30 seconds. Stir in broccoli rabe, water, and salt. Cover and cook until broccoli rabe is bright green and crisp-tender, 3 to 4 minutes. Off heat, stir in vinegar, then transfer to bowl.

2. Heat remaining 2 tablespoons oil in now-empty skillet over medium-high heat until shimmering. Add mushrooms (skillet will be very full), cover, and cook, stirring occasionally, until mushrooms release their liquid, 6 to 8 minutes. Uncover and continue to cook until moisture has evaporated and mushrooms begin to brown, 6 to 8 minutes. Stir in cooked broccoli rabe and season with salt and pepper to taste.

3. TO FINISH Reduce heat to low and shingle cheese over vegetables. Cook until cheese is melted, about 2 minutes, then fold melted cheese thoroughly into mushroom mixture. Divide evenly among rolls. Serve.

PREP AHEAD

- Trim and cut broccoli rabe
- Remove gills, halve, and slice mushrooms

MAKE AHEAD

- Refrigerate cooked broccoli rabe and mushrooms for up to 1 day

NOTES FROM THE TEST KITCHEN

- Sub broccolini for broccoli rabe
- Sub 18 ounces cremini mushrooms for portobello mushroom caps
- Sub provolone for American cheese

MEAL PLAN 12

WHY THIS MEAL PLAN WORKS

Rich, bright flavors of spices and herbs infuse these meals. The cod foil packets (enlivened with chipotles and cilantro) can be fully assembled ahead, so all you need to do is bake them for 15 minutes before dinner is served. The light but satisfying tortellini salad, which is entirely make ahead, uses convenient store-bought cheese tortellini and helps use up the bunch of mint you buy this week (you also use it in the chicken). The flavor-packed make-ahead sauces for the chicken and steak elevate those meals far beyond the minimal work required. We recommend cooking the cod within 2 days of purchase (or see page 14 for short-term freezing).

GROCERY LIST

PROTEIN		Substitutions
☐ Skinless cod fillets	4 (6 to 8 ounces each), 1 inch thick	*Black sea bass, haddock, hake, or pollack*
☐ Bone-in chicken thighs	8 (5 to 7 ounces each)	
☐ Strip steaks	2 (1 pound each), 1½ inches thick	
PRODUCE		
☐ Cauliflower	1 head (2 pounds)	
☐ Asparagus	2 pounds	
☐ Cherry tomatoes	22 ounces	*Grape or vine-ripened tomatoes*
☐ Cremini mushrooms	12 ounces	*Shiitake or white mushrooms*
☐ Cilantro	1 small bunch (enough for ¼ cup chopped)	*Parsley*
☐ Mint	2 bunches (enough for 1½ cups chopped)	*Basil or parsley*
DAIRY		
☐ Sour cream	½ cup	
OTHER		
☐ Prepared horseradish	2 tablespoons	

PREP AHEAD

Cut potatoes into ¾-inch pieces

Core cauliflower and cut into 1-inch florets

Trim asparagus; cut 1 pound into 1-inch lengths

Halve 12 ounces cherry tomatoes

Quarter 10 ounces cherry tomatoes

Trim and quarter mushrooms

Wash and pick cilantro

Wash and pick mint

Juice 2 lemons (¼ cup)

Grate orange zest (¼ teaspoon)

Juice orange (2 tablespoons)

Grate Parmesan (½ cup)

Toast pine nuts

Trim and halve steaks crosswise

MAKE AHEAD

UP TO 2 DAYS	Make yogurt sauce for chicken thighs	
	Make sour cream sauce for steak	
	Make Tortellini Salad with Asparagus and Mint	
UP TO 1 DAY	Assemble packets for foil-baked cod	

PANTRY ITEMS

CUPBOARD & COUNTER		Substitutions
☐ Dried cheese tortellini	1 pound	
☐ Black beans	1 (15-ounce) can	*Pinto beans*
☐ Canned chipotle chile in adobo	2 teaspoons	
☐ Oil	10 tablespoons	
☐ Ground coriander	1½ teaspoons	
☐ Yukon Gold potatoes	1 pound	*Red potatoes*
☐ Garlic cloves	8	
REFRIGERATOR		
☐ Unsalted butter	8 tablespoons	
☐ Parmesan cheese	1 ounce	*Pecorino Romano*
☐ Plain whole-milk yogurt	½ cup	
☐ Lemons	2	
☐ Orange	1	*2 limes*
FREEZER		
☐ Frozen corn	2 cups	*Fresh corn*
☐ Pine nuts	¼ cup	*Walnuts*

CORIANDER CHICKEN
with **CAULIFLOWER** *and*
YOGURT SAUCE

SERVES 4 | ACTIVE TIME 45 MINUTES

½ cup plain whole-milk yogurt

3 tablespoons plus ½ cup chopped fresh mint, divided

1 tablespoon lemon juice

1¾ teaspoons table salt, divided

1 teaspoon pepper, divided

8 (5- to 7-ounce) bone-in chicken thighs, trimmed

1½ teaspoons ground coriander

2 tablespoons oil

1 head cauliflower (2 pounds), cored and cut into 1-inch florets

10 ounces cherry tomatoes, quartered

1 garlic clove, minced

1. FOR THE YOGURT SAUCE Combine yogurt, 3 tablespoons mint, lemon juice, ¼ teaspoon salt, and ¼ teaspoon pepper in bowl; set aside.

2. FOR THE CHICKEN AND CAULIFLOWER Adjust oven rack to middle position and heat oven to 450 degrees. Pat chicken dry, then sprinkle with coriander, ¾ teaspoon salt, and ½ teaspoon pepper. Heat oil in 12-inch nonstick skillet over medium-high heat until just smoking. Cook chicken skin side down until skin is browned and crispy, about 7 minutes. Flip chicken and continue to cook 3 minutes longer. Transfer chicken skin side up to rimmed baking sheet and roast until chicken registers 175 degrees, about 17 minutes.

3. Meanwhile, heat fat left in skillet over medium-high heat until shimmering. Add cauliflower, remaining ¾ teaspoon salt, and remaining ¼ teaspoon pepper and cook until tender and browned, stirring occasionally, 12 to 14 minutes. Off heat, stir in tomatoes and garlic. Transfer cauliflower to platter and sprinkle with remaining ½ cup mint. Serve chicken with cauliflower and reserved yogurt sauce.

PREP AHEAD

- Wash and pick mint
- Juice lemon
- Core and cut cauliflower
- Quarter cherry tomatoes

MAKE AHEAD

- Refrigerate yogurt sauce for up to 2 days

NOTES FROM THE TEST KITCHEN

- Sub grape tomatoes or vine-ripened tomatoes for cherry tomatoes
- Sub basil or parsley for mint

ONE-PAN STEAK *with* POTATOES, MUSHROOMS, *and* ASPARAGUS

SERVES 4 | ACTIVE TIME 45 MINUTES

- ½ cup sour cream
- 2 tablespoons prepared horseradish
- 2 tablespoons water
- 1½ plus ⅛ teaspoons table salt, divided
- 1¼ teaspoons pepper, divided
- 2 (1-pound) strip steaks, about 1½ inches thick, trimmed and halved crosswise
- 3 tablespoons unsalted butter, divided, plus 1 tablespoon melted
- 1 pound Yukon Gold potatoes, unpeeled, cut into ¾-inch pieces
- 12 ounces cremini mushrooms, trimmed and quartered
- 3 garlic cloves, sliced thin
- 1 pound asparagus, trimmed

1. FOR THE SOUR CREAM SAUCE Combine sour cream, horseradish, water, ¼ teaspoon salt, and ¼ teaspoon pepper in bowl; set aside.

2. FOR THE STEAK Adjust oven rack to middle position and heat oven to 400 degrees. Heat 12-inch cast-iron skillet over medium-high heat for 5 minutes. Pat steaks dry with paper towels and sprinkle with ¾ teaspoon salt and ½ teaspoon pepper. Melt 1 tablespoon butter in preheated skillet. Add steaks and cook until well browned on both sides, about 3 minutes per side. Transfer steaks to plate; set aside.

3. FOR THE VEGETABLES Add 2 tablespoons butter to now-empty skillet over medium-high heat. Stir in potatoes, mushrooms, ½ teaspoon salt, and remaining ½ teaspoon pepper. Cook, stirring occasionally, until vegetables are lightly browned, about 10 minutes. Add garlic and cook until fragrant, about 30 seconds.

4. Off heat, place asparagus in single layer on top of vegetables in skillet. Drizzle asparagus with melted butter and sprinkle with remaining ⅛ teaspoon salt. Place reserved steaks on top of asparagus.

5. TO FINISH Transfer skillet to oven and roast until steaks register 120 to 125 degrees (for medium-rare), 10 to 15 minutes. Tent skillet with aluminum foil and let steaks rest for 5 minutes. Serve with reserved sour cream sauce.

PREP AHEAD
- Cut potatoes
- Trim and quarter mushrooms
- Slice garlic
- Trim asparagus
- Trim and halve steaks

MAKE AHEAD
- Refrigerate sour cream sauce for up to 2 days

NOTES FROM THE TEST KITCHEN
- You can use a 12-inch nonstick skillet instead of cast iron, but make sure it's ovensafe to 400 degrees
- Sub red potatoes for Yukon Gold
- Sub shiitake or white mushrooms for cremini

FOIL-BAKED COD *with* BLACK BEANS *and* CORN

SERVES 4 | ACTIVE TIME 20 MINUTES

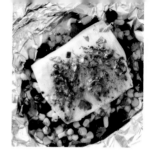

4 (6- to 8-ounce) skinless cod fillets, 1 inch thick

1½ teaspoons table salt, divided

¾ teaspoon pepper, divided

4 tablespoons unsalted butter, softened

2 teaspoons minced canned chipotle chile in adobo sauce, divided

¼ teaspoon grated orange zest plus 2 tablespoons juice

2 garlic cloves, minced, divided

1 (15-ounce) can black beans, rinsed

2 cups frozen corn

¼ cup chopped fresh cilantro, divided

1. FOR THE COD PACKETS Adjust oven rack to lower-middle position and heat oven to 450 degrees. Pat cod dry with paper towels and sprinkle with ½ teaspoon salt and ¼ teaspoon pepper. Using fork, mash butter, 1 teaspoon chipotle, orange zest, half of garlic, ½ teaspoon salt, and ¼ teaspoon pepper in bowl until combined. Spread butter mixture over tops of fillets.

2. Combine beans, corn, 2 tablespoons cilantro, orange juice, remaining 1 teaspoon chipotle, remaining garlic, remaining ½ teaspoon salt, and remaining ¼ teaspoon pepper in bowl. Arrange four 12-inch sheets of aluminum foil flat on counter. Divide bean mixture among foil sheets, arranging in center of each sheet, then top with fish. Top each with 12-inch sheet foil and tightly crimp edges of foil together until packet is well sealed, leaving as much headroom as possible so steam can circulate. Place packets on rimmed baking sheet, overlapping as needed.

3. TO FINISH Bake packets until cod registers 135 degrees, 15 to 20 minutes (insert thermometer through packet into thick part of fish). Carefully open packets, allowing steam to escape away from you. Using thin metal spatula, gently slide cod and vegetables, and any accumulated juices, onto individual plates. Sprinkle with remaining 2 tablespoons cilantro and serve.

PREP AHEAD

• Grate orange zest and juice orange

• Wash and pick cilantro

MAKE AHEAD

• Refrigerate assembled cod packets for up to 1 day

NOTES FROM THE TEST KITCHEN

• Sub black sea bass, haddock, hake, or pollock for cod

• Sub lime for orange

• Sub pinto beans for black beans

• Sub fresh corn for frozen

• Sub parsley for cilantro

TORTELLINI SALAD *with* ASPARAGUS *and* MINT

SERVES 4 TO 6 | ACTIVE TIME 30 MINUTES

1 pound asparagus, trimmed and cut into 1-inch lengths

1 teaspoon table salt, plus salt for cooking pasta and blanching asparagus

1 pound dried cheese tortellini

½ cup extra-virgin olive oil

3 tablespoons lemon juice

2 garlic cloves, minced

¾ teaspoon pepper

12 ounces cherry tomatoes, halved

1 ounce Parmesan cheese, grated (½ cup)

¾ cup chopped fresh mint

¼ cup pine nuts, toasted

1. Bring 4 quarts water to boil in large pot. Fill large bowl halfway with ice and water. Add asparagus and 1 tablespoon salt to boiling water and cook until crisp-tender, about 2 minutes. Using slotted spoon, transfer asparagus to ice water and let cool, about 2 minutes; drain and pat dry.

2. Return pot of water to boil. Add pasta and cook, stirring often, until tender. Drain pasta, rinse with cold water, and drain again, leaving pasta slightly wet.

3. Whisk oil, lemon juice, garlic, salt, and pepper together in large bowl. Add tortellini, asparagus, tomatoes, Parmesan, mint, and pine nuts and toss gently to combine. Season with salt and pepper to taste. Serve.

PREP AHEAD

- Trim and cut asparagus
- Juice lemon
- Halve cherry tomatoes
- Grate Parmesan
- Wash and pick mint
- Toast pine nuts

MAKE AHEAD

- Refrigerate tortellini salad for up to 2 days

NOTES FROM THE TEST KITCHEN

- Sub grape tomatoes or vine-ripened tomatoes for cherry tomatoes
- Sub Pecorino Romano for Parmesan
- Sub basil or parsley for mint
- Sub walnuts for pine nuts

MEAL PLAN 13

MEAL 1   Steak, Mushroom, and Spinach Rice Bowl

MEAL 2   Roasted Pork Tenderloin with Asparagus Salad

MEAL 3   Tortellini and Vegetable Soup with Pesto

MEAL 4   Shrimp Burgers

MEAL 5   Choose a Pantry Recipe *(we suggest Lentil Salad with Oranges, Celery, and Feta)*

Steak, Mushroom, and Spinach Rice Bowl
(page 136)

Roasted Pork Tenderloin with Asparagus Salad
(page 137)

Tortellini and Vegetable Soup with Pesto
(page 138)

Shrimp Burgers
(page 139)

Choose a Pantry Recipe
(we suggest Lentil Salad with Oranges, Celery, and Feta, page 251)

WHY THIS MEAL PLAN WORKS

A family-pleasing mix of comfort foods that are satisfying but not too heavy features in this plan. Prepared pesto transforms into a dressing for the asparagus salad and also serves as a rich finishing dollop for the tortellini and vegetable soup (which ingeniously uses V8 juice in the base). If you would like to make your own pesto, see page 33. Simply slicing steak and mushrooms, cooking rice for the rice bowl, and making the minestrone base in advance gets you far ahead on your meal prepping. The shrimp burger patties can be made entirely ahead of time, and since that recipe is easily doubled, you can freeze an extra batch of burgers for another meal down the road or for family members to pull out of the freezer anytime they need a quick meal.

GROCERY LIST

PROTEIN		Substitutions
☐ Sirloin steak tips	1 pound	
☐ Pork tenderloins	2 (12 to 16 ounces each)	
PRODUCE		
☐ Asparagus	1 pound	*Snap peas*
☐ Baby spinach	10 ounces	*Frozen spinach*
☐ Shiitake mushrooms	8 ounces	*Cremini mushrooms*
☐ Zucchini	1	*Summer squash*
☐ Scallions	4	
☐ Bibb lettuce	4 leaves	
OTHER		
☐ Fresh cheese tortellini (not frozen or dried)	9 ounces	
☐ Prepared pesto	1½ cups (12 ounces)	
☐ V8 juice	2½ cups	

PREP AHEAD

Finely chop onion

Trim and thinly slice asparagus

Stem and thinly slice shiitake mushrooms

Finely chop 3 scallions

Thinly slice 1 scallion

Peel and chop carrots

Halve zucchini lengthwise, seed, and chop

Separate and wash lettuce leaves

Juice lemon (3 tablespoons)

Thaw, peel, and devein shrimp

Trim and thinly slice steak tips

Finely chop bacon

MAKE AHEAD

UP TO 3 DAYS	Cook rice for rice bowl
	Make tortellini and vegetable soup base
UP TO 1 DAY	Shape shrimp burger patties (or freeze for up to 1 month)

PANTRY ITEMS

CUPBOARD & COUNTER		Substitutions
☐ Short-grain white rice	2 cups	
☐ Panko bread crumbs	1 cup	
☐ Cannellini beans	2 (15-ounce) cans	*Small white beans or chickpeas*
☐ Oil	⅔ cup	
☐ Seasoned rice vinegar	2 teaspoons	
☐ Brown sugar	1 tablespoon packed	
☐ Dry mustard	1 teaspoon	
☐ Dried oregano	1 teaspoon	*1 tablespoon chopped fresh oregano*
☐ Cayenne pepper	⅛ teaspoon	
☐ Garlic cloves	3	
☐ Onion	1	
REFRIGERATOR		
☐ Feta cheese	4 ounces	*Goat cheese*
☐ Eggs	4 large	
☐ Broth	3½ cups	
☐ Soy sauce	3 tablespoons	*Tamari*
☐ Mayonnaise	2 tablespoons	
☐ Sriracha	To taste	
☐ Carrots	2	
☐ Lemon	1	
FREEZER		
☐ Hamburger buns	4	
☐ Shrimp	1½ pounds, large (26 to 30 per pound)	
☐ Bacon	2 slices	*2 ounces pancetta or salt pork*

STEAK, MUSHROOM, *and* SPINACH RICE BOWL

SERVES 4 | ACTIVE TIME 35 MINUTES

2 cups water

2 cups short-grain white rice

2 teaspoons seasoned rice vinegar

1½ teaspoons table salt, divided

1 pound sirloin steak tips,
   trimmed and sliced thin

3 tablespoons soy sauce, divided

1 tablespoon packed brown sugar

¼ cup oil, divided

8 ounces shiitake mushrooms,
   stemmed and sliced thin

10 ounces (10 cups) baby spinach

4 large eggs

   Sriracha, for serving

1. FOR THE RICE Adjust oven rack to lower-middle position and heat oven to 200 degrees. Bring water, rice, vinegar, and 1¼ teaspoons salt to boil in medium saucepan over high heat. Cover, reduce heat to low, and cook until liquid is absorbed, 7 to 9 minutes. Remove rice from heat and let sit, covered, until tender, about 15 minutes. Fluff rice with fork and set aside.

2. FOR THE STEAK Toss steak with 2 tablespoons soy sauce and sugar in large bowl. Heat 1 tablespoon oil in 12-inch nonstick skillet over medium-high heat until just smoking. Add half of steak mixture and cook until well browned, 2 to 4 minutes. Transfer to clean bowl, tent loosely with aluminum foil, and repeat with 1 tablespoon oil and remaining steak.

3. TO FINISH Add 1 tablespoon oil, mushrooms, and remaining 1 tablespoon soy sauce to now-empty skillet and cook until mushrooms are soft, about 2 minutes. Add spinach and cook until wilted, 2 to 3 minutes; remove from heat. Portion rice into bowls and top with beef and mushroom-spinach mixture. Keep bowls warm in oven.

4. Wipe out skillet and heat remaining 1 tablespoon oil over medium heat until shimmering. Crack eggs into 2 small bowls (2 eggs in each) and sprinkle with remaining ¼ teaspoon salt. Working quickly, pour 1 bowl of eggs in 1 side of skillet and second bowl of eggs in other side. Cover and cook until whites are set, 2 to 3 minutes. Remove bowls from oven and top each with 1 egg. Serve with sriracha.

PREP AHEAD

- Stem and slice mushrooms
- Trim and slice steak tips

MAKE AHEAD

- Refrigerate cooked rice for up to 3 days

NOTES FROM THE TEST KITCHEN

- Serve with kimchi, if you have it
- Sub cremini mushrooms for shiitakes
- Sub frozen spinach for fresh
- Sub tamari for soy sauce

ROASTED PORK TENDERLOIN
with ASPARAGUS SALAD

SERVES 4 | ACTIVE TIME 30 MINUTES

1 cup pesto

3 tablespoons lemon juice

3 tablespoons oil, divided

2 teaspoons table salt, divided

1½ teaspoons pepper, divided

1 pound asparagus, trimmed and sliced thin on bias

1 (15-ounce) can cannellini beans, rinsed

2 (12- to 16-ounce) pork tenderloins, trimmed

1 teaspoon dry mustard

4 ounces feta cheese, crumbled (1 cup)

1 scallion, sliced thin

1. Adjust oven rack to middle position and heat oven to 375 degrees. Whisk pesto, lemon juice, 2 tablespoons oil, 1 teaspoon salt, and ½ teaspoon pepper in large bowl. Add asparagus and beans and toss to combine. Transfer to platter and set aside.

2. Pat pork dry with paper towels and sprinkle with mustard, remaining 1 teaspoon salt, and remaining 1 teaspoon pepper. Heat remaining 1 tablespoon oil in 12-inch nonstick skillet over medium-high heat until just smoking. Cook pork until well browned all over, about 8 minutes; transfer to rimmed baking sheet. Roast until pork registers 135 to 140 degrees, 12 to 15 minutes. Transfer pork to cutting board, tent with aluminum foil, and let rest for 5 minutes.

3. Slice pork on bias ½ inch thick and arrange alongside salad on platter. Sprinkle salad with feta and scallion. Serve.

PREP AHEAD

- Juice lemon
- Trim and slice asparagus
- Slice scallion

NOTES FROM THE TEST KITCHEN

- Sub snap peas for asparagus
- Sub small white beans or chickpeas for cannellini beans
- Sub goat cheese for feta

TORTELLINI *and* VEGETABLE SOUP *with* PESTO

SERVES 4 TO 6 | ACTIVE TIME 30 MINUTES

2 slices bacon, chopped fine

2 carrots, peeled and chopped

1 onion, chopped fine

3 garlic cloves, minced

1 teaspoon dried oregano

3½ cups broth

2½ cups V8 juice

1 (15-ounce) can cannellini beans, rinsed

9 ounces fresh cheese tortellini

1 zucchini, halved lengthwise, seeded, and chopped

½ cup pesto

1. FOR THE SOUP BASE Cook bacon in Dutch oven over medium heat until crispy, 5 to 7 minutes. Stir in carrots and onion and cook until onion is softened, about 5 minutes. Stir in garlic and oregano and cook until fragrant, about 30 seconds.

2. Stir in broth, juice, and beans, scraping up any browned bits. Bring to simmer and cook until beans are heated through and flavors meld, about 10 minutes.

3. TO FINISH Stir in tortellini and zucchini and simmer until tender, 5 to 7 minutes. Season with salt and pepper to taste. Dollop individual portions with pesto before serving.

PREP AHEAD

- Peel and chop carrots
- Chop onion
- Halve, seed, and chop zucchini
- Chop bacon

MAKE AHEAD

- Refrigerate soup base for up to 3 days

NOTES FROM THE TEST KITCHEN

- Sub 2 ounces pancetta or salt pork for bacon
- Sub 1 tablespoon chopped fresh oregano for dried
- Sub small white beans or chickpeas for cannellini beans
- Sub summer squash for zucchini

SHRIMP BURGERS

SERVES 4 | ACTIVE TIME 30 MINUTES

1 cup panko bread crumbs

1½ pounds large shrimp (26 to 30 per pound), thawed, peeled, and deveined

2 tablespoons mayonnaise

½ teaspoon table salt

¼ teaspoon pepper

⅛ teaspoon cayenne pepper

3 scallions, chopped fine

3 tablespoons oil

4 hamburger buns

4 leaves Bibb lettuce

1. FOR THE SHRIMP BURGERS Place panko in shallow dish. Place one-third of shrimp (1 cup), mayonnaise, salt, pepper, and cayenne in food processor and pulse until shrimp are finely chopped, about 8 pulses. Add remaining two-thirds of shrimp (2 cups) to shrimp mixture in processor and pulse until coarsely chopped, about 4 pulses, scraping down sides of bowl as needed. Transfer shrimp mixture to bowl and stir in scallions.

2. Divide shrimp mixture into 4 equal portions and pack into 3½-inch-wide patties. Working with one patty at a time, dredge both sides of patties in panko, pressing lightly to adhere, and transfer to plate.

3. TO FINISH Heat oil in 12-inch nonstick skillet over medium heat until shimmering. Place patties in skillet and cook until golden brown on first side, 3 to 5 minutes. Carefully flip and continue to cook until shrimp registers 140 to 145 degrees and second side is golden brown, 3 to 5 minutes longer. Transfer burgers to paper towel–lined plate and let drain, about 30 seconds per side. Serve burgers on buns with lettuce.

PREP AHEAD

- Chop scallions
- Separate and wash lettuce leaves
- Thaw, peel, and devein shrimp

MAKE AHEAD

- Refrigerate shaped burgers for up to 1 day (or freeze for up to 1 month)

NOTES FROM THE TEST KITCHEN

- Serve with lemon wedges, tartar sauce, cocktail sauce, or condiments of your choice
- This recipe can be easily doubled

MEAL PLAN 14

WHY THIS MEAL PLAN WORKS

Entire bunches of fresh dill and mint infuse this week's recipes with fragrance as well as flavor. This is a nice plan to tackle during a week when you have a bit more breathing room at dinnertime (although the poached salmon and the dressing for its cucumber salad can be made ahead, turning that into a superfast meal). Since the meatballs freeze so well and can be plucked from the freezer in whatever amount you need, it really pays off to make a double batch if you have time on the weekend. (Your family will thank you.) If you have leftover ginger from making the stir-fry, it keeps well in an airtight container in the freezer, and you can grate it next time right from frozen. We recommend cooking the salmon within 2 days of purchasing the fish (or see page 14 for short-term freezing).

GROCERY LIST

PROTEIN		Substitutions
☐ Skin-on salmon fillets	4 (6 to 8 ounces each), 1 inch thick	*Wild salmon or arctic char*
☐ Bone-in split chicken breasts	4 (10 to 12 ounces each)	
☐ Flank steak	1½ pounds	*Skirt steak*
☐ 85 percent lean ground beef	1½ pounds	*Ground lamb*
PRODUCE		
☐ Green beans	1 pound	
☐ Cucumbers	2	
☐ Scallions	4	
☐ Dill	1 bunch (enough for ½ cup chopped)	*Parsley (for salmon)*
☐ Mint	1 small bunch (enough for ¼ cup chopped)	*Parsley (for chicken)*
☐ Fresh ginger	1 small knob (enough for 1 tablespoon grated)	
OTHER		
☐ Harissa	2 tablespoons	

PREP AHEAD

Trim green beans and halve crosswise

Peel and shred carrots

Cut scallions into 1½-inch pieces, then quarter white parts lengthwise

Cut peel and pith from oranges and cut into segments; reserve juice

Grate lemon zest (2 teaspoons)

Juice lemons (¼ cup)

Peel cucumbers, then halve lengthwise, seed, and thinly slice

Wash and pick dill

Wash and pick mint

Trim flank steak, then cut lengthwise with grain into thirds and slice crosswise ⅛ inch thick

MAKE AHEAD

UP TO 3 DAYS	Cook meatballs (or freeze for up to 1 month)
UP TO 2 DAYS	Poach salmon fillets
	Make yogurt dressing for cucumber-dill salad
UP TO 1 DAY	Make lemon orzo
	Shape meatballs (or freeze for up to 1 month)

PANTRY ITEMS

CUPBOARD & COUNTER		Substitutions
☐ Orzo	1⅓ cups	White rice
☐ Chickpeas	1 (15-ounce) can	Small white beans
☐ Oil	¾ cup	
☐ Sugar	2 tablespoons	
☐ Cornstarch	1¾ teaspoons	
☐ Red pepper flakes	¼ teaspoon	
☐ Garlic	5 cloves	
REFRIGERATOR		
☐ Plain Greek yogurt	⅔ cup	
☐ Feta cheese	5 ounces	Goat cheese
☐ Broth	½ cup	
☐ Soy sauce	3 tablespoons	Tamari
☐ Mayonnaise	2 tablespoons	
☐ Mirin	1 tablespoon	
☐ Carrots	1 pound	
☐ Lemons	3	
☐ Oranges	2	
FREEZER		
☐ Hearty white sandwich bread	2 slices	

HERB-POACHED SALMON
with CUCUMBER-DILL SALAD

SERVES 4 | ACTIVE TIME 20 MINUTES

- 4 (6- to 8-ounce) skin-on salmon fillets, 1 inch thick

- ¼ cup chopped fresh dill, divided

- 1 tablespoon oil

- 1 teaspoon grated lemon zest plus 2 tablespoons juice, divided, plus lemon wedges for serving

- ¾ teaspoon table salt

- ¼ teaspoon pepper

- ¼ cup plain Greek yogurt

- 2 tablespoons mayonnaise

- 2 cucumbers, peeled, halved lengthwise, seeded, and sliced thin

1. FOR THE SALMON Adjust oven rack to middle position and heat oven to 250 degrees. Place 18 by 12-inch sheet aluminum foil flat on counter and spray center with vegetable oil spray. Pat salmon dry with paper towels and place fillets skin side down in center of foil. Top salmon with 2 tablespoons dill, oil, lemon zest and 1 tablespoon juice, salt, and pepper. Top with second 18 by 12-inch sheet foil and tightly crimp edges of foil together until packet is well sealed, leaving as much headroom as possible so steam can circulate.

2. Place packet on rimmed baking sheet, transfer to oven, and cook until salmon registers 125 degrees (for medium-rare), 45 minutes to 1 hour (insert thermometer through packet into thick part of fish). Carefully open packet, allowing steam to escape away from you, and let salmon cool to room temperature, about 30 minutes.

3. Pour off any accumulated liquid from packet, and using thin metal spatula, gently slide salmon to serving platter, discarding skin if desired.

4. FOR THE YOGURT DRESSING Whisk yogurt, mayonnaise, remaining 1 tablespoon lemon juice, and remaining 2 tablespoons dill together in bowl.

5. TO FINISH Stir cucumbers into yogurt dressing and season with salt and pepper to taste. Serve salmon with salad and lemon wedges.

PREP AHEAD

- Wash and pick dill

- Grate lemon zest and juice lemon

- Peel, seed, and slice cucumbers

MAKE AHEAD

- Refrigerate cooked salmon for up to 2 days

- Refrigerate yogurt dressing for up to 2 days

NOTES FROM THE TEST KITCHEN

- Sub wild salmon or arctic char for salmon (cook to 120 degrees)

- Sub parsley for dill

CRISPY CHICKEN *with* CARROT, ORANGE, *and* CHICKPEA SALAD

SERVES 4 | ACTIVE TIME 45 MINUTES

4 (10- to 12-ounce) bone-in split chicken breasts, trimmed

1 teaspoon table salt, divided

½ teaspoon pepper

2 oranges

2 tablespoons harissa

1 tablespoon lemon juice

1 pound carrots, peeled and shredded

1 (15-ounce) can chickpeas, rinsed

3 ounces feta cheese, cut into ½-inch pieces (¾ cup)

2 tablespoons chopped fresh mint

2 tablespoons oil

1. Pound thicker end of chicken breasts between 2 sheets of plastic wrap to ¾- to 1-inch thickness. Pat chicken dry with paper towels and sprinkle with ½ teaspoon salt and pepper. Place chicken skin side down in cold 12-inch nonstick skillet. Cover skillet, place over medium heat, and cook chicken, without moving, until skin is light golden brown, about 15 minutes.

2. Increase heat to medium-high and continue to cook chicken, covered, until skin is deep golden brown and crispy and breasts register 160 degrees, 10 to 15 minutes, rotating skillet halfway through cooking. Transfer chicken skin side up to serving platter, tent with aluminum foil, and let rest while finishing salad.

3. While chicken rests, cut away peel and pith from oranges. Holding fruit over bowl, use paring knife to slice between membranes to release segments. Cut segments in half crosswise and let drain in fine-mesh strainer set over large bowl, reserving juice. Whisk harissa, lemon juice, and remaining ½ teaspoon salt into reserved juice. Add orange segments and carrots and toss to combine.

4. Drain salad in fine-mesh strainer and return to now-empty bowl. Stir in chickpeas, feta, mint, and oil and season with salt and pepper to taste. Serve with chicken.

PREP AHEAD

- Cut peel and pith from oranges and segment oranges; reserve juice
- Juice lemon
- Peel and shred carrots
- Wash and pick mint

NOTES FROM THE TEST KITCHEN

- You will need a 12-inch nonstick skillet with a tight-fitting lid
- Sub small white beans for chickpeas
- Sub goat cheese for feta
- Sub parsley for mint

MEATBALLS *and* LEMON ORZO *with* MINT *and* DILL

SERVES 4 | ACTIVE TIME 40 MINUTES

1½ cups orzo

1 teaspoon table salt, plus salt for cooking orzo

1 teaspoon grated lemon zest plus 1 tablespoon juice

2 tablespoons chopped fresh mint, divided

2 tablespoons chopped fresh dill, divided

2 garlic cloves, minced, divided

6 tablespoons oil, divided

2 slices hearty white sandwich bread, torn into 1-inch pieces

⅓ cup plain Greek yogurt

1½ pounds 85 percent lean ground beef

½ teaspoon pepper

2 ounces feta cheese, crumbled (½ cup)

1. FOR THE ORZO Bring 3 quarts water to boil in large saucepan. Add orzo and 1 teaspoon salt and cook over medium heat until just tender, about 10 minutes. Drain and toss with lemon zest and juice, 1 tablespoon mint, 1 tablespoon dill, half of garlic, and 2 tablespoons oil. Season orzo with salt and pepper to taste.

2. FOR THE SHAPED MEATBALLS Using fork, mash bread with yogurt and 2 tablespoons water into paste in large bowl until smooth. Add beef, salt, pepper, remaining garlic, remaining 1 tablespoon mint, and remaining 1 tablespoon dill and, using hands, knead gently until combined. Pinch off and roll mixture into 24 tightly packed 1½-inch meatballs.

3. FOR THE COOKED MEATBALLS Heat remaining ¼ cup oil in 12-inch nonstick skillet over medium-high heat until just smoking. Add meatballs and cook until browned on all sides, 8 to 10 minutes.

4. TO FINISH Sprinkle orzo with feta and serve with meatballs.

PREP AHEAD

- Grate lemon zest and juice lemon
- Wash and pick mint
- Wash and pick dill

MAKE AHEAD

- Refrigerate orzo for up to 1 day
- Refrigerate shaped uncooked meatballs for up to 1 day (or freeze for up to 1 month)
- Refrigerate cooked meatballs for up to 3 days (or freeze for up to 1 month)

NOTES FROM THE TEST KITCHEN

- This recipe is easily doubled
- Sub rice (pages 34–35) for orzo
- Sub lamb for beef
- Sub goat cheese for feta

TERIYAKI STIR-FRIED BEEF
with GREEN BEANS

SERVES 4 | ACTIVE TIME 40 MINUTES

3 garlic cloves, minced

1 tablespoon grated fresh ginger

3 tablespoons oil, divided

½ cup broth

3 tablespoons soy sauce, divided

2 tablespoons sugar

1 tablespoon mirin

1¾ teaspoons cornstarch, divided

¼ teaspoon red pepper flakes

1½ pounds flank steak, trimmed, cut lengthwise with grain into thirds, then sliced crosswise ⅛ inch thick

1 pound green beans, trimmed and halved

2 tablespoons water

4 scallions, cut into 1½-inch pieces, white parts quartered lengthwise

1. Combine garlic, ginger, and 1 tablespoon oil in small bowl; set aside. Whisk broth, 2 tablespoons soy sauce, sugar, mirin, 1 teaspoon cornstarch, and pepper flakes in second bowl until sugar has dissolved; set aside. Toss beef with remaining 1 tablespoon soy sauce and remaining ¾ teaspoon cornstarch in third bowl.

2. Heat 2 teaspoons oil in 12-inch nonstick skillet over high heat until just smoking. Add half of beef and cook, tossing slowly but constantly, until no longer pink, 2 to 6 minutes; transfer to clean bowl. Repeat with 2 teaspoons oil and remaining beef.

3. Heat remaining 2 teaspoons oil in now-empty skillet over high heat until just smoking. Add green beans and cook, tossing slowly but constantly, until spotty brown, 2 to 6 minutes. Add water (water will spatter), cover, and cook until green beans are crisp-tender, 2 to 3 minutes.

4. Push green beans to one side of skillet and reduce heat to medium. Add garlic mixture to clearing and cook, mashing mixture into skillet, until fragrant, about 30 seconds. Stir garlic mixture into vegetables.

5. Whisk stir-fry sauce to recombine, then add to skillet along with scallions and beef with any accumulated juices. Increase heat to high and cook, tossing constantly, until sauce has thickened, about 30 seconds. Serve.

PREP AHEAD

- Trim and halve green beans
- Cut scallions
- Trim and cut flank steak

NOTES FROM THE TEST KITCHEN

- Instead of a 12-inch nonstick skillet with a tight-fitting lid, you can use a 14-inch flat-bottomed wok
- Serve with rice (pages 34–35), if you like
- Sub skirt steak for flank steak
- Sub tamari for soy sauce

MEAL PLAN 15

Green Chicken Chili
(page 152)

Pan-Seared Chicken with Warm Bulgur Pilaf
(page 153)

Chorizo and Bell Pepper Tacos with Salsa Verde
(page 154)

Spaghetti with Spring Vegetables
(page 155)

Choose a Pantry Recipe
(we suggest Garlicky White Beans with Shrimp, page 276)

WHY THIS MEAL PLAN WORKS

Chili is usually out of reach on weeknights because it requires too much simmering time, but we speed it up in our superflavorful chicken chili by using store-bought rotisserie chicken. (You can also make the entire chili up to three days ahead.) Between the chili and the chorizo tacos, we use a whole jar of green salsa. Sour cream lends creamy richness to these two recipes as well; you'll have some left over if you buy an 8-ounce carton, so if you prefer, substitute a container of Greek yogurt. Fresh tomatoes make a double appearance this week: in the hearty bulgur pilaf and the spaghetti (plus, our pantry recipe includes canned tomatoes).

GROCERY LIST

PROTEIN		Substitutions
☐ Boneless, skinless chicken breasts	4 (6 to 8 ounces each)	
☐ Rotisserie chicken	1 (2½ pounds)	
☐ Mexican-style chorizo sausage	1 pound	
PRODUCE		
☐ Cherry tomatoes	1 pound	*Grape or vine-ripened tomatoes*
☐ Asparagus	1 pound	
☐ Zucchini	1	
☐ Red bell pepper	1	*Poblano chile*
☐ Cilantro	1 bunch (enough for 1 cup chopped)	
☐ Parsley	1 bunch (enough for ¾ cup minced)	*Scallions*
☐ Chives	1 small bunch (enough for ¼ cup minced)	*Parsley or mint*
DAIRY		
☐ Sour cream	½ cup (4 ounces)	*Greek yogurt*
OTHER		
☐ Green salsa	1½ cups (16-ounce jar)	

PREP AHEAD

Trim asparagus and cut on bias into 1-inch lengths

Halve cherry tomatoes

Halve zucchini lengthwise and slice crosswise ¼ inch thick

Stem, seed, and thinly slice bell pepper

Finely chop onion

Juice lemon (2 tablespoons)

Juice lime (1 tablespoon)

Wash and pick cilantro

Wash and pick parsley

Grate Pecorino Romano (½ cup)

Halve olives

Pick rotisserie chicken and shred meat into bite-size pieces, discarding skin and bones

Remove casings from chorizo

MAKE AHEAD

UP TO 3 DAYS	Make chicken chili (or freeze for up to 1 month)	
	Cook bulgur for pilaf	
	Sear chicken breasts	
UP TO 2 DAYS	Make sour cream sauce for tacos	
	Cook taco filling	

PANTRY ITEMS

CUPBOARD & COUNTER

		Substitutions
☐ Spaghetti	1 pound	*Any strand pasta*
☐ Medium-grind bulgur (not cracked wheat)	1½ cups	
☐ Cannellini beans	2 (15-ounce) cans	*Small white beans*
☐ Oil	¾ cup	
☐ Ground cumin	1 tablespoon	
☐ Red pepper flakes	⅛ teaspoon	
☐ Garlic cloves	8	
☐ Onion	1	*4 large shallots*

REFRIGERATOR

☐ Feta cheese	4 ounces	*Goat cheese*
☐ Pecorino Romano cheese	1 ounce	*Parmesan*
☐ Broth	4 cups	
☐ Pitted kalamata olives	½ cup	*Any variety olives*
☐ Lemons	2	*Red wine vinegar (for chicken)*
☐ Lime	2	

FREEZER

☐ Corn tortillas	8 (6-inch) tortillas	*Flour tortillas*
☐ Frozen peas	1 cup	

GREEN CHICKEN CHILI

SERVES 4 | ACTIVE TIME 40 MINUTES

1 tablespoon oil

1 onion, chopped fine

¾ teaspoon pepper

½ teaspoon table salt

3 garlic cloves, minced

2 teaspoons ground cumin

4 cups broth

2 (15-ounce) cans cannellini beans, rinsed

1 cup jarred green salsa

1 (2½-pound) rotisserie chicken, skin and bones discarded, meat shredded into bite-size pieces (3 cups)

½ cup chopped fresh cilantro

¼ cup sour cream

1. FOR THE CHILI Heat oil in Dutch oven over medium heat until shimmering. Add onion, pepper, and salt and cook until softened, about 4 minutes. Stir in garlic and cumin and cook until fragrant, about 1 minute.

2. Increase heat to medium-high. Stir in broth, beans, and salsa and bring to boil. Reduce heat to medium-low and simmer until flavors have melded, about 10 minutes.

3. Using back of wooden spoon, mash some beans against side of pot until chili is slightly thickened. Stir in chicken and cilantro and cook until warmed through, about 2 minutes.

4. TO FINISH Dollop each bowl with 1 tablespoon sour cream and serve.

PREP AHEAD

- Chop onion
- Wash and pick cilantro
- Pick chicken and shred into pieces, discarding skin and bones

MAKE AHEAD

- Refrigerate chili for up to 3 days (or freeze for up to 1 month)

NOTES FROM THE TEST KITCHEN

- Serve with lime wedges, if you have them
- Sub 4 large shallots for onion
- Sub small white beans for cannellini beans

PAN-SEARED CHICKEN
with WARM BULGUR PILAF

SERVES 4 | ACTIVE TIME 40 MINUTES

1½ cups medium-grind bulgur, rinsed

½ teaspoon table salt, plus salt for cooking bulgur

4 (6- to 8-ounce) boneless, skinless chicken breasts, trimmed

¼ teaspoon pepper

3 tablespoons oil, divided

10 ounces cherry tomatoes, halved

4 ounces feta cheese, crumbled (1 cup)

¾ cup minced fresh parsley

½ cup pitted kalamata olives, halved

1 tablespoon lemon juice, plus lemon wedges for serving

1. FOR THE BULGUR Bring 2¼ cups water, bulgur, and ¼ teaspoon salt to boil in large saucepan over medium-high heat. Reduce heat to low, cover, and simmer gently until bulgur is tender, 16 to 18 minutes. Remove pot from heat and let sit, covered, for 10 minutes.

2. FOR THE CHICKEN Pat chicken dry with paper towels and sprinkle with salt and pepper. Heat 1 tablespoon oil in 12-inch skillet over medium-high heat until just smoking. Cook chicken until golden brown and meat registers 160 degrees, 6 to 8 minutes per side. Transfer to cutting board, tent with aluminum foil, and let rest for 5 minutes.

3. TO FINISH Fluff bulgur with fork, add tomatoes, feta, parsley, olives, lemon juice, and remaining 2 tablespoons oil and stir gently to combine. Season with salt and pepper to taste. Slice chicken breasts ¼ inch thick on bias. Serve with bulgur and lemon wedges.

PREP AHEAD

- Halve cherry tomatoes
- Wash and pick parsley
- Juice lemon

MAKE AHEAD

- Refrigerate cooked bulgur for up to 3 days
- Refrigerate seared chicken for up to 3 days

NOTES FROM THE TEST KITCHEN

- Sub grape or vine-ripened tomatoes for cherry tomatoes
- Sub goat cheese for feta
- Sub scallions for parsley
- Sub any variety olive for kalamata
- Sub red wine vinegar for lemon juice

CHORIZO *and* BELL PEPPER TACOS *with* SALSA VERDE

SERVES 4 | ACTIVE TIME 25 MINUTES

- ¼ cup sour cream
- 1 tablespoon water
- 1 tablespoon lime juice, plus lime wedges for serving
- ½ teaspoon table salt, divided
- 1 pound Mexican-style chorizo sausage, casings removed
- 1 red bell pepper, stemmed, seeded, and sliced thin
- 1 teaspoon ground cumin
- ⅛ teaspoon pepper
- ½ cup jarred green salsa, plus extra for serving
- 8 (6-inch) corn tortillas, warmed
- ½ cup chopped fresh cilantro

1. FOR THE SOUR CREAM SAUCE Combine sour cream, water, lime juice, and ¼ teaspoon salt in bowl; set aside.

2. FOR THE TACO FILLING Cook chorizo in 12-inch nonstick skillet over medium-high heat, breaking up meat with wooden spoon, until no longer pink, about 4 minutes. Stir in bell pepper, cumin, pepper, and remaining ¼ teaspoon salt. Continue to cook until bell pepper is just softened and meat is cooked through, about 4 minutes longer. Stir in salsa and cook until heated through, about 1 minute.

3. TO FINISH Divide filling among tortillas. Top with sour cream sauce, cilantro, and extra salsa. Serve with lime wedges.

PREP AHEAD

- Juice lime
- Stem, seed, and slice bell pepper
- Wash and pick cilantro
- Remove casings from chorizo

MAKE AHEAD

- Refrigerate sour cream sauce for up to 2 days
- Refrigerate taco filling for up to 2 days

NOTES FROM THE TEST KITCHEN

- Garnish with thinly sliced onion, if you have it
- Sub Greek yogurt for sour cream
- Sub poblano chile for bell pepper
- Sub flour tortillas for corn tortillas

SPAGHETTI *with* SPRING VEGETABLES

SERVES 4 TO 6 | ACTIVE TIME 45 MINUTES

6 tablespoons extra-virgin olive oil, divided, plus extra for drizzling

6 ounces cherry tomatoes, halved

5 garlic cloves (1 clove minced, 4 cloves sliced thin)

¾ teaspoon table salt, divided, plus salt for cooking pasta

1 zucchini, halved lengthwise then sliced crosswise ¼ inch thick

⅛ teaspoon red pepper flakes

1 cup frozen peas, thawed

1 pound asparagus, trimmed and cut on bias into 1-inch lengths

1 pound spaghetti

¼ cup minced fresh chives

1 tablespoon lemon juice

1 ounce Pecorino Romano cheese, grated (½ cup), divided

1. Toss 1 tablespoon oil, tomatoes, minced garlic, and ¼ teaspoon salt together in bowl; set aside.

2. Heat 3 tablespoons oil in 12-inch nonstick skillet over medium-low heat until shimmering. Add zucchini, pepper flakes, sliced garlic, and remaining ½ teaspoon salt; cover and cook, stirring occasionally, until zucchini softens and breaks down, 10 to 15 minutes. Add peas, asparagus, and ¾ cup water and bring to simmer over medium-high heat. Cover and cook until asparagus is crisp-tender, about 2 minutes.

3. Meanwhile, bring 4 quarts water to boil in large pot. Add pasta and 1 tablespoon salt and cook, stirring often, until al dente. Reserve ½ cup cooking water, then drain pasta and return it to pot.

4. Add remaining 2 tablespoons oil, vegetable mixture, chives, and lemon juice to pasta and toss to combine. Adjust consistency with reserved cooking water as needed. Transfer to serving bowl, sprinkle with ¼ cup Pecorino, and drizzle with extra oil to taste. Spoon tomatoes and their juices over top. Serve, passing remaining ¼ cup Pecorino separately.

PREP AHEAD

- Halve cherry tomatoes
- Halve and slice zucchini
- Trim and cut asparagus
- Juice lemon
- Grate Pecorino

NOTES FROM THE TEST KITCHEN

- Sub any strand pasta for spaghetti
- Sub grape or vine-ripened tomatoes for cherry tomatoes
- Sub parsley or mint for chives
- Sub Parmesan for Pecorino Romano

MEAL PLAN 16

MEAL 1 Roasted Salmon and Broccoli Rabe with Gremolata

MEAL 2 Chicken with Parsley Sauce and Celery Root Slaw

MEAL 3 Chicken Thighs with White Beans, Pancetta, and Kale

MEAL 4 Ground Beef Stroganoff with Egg Noodles

MEAL 5 Choose a Pantry Recipe
(we suggest 5-Ingredient Black Bean Soup)

WHY THIS MEAL PLAN WORKS

One-pot dishes can lighten the burden of weeknight cooking, and two of the recipes in this week's plan are just that: The elegant roasted salmon and broccoli rabe, in addition to being superfast, cooks all together on a sheet pan (and can also be assembled ahead and transferred directly from refrigerator to oven), while the hearty stroganoff is made entirely in a Dutch oven—noodles and all. You'll want your food processor for the bright parsley sauce that tops the chicken, but even so, that meal is on the table in less than half an hour. We recommend cooking the salmon within 2 days of purchasing the fish (or see page 14 for short-term freezing).

GROCERY LIST

PROTEIN		Substitutions
☐ Skinless salmon fillets	4 (6 to 8 ounces each), 1 inch thick	*Wild salmon or arctic char*
☐ Chicken cutlets	8 (4 ounces each)	
☐ Bone-in chicken thighs	8 (5 to 7 ounces each)	
☐ 85 percent lean ground beef	1 pound	*Ground pork*
☐ Pancetta	2 ounces	*2 slices bacon*
PRODUCE		
☐ Broccoli rabe	1 pound	*Broccolini*
☐ Celery root	1 large head (1 pound)	
☐ White mushrooms	8 ounces	*Cremini mushrooms*
☐ Baby kale	6 ounces (6 cups)	*Baby spinach*
☐ Parsley	2 large bunches (enough for 1 cup chopped plus 1½ cups leaves)	*Basil (for salmon)*
DAIRY		
☐ Sour cream	1 cup	*Greek yogurt*
OTHER		
☐ Prepared horseradish	2 tablespoons	

PREP AHEAD

Trim broccoli rabe and cut into 1½-inch pieces

Peel and shred celery root

Trim and thinly slice white mushrooms

Grate lemon zest (1 teaspoon)

Juice lemons (¼ cup)

Core apple and cut into ¼-inch-thick matchsticks

Finely chop onion

Wash and pick parsley

Toast and finely chop pistachios

Finely chop pancetta

MAKE AHEAD

UP TO 1 DAY	Assemble salmon and broccoli rabe on sheet pan
	Make gremolata for roasted salmon
	Make parsley sauce for chicken cutlets
	Cook ground beef for stroganoff (or freeze for up to 1 month)

PANTRY ITEMS

CUPBOARD & COUNTER		Substitutions
☐ Egg noodles	8 ounces (4 cups)	
☐ Cannellini beans	2 (15-ounce) cans	*Small white beans*
☐ Oil	⅔ cup	
☐ Dried rosemary	½ teaspoon	*1½ teaspoons chopped fresh rosemary*
☐ Red pepper flakes	Pinch	
☐ All-purpose flour	3 tablespoons	
☐ Garlic cloves	10	
☐ Granny Smith apple	1	*Any variety apple*
☐ Onion	1	*4 large shallots*
REFRIGERATOR		
☐ Broth	5¼ cups	
☐ Lemons	3	
FREEZER		
☐ Shelled pistachios	¼ cup	*Pine nuts*

ROASTED SALMON *and* BROCCOLI RABE *with* GREMOLATA

SERVES 4 | ACTIVE TIME 15 MINUTES

¼ cup shelled pistachios, toasted and chopped fine

2 tablespoons chopped fresh parsley

1 teaspoon grated lemon zest

2 garlic cloves, minced, divided

1 pound broccoli rabe, trimmed and cut into 1½-inch pieces

2 tablespoons plus 2 teaspoons oil, divided

¾ teaspoon table salt, divided

½ teaspoon pepper, divided

Pinch red pepper flakes

4 (6- to 8-ounce) skinless salmon fillets, 1 inch thick

1. FOR THE GREMOLATA Adjust oven rack to middle position and heat oven to 450 degrees. Combine pistachios, parsley, lemon zest, and half of garlic in small bowl; set aside.

2. FOR THE BROCCOLI RABE AND SALMON Toss broccoli rabe with 2 tablespoons oil, ¼ teaspoon salt, ¼ teaspoon pepper, pepper flakes, and remaining garlic in bowl. Arrange on one half of rimmed baking sheet. Pat salmon dry with paper towels, then rub with remaining 2 teaspoons oil and sprinkle with remaining ½ teaspoon salt and remaining ¼ teaspoon pepper. Arrange salmon on empty half of baking sheet, skin side down.

3. TO FINISH Roast until salmon registers 125 degrees (for medium-rare) and broccoli rabe is tender, about 10 minutes. Sprinkle individual portions with gremolata before serving.

PREP AHEAD

- Toast and chop pistachios
- Wash and pick parsley
- Grate lemon zest
- Trim and cut broccoli rabe

MAKE AHEAD

- Refrigerate gremolata for up to 1 day
- Refrigerate broccoli rabe and salmon on sheet pan for up to 1 day

NOTES FROM THE TEST KITCHEN

- Sub broccolini for broccoli rabe
- Sub basil for parsley
- Sub pine nuts for pistachios
- Sub wild salmon or arctic char for salmon (cook to 120 degrees)

CHICKEN *with* PARSLEY SAUCE *and* CELERY ROOT SLAW

SERVES 4 | ACTIVE TIME 25 MINUTES

½ cup chopped fresh parsley plus
   1½ cups leaves

¼ cup oil, divided

¼ cup lemon juice (2 lemons), divided

1 garlic clove, minced

½ cup sour cream

½ cup water

2 tablespoons prepared horseradish

1 large head celery root (1 pound),
   peeled and shredded

1 Granny Smith apple, cored and
   cut into ¼-inch-thick matchsticks

8 (4-ounce) chicken cutlets, trimmed

½ teaspoon table salt

¼ teaspoon pepper

1. FOR THE PARSLEY SAUCE Process parsley leaves, 3 tablespoons oil, 3 tablespoons lemon juice, and garlic in food processor until smooth, about 30 seconds, scraping down sides of bowl as needed. Season with salt and pepper to taste; set aside.

2. FOR THE SLAW AND CHICKEN Combine sour cream, water, chopped parsley, horseradish, and remaining 1 tablespoon lemon juice in medium bowl. Stir in celery root and apple and season with salt and pepper to taste.

3. Pat chicken dry with paper towels and sprinkle with salt and pepper. Heat remaining 1 tablespoon oil in 12-inch nonstick skillet over medium-high heat until just smoking. Add chicken and cook until golden, 3 to 5 minutes per side. Transfer to platter, top with parsley sauce, and serve with celery root slaw.

PREP AHEAD

- Wash and pick parsley
- Juice lemons
- Peel and shred celery root
- Core and cut apple

MAKE AHEAD

- Refrigerate parsley sauce for up to 1 day

NOTES FROM THE TEST KITCHEN

- Shred celery root on the large holes of a box grater or in a food processor fitted with the shredding disk
- Sub any variety apple for Granny Smith
- Sub Greek yogurt for sour cream

CHICKEN THIGHS *with* WHITE BEANS, PANCETTA, *and* KALE

SERVES 4 | ACTIVE TIME 40 MINUTES

8 (5- to 7-ounce) bone-in chicken thighs, trimmed

½ teaspoon table salt

½ teaspoon pepper, divided

2 teaspoons oil

2 ounces pancetta, chopped fine

5 garlic cloves, smashed and peeled

½ teaspoon dried rosemary

2 (15-ounce) cans cannellini beans, rinsed

1 cup broth

6 ounces (6 cups) baby kale

2 tablespoons chopped fresh parsley

Lemon wedges

1. Adjust oven rack to upper-middle position and heat oven to 450 degrees. Pat chicken dry with paper towels and sprinkle with salt and ¼ teaspoon pepper. Heat oil in 12-inch skillet over medium-high heat until just smoking. Add chicken skin side down and cook until well browned, 6 to 8 minutes.

2. Transfer chicken to rimmed baking sheet, skin side up (do not wipe out skillet), then transfer to oven and roast until chicken registers 175 degrees, 15 to 20 minutes. Remove chicken from oven, tent with aluminum foil, and let rest while finishing dish.

3. Meanwhile, pour off all but 1 tablespoon fat from skillet and heat over medium heat until shimmering. Add pancetta, garlic, and rosemary and cook until garlic is golden brown, about 3 minutes. Stir in beans, broth, and remaining ¼ teaspoon pepper. Bring to simmer and cook until slightly thickened, 5 to 7 minutes.

4. Stir in baby kale, reduce heat to medium-low, and cook until mostly wilted, about 2 minutes. Season with salt and pepper to taste. Top with chicken, sprinkle with parsley, and serve with lemon wedges.

PREP AHEAD

- Wash and pick parsley
- Chop pancetta

NOTES FROM THE TEST KITCHEN

- Sub small white beans for cannellini beans
- Sub baby spinach for baby kale
- Sub 1½ teaspoons chopped fresh rosemary for dried
- Sub bacon for pancetta

GROUND BEEF STROGANOFF
with EGG NOODLES

SERVES 4 | ACTIVE TIME 45 MINUTES

2 tablespoons oil, divided

8 ounces white mushrooms, trimmed and sliced thin

1 teaspoon table salt, divided

2 garlic cloves, minced

1 onion, chopped fine

¾ teaspoon pepper, divided

1 pound 85 percent lean ground beef

3 tablespoons all-purpose flour

4¼ cups broth

8 ounces (4 cups) egg noodles

½ cup sour cream

2 tablespoons chopped fresh parsley

1. FOR THE BEEF Heat 1 tablespoon oil in Dutch oven over medium-high heat until shimmering. Add mushrooms and ¼ teaspoon salt and cook until mushrooms begin to brown, 5 to 7 minutes; transfer to bowl.

2. Add remaining 1 tablespoon oil to now-empty pot and heat until shimmering. Add garlic, onion, ½ teaspoon salt, and ½ teaspoon pepper and cook, stirring occasionally, until beginning to soften, about 3 minutes. Add beef, remaining ¼ teaspoon salt, and remaining ¼ teaspoon pepper and cook, breaking up meat with wooden spoon, until no longer pink, 5 to 7 minutes.

3. FOR THE STROGANOFF Add flour and stir until beef is well coated; cook for 1 minute. Stir in broth and bring to simmer, scraping up any browned bits. Cook until mixture is slightly thickened, about 3 minutes. Stir in noodles, reduce heat to medium, and cook, uncovered, until noodles are tender, 10 to 12 minutes, stirring occasionally.

4. Off heat, stir in sour cream and mushrooms, and season with salt and pepper to taste. Sprinkle with parsley and serve.

PREP AHEAD

- Trim and slice mushrooms
- Chop onion
- Wash and pick parsley

MAKE AHEAD

- Refrigerate cooked beef for up to 1 day (or freeze for up to 1 month)

NOTES FROM THE TEST KITCHEN

- The ground beef mixture is easily doubled
- Sub cremini mushrooms for white mushrooms
- Sub 4 large shallots for onion
- Sub ground pork for ground beef
- Sub Greek yogurt for sour cream

MEAL PLAN 17

MEAL 1   **Curried Chicken Sandwiches with Apple-Yogurt Slaw**

MEAL 2   **Spicy Beef Lettuce Wraps with Oyster Sauce**

MEAL 3   **Spicy Pork Chops with Summer Vegetable Sauté**

MEAL 4   **Soba Noodles with Roasted Eggplant and Sesame**

MEAL 5   **Choose a Pantry Recipe**
(we suggest Black Beans and Rice with Eggs)

WHY THIS MEAL PLAN WORKS

Tell your family this is an eat-with-your-hands kind of week, since it includes the chicken sandwiches, the beef and lettuce wraps, and even the (shh, we won't tell) bone-in pork chops served with a modern succotash (you'll want a fork for that, but you'll use your hands to get every last morsel off the bones). This plan also has a summery feel—and it's even more fun to eat with your hands if you can do it outside. We use chili-garlic sauce and oyster sauce in two very different meals: first, a well-seasoned ground beef mixture served family-style, to be scooped into lettuce leaves by each diner, and second, simple yet substantial buckwheat noodles with eggplant that are just as good at room temperature as they are warm.

GROCERY LIST

PROTEIN		Substitutions
☐ Chicken cutlets	4 (4 ounces each)	
☐ 85 percent lean ground beef	1 pound	*Ground chicken or turkey (not 99 percent lean)*
☐ Bone-in pork rib or center-cut chops	4 (8 to 10 ounces each), ¾ to 1 inch thick	
PRODUCE		
☐ Eggplant	3 pounds	
☐ Summer squash	1 pound	*Zucchini*
☐ Bibb lettuce	1 head (8 ounces)	*Boston lettuce*
☐ Scallions	5	
☐ Corn	2 ears	*1½ cups frozen corn*
☐ Poblano chiles	2	*Green bell peppers*
☐ Red bell pepper	1	*Poblano chile*
☐ Jalapeño chile	1	*Habanero chile*
☐ Cilantro	1 bunch (enough for ¾ cup leaves plus ¼ cup chopped)	*Mint (for chicken); parsley (for pork chops)*
☐ Fresh ginger	1 knob (enough for 4 teaspoons grated)	

PREP AHEAD

Cut eggplant into 1-inch pieces

Cut summer squash into ½-inch pieces

Separate and wash Bibb lettuce leaves

Thinly slice scallions

Cut kernels from ears of corn

Stem, seed, and thinly slice poblanos

Stem, seed, and finely chop
red bell pepper

Stem, seed, and mince jalapeño

Chop onion

Peel and shred apple

Wash and pick cilantro

Toast sesame seeds

Trim pork chops, then cut slits about
2 inches apart into fat and underlying
silverskin, opposite bone

MAKE AHEAD

UP TO 3 DAYS	Cook chicken for chicken sandwiches
UP TO 2 DAYS	Roast eggplant for soba noodles
UP TO 1 DAY	Cook beef mixture for spicy beef lettuce wraps (or freeze for up to 1 month)
	Rub spice rub on pork chops

PANTRY ITEMS

CUPBOARD & COUNTER		Substitutions
☐ Dried soba noodles	12 ounces	
☐ Oil	¾ cup	
☐ All-purpose flour	½ cup	
☐ Sugar	⅓ cup	
☐ Curry powder	2 tablespoons	
☐ Paprika	1 teaspoon	
☐ Chili powder	1 teaspoon	
☐ Cayenne pepper	¼ teaspoon	
☐ Onion	1 small	*3 shallots*
☐ Granny Smith apple	1	*Any variety apple*
REFRIGERATOR		
☐ Plain Greek yogurt	1 cup	
☐ Oyster sauce	6 tablespoons	
☐ Soy sauce	⅓ cup	*Tamari*
☐ Toasted sesame oil	3 tablespoons	
☐ Asian chili-garlic sauce	2½ tablespoons	
☐ Shaoxing wine	2 tablespoons	*Dry sherry*
☐ Sake	5 teaspoons	*Dry vermouth*
☐ Lime	1	
FREEZER		
☐ Naan breads	4	*Pita or crusty bread*
☐ Sesame seeds	2 teaspoons	

CURRIED CHICKEN SANDWICHES *with* APPLE-YOGURT SLAW

SERVES 4 | ACTIVE TIME 30 MINUTES

1 Granny Smith apple, peeled and shredded

1¼ teaspoons table salt, divided

4 naan breads

½ cup all-purpose flour

2 tablespoons curry powder

¼ teaspoon cayenne pepper

4 (4-ounce) chicken cutlets, trimmed

3 tablespoons oil

1 cup plain Greek yogurt

1 jalapeño chile, stemmed, seeded, and minced

2 tablespoons chopped fresh cilantro

1 teaspoon grated fresh ginger

1. Adjust oven rack to middle position and heat oven to 400 degrees. Toss apple with ¼ teaspoon salt in colander, then set aside to drain for 10 minutes. Press to release excess liquid. Meanwhile, bake naan on rimmed baking sheet until light golden brown and beginning to crisp, about 10 minutes.

2. FOR THE CHICKEN Combine flour, curry powder, cayenne, and remaining 1 teaspoon salt in shallow dish. Pat chicken dry, then dredge cutlets in flour mixture, shaking off excess. Heat oil in 12-inch nonstick skillet over medium-high heat until just smoking. Add cutlets and cook until golden, 2 to 3 minutes per side. Transfer to cutting board, tent loosely with aluminum foil, and let rest for 5 minutes. Slice chicken ½ inch thick on bias.

3. TO FINISH Combine drained apple, yogurt, jalapeño, cilantro, and ginger in bowl, then season with salt and pepper to taste. Divide chicken evenly among naan, arranging slices over half of each naan, then top with apple slaw. Fold naan to cover filling and serve.

PREP AHEAD

- Peel and shred apple
- Stem, seed, and mince jalapeño
- Wash and pick cilantro

MAKE AHEAD

- Refrigerate cooked chicken for up to 3 days

NOTES FROM THE TEST KITCHEN

- Serve with Simplest Salad (page 32), if you like
- Sub any variety apple for Granny Smith
- Sub habanero chile for jalapeño (to taste)
- Sub mint for cilantro
- Sub pita or crusty bread for naan

SPICY BEEF LETTUCE WRAPS
with OYSTER SAUCE

SERVES 4 | ACTIVE TIME 20 MINUTES

¼ cup water

3 tablespoons oyster sauce

2 tablespoons Shaoxing wine

1 pound 85 percent lean ground beef

1 red bell pepper, stemmed, seeded, and chopped fine

5 scallions, sliced thin

1 tablespoon Asian chili-garlic sauce

1 tablespoon grated fresh ginger

1 head Bibb lettuce (8 ounces), leaves separated

1. FOR THE SAUCE Whisk water, oyster sauce, and Shaoxing wine together in bowl; set aside.

2. FOR THE BEEF Cook beef in 12-inch nonstick skillet over medium-high heat, breaking up meat with wooden spoon, until no longer pink, 3 to 5 minutes. Using slotted spoon, transfer beef to separate bowl.

3. Add bell pepper and scallions to fat left in skillet and cook until softened, about 3 minutes. Push vegetables to sides of skillet. Add chili-garlic sauce and ginger and cook, mashing mixture into skillet, until fragrant, about 30 seconds. Stir in beef and reserved oyster sauce mixture and cook until thickened, about 1 minute.

4. TO FINISH Serve with lettuce leaves as wraps or cups for beef.

PREP AHEAD

- Stem, seed, and chop red bell pepper
- Slice scallions
- Separate and wash lettuce leaves

MAKE AHEAD

- Refrigerate cooked beef for up to 1 day (or freeze for up to 1 month)

NOTES FROM THE TEST KITCHEN

- Serve with rice (pages 34–35), if you like
- Sub dry sherry for Shaoxing wine
- Sub ground chicken or turkey for ground beef
- Sub poblano chile for red bell pepper
- Sub Boston lettuce for Bibb

SPICY PORK CHOPS *with* SUMMER VEGETABLE SAUTÉ

SERVES 4 | ACTIVE TIME 35 MINUTES

1 teaspoon paprika

1 teaspoon chili powder

½ teaspoon table salt

½ teaspoon pepper

4 (8- to 10-ounce) bone-in pork rib or center-cut chops, ¾ to 1 inch thick, trimmed

2 tablespoons oil, divided

1 small onion, chopped

1 pound summer squash, cut into ½-inch pieces

2 poblano chiles, stemmed, seeded, and sliced thin

2 ears corn, kernels cut from cobs

2 tablespoons chopped fresh cilantro

Lime wedges

1. FOR THE SEASONED PORK CHOPS Combine paprika, chili powder, salt, and pepper in small bowl. Cut slits about 2 inches apart into fat and underlying silverskin, opposite bone of chops. Pat chops dry with paper towels and rub with spice mixture.

2. FOR THE CHOPS AND VEGETABLE SAUTÉ Heat 1 tablespoon oil in 12-inch nonstick skillet over medium heat until just smoking. Add chops and cook until well browned and chops register 140 to 145 degrees, about 5 minutes per side. Transfer to serving platter, tent with aluminum foil, and let rest while cooking vegetables.

3. Add remaining 1 tablespoon oil, onion, squash, poblanos, and corn to now-empty skillet and cook until softened, about 6 minutes. Stir in cilantro and season with salt and pepper to taste. Serve with pork chops and lime wedges.

PREP AHEAD

- Chop onion
- Cut summer squash
- Stem, seed, and slice poblanos
- Cut kernels from corn
- Wash and pick cilantro
- Trim pork chops, then cut slits about 2 inches apart into fat and underlying silverskin, opposite bone

MAKE AHEAD

- Refrigerate seasoned pork chops for up to 1 day

NOTES FROM THE TEST KITCHEN

- Sub zucchini for summer squash
- Sub green bell peppers for poblanos
- Sub 1½ cups frozen corn for fresh
- Sub 3 shallots for onion
- Sub parsley for cilantro

SOBA NOODLES *with* ROASTED EGGPLANT *and* SESAME

SERVES 4 | ACTIVE TIME 30 MINUTES

3 pounds eggplant, cut into 1-inch pieces

¼ cup oil

⅓ cup soy sauce, divided

12 ounces dried soba noodles

⅓ cup sugar

3 tablespoons oyster sauce

3 tablespoons toasted sesame oil

5 teaspoons sake

1½ tablespoons Asian chili-garlic sauce

¾ cup fresh cilantro leaves

2 teaspoons sesame seeds, toasted

1. FOR THE ROASTED EGGPLANT Adjust oven racks to upper-middle and lower-middle positions and heat oven to 450 degrees. Line 2 rimmed baking sheets with aluminum foil and spray with vegetable oil spray. Toss eggplant with oil and 1 tablespoon soy sauce, then spread evenly on prepared baking sheets. Roast until eggplant is well browned and tender, 25 to 30 minutes, stirring eggplant and switching sheets halfway through roasting.

2. FOR THE NOODLES Meanwhile, bring 4 quarts water to boil in large pot. Add noodles and cook, stirring often, until tender. Reserve ½ cup cooking water, then drain noodles.

3. Cook sugar, oyster sauce, sesame oil, sake, chili-garlic sauce, and remaining soy sauce in now-empty pot over medium heat, whisking often, until sugar has dissolved, about 1 minute. Add roasted eggplant and noodles to pot with sauce and toss gently to combine. Adjust consistency with reserved cooking water as needed. Sprinkle with cilantro and sesame seeds. Serve.

PREP AHEAD

- Cut eggplant
- Wash and pick cilantro
- Toast sesame seeds

MAKE AHEAD

- Refrigerate roasted eggplant for up to 2 days

NOTES FROM THE TEST KITCHEN

- Sub tamari for soy sauce
- Sub dry vermouth for sake

MEAL PLAN 18

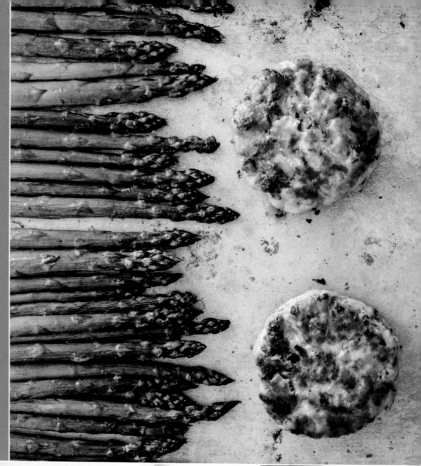

MEAL 1 Salmon Burgers with Asparagus and Lemon Mayo

MEAL 2 Chicken with Spring Vegetables, Capers, and Lemon

MEAL 3 Herbed Steaks with Lemon-Garlic Potatoes

MEAL 4 Grilled Pork Tenderloin and Summer Squash with Chimichurri

MEAL 5 Choose a Pantry Recipe
(we suggest Creamy Stovetop Macaroni and Cheese)

WHY THIS MEAL PLAN WORKS

Our heads were filled with thoughts of early summer when we designed this meal plan, making the most of ingredients including salmon, asparagus (used in two recipes), summer squash, bright herbs, and zesty lemon. We extended the summery feel of these meals by turning the salmon into burgers and grilling our pork tenderloin and summer squash before topping them with a potent chimichurri sauce. The salmon burgers can be shaped ahead of time and refrigerated, along with their bright lemony topping. And the baked chicken-and-vegetables dinner can be fully assembled in its baking dish and refrigerated, ready to pop into the oven for hands-free cooking on a particularly busy evening.

GROCERY LIST

PROTEIN		Substitutions
☐ Skinless salmon	1 pound	*Wild salmon or arctic char*
☐ Bone-in split chicken breasts	4 (10 to 12 ounces each)	
☐ Strip steaks	2 (1 pound each)	
☐ Pork tenderloins	2 (12 to 16 ounces each)	
PRODUCE		
☐ Asparagus	1½ pounds	
☐ Cherry tomatoes	8 ounces	*Grape tomatoes*
☐ Summer squash	4	*Zucchini*
☐ Bibb lettuce	1 small head	
☐ Parsley	2 bunches (enough for ¾ cup minced plus ⅔ cup chopped)	*Basil (for chicken); basil or cilantro (for steaks)*
☐ Cilantro	1 bunch (enough for ¼ cup minced)	

PREP AHEAD

Trim asparagus; halve 8 ounces crosswise

Cut potatoes into 1-inch pieces

Cut summer squashes into ½-inch-thick lengths

Juice lemons (3 tablespoons plus 2 teaspoons)

Chop shallot

Wash and pick cilantro

Wash and pick parsley

Cut salmon into 1-inch pieces

Trim pork tenderloins and pound ½ inch thick

MAKE AHEAD

UP TO 2 DAYS	Shape salmon patties (or freeze for up to 1 month)
	Assemble chicken and vegetables in baking dish
UP TO 1 DAY	Make lemon mayo for salmon burgers
	Make chimichurri for pork tenderloin

PANTRY ITEMS

CUPBOARD & COUNTER		Substitutions
☐ Oil	1¼ cups	
☐ Red wine vinegar	3 tablespoons	
☐ Brown sugar	1 tablespoon packed	
☐ Dried oregano	½ teaspoon	
☐ Red potatoes	1¼ pounds	*Yukon Gold potatoes*
☐ Garlic cloves	9	
☐ Shallot	1	
REFRIGERATOR		
☐ Jarred whole artichoke hearts packed in water	10-ounce jar (enough for 1½ cups)	*Frozen artichoke hearts*
☐ Capers	3 ½-ounce jar (enough for 5 tablespoons)	
☐ Mayonnaise	6 tablespoons	
☐ Dijon mustard	5 teaspoons	*Spicy brown mustard*
☐ Lemons	2	*White wine vinegar (for salmon)*
FREEZER		
☐ Hamburger buns	5	

SALMON BURGERS *with* ASPARAGUS *and* LEMON MAYO

SERVES 4 | ACTIVE TIME 25 MINUTES

- 6 tablespoons mayonnaise, divided
- 3 tablespoons chopped fresh parsley, divided
- 1 tablespoon lemon juice
- 5 hamburger buns, 1 bun torn into 1-inch pieces, 4 buns toasted, if desired
- 1 pound skinless salmon, cut into 1-inch pieces
- 1 tablespoon Dijon mustard
- 2 teaspoons capers, rinsed and minced
- ½ teaspoon table salt, divided
- ⅛ teaspoon plus ¼ teaspoon pepper, divided
- 1 pound asparagus, trimmed
- 1 teaspoon oil
- 4 leaves Bibb lettuce

1. Adjust oven rack 4 inches from broiler element and heat broiler. Line rimmed baking sheet with aluminum foil.

2. FOR THE LEMON MAYO Whisk ¼ cup mayonnaise, 1 tablespoon parsley, and lemon juice together in bowl. Season with salt and pepper to taste; set aside for serving.

3. FOR THE SALMON BURGERS Pulse bun pieces in food processor to fine crumbs, about 4 pulses; transfer to large bowl. Working in 2 batches, pulse salmon in now-empty food processor until coarsely ground, about 4 pulses; transfer to bowl with bread crumbs and toss to combine. Add mustard, capers, ¼ teaspoon salt, ⅛ teaspoon pepper, remaining 2 tablespoons mayonnaise, and remaining 2 tablespoons parsley and, using hands, knead gently until combined. Divide salmon mixture into 4 equal portions and pack gently into 1-inch-thick patties. Place patties on 1 side of prepared sheet.

4. TO FINISH Toss asparagus with oil, remaining ¼ teaspoon salt, and remaining ¼ teaspoon pepper and spread in single layer on empty side of sheet. Broil until burgers are lightly browned on top, 4 to 6 minutes. Flip burgers and asparagus and continue to broil until burgers register 125 degrees (for medium-rare) and asparagus is lightly browned and tender, 3 to 6 minutes.

5. Spread reserved lemon mayo on bun tops. Place burgers on buns and top with lettuce. Serve with asparagus.

PREP AHEAD

- Wash and pick parsley
- Juice lemon
- Trim asparagus
- Cut salmon

MAKE AHEAD

- Refrigerate shaped salmon patties for up to 2 days (or freeze for up to 1 month)
- Refrigerate lemon mayo for up to 1 day

NOTES FROM THE TEST KITCHEN

- Sub white wine vinegar for lemon juice
- Sub wild salmon or arctic char for salmon (cook to 120 degrees)
- Sub spicy brown mustard for Dijon

CHICKEN *with* SPRING VEGETABLES, CAPERS, *and* LEMON

SERVES 4 | ACTIVE TIME 20 MINUTES

½ cup oil

6 tablespoons chopped fresh parsley, divided

1 shallot, chopped

6 garlic cloves, minced

1½ teaspoons salt, divided

½ teaspoon pepper, divided

2 tablespoons lemon juice plus ½ lemon sliced into ¼-inch-thick rounds

1½ cups jarred whole artichoke hearts packed in water, drained and patted dry

8 ounces cherry tomatoes

¼ cup capers, rinsed

4 (10- to 12-ounce) bone-in split chicken breasts, trimmed

8 ounces asparagus, trimmed and halved crosswise

1. FOR THE CHICKEN AND VEGETABLES Adjust oven rack to middle position and heat oven to 450 degrees. Process oil, ¼ cup parsley, shallot, garlic, 1 teaspoon salt, and ¼ teaspoon pepper in food processor until smooth, about 20 seconds, scraping down sides of bowl as needed. Transfer ¼ cup marinade to bowl and stir in lemon juice; set dressing aside for serving.

2. In large bowl, toss 2 tablespoons marinade with artichokes, tomatoes, capers, lemon slices, remaining ½ teaspoon salt, and remaining ¼ teaspoon pepper; transfer to 13 by 9-inch baking dish. Toss chicken with remaining marinade in now-empty bowl, then lay chicken skin side up on top of vegetables in dish.

3. TO FINISH Bake until chicken registers 160 degrees, about 45 minutes. Transfer chicken to cutting board, tent with aluminum foil, and let rest while finishing vegetables. Stir asparagus into vegetables in dish and bake until asparagus is crisp-tender, about 10 minutes. Sprinkle vegetables with remaining 2 tablespoons parsley and whisk reserved dressing to recombine. Serve vegetables with chicken, drizzling with dressing.

PREP AHEAD

- Wash and pick parsley
- Chop shallot
- Juice lemon
- Trim and halve asparagus

MAKE AHEAD

- Refrigerate assembled chicken and vegetables for up to 2 days

NOTES FROM THE TEST KITCHEN

- Sub basil for parsley
- Sub frozen artichoke hearts for jarred
- Sub grape tomatoes for cherry tomatoes

HERBED STEAKS *with* LEMON-GARLIC POTATOES

SERVES 4 | ACTIVE TIME 35 MINUTES

2 (1-pound) strip steaks, trimmed and halved crosswise

1¼ teaspoon table salt, divided

¾ teaspoon pepper, divided

3 tablespoons oil, divided

1¼ pounds red potatoes, unpeeled, cut into 1-inch pieces

2 garlic cloves, minced

2 teaspoons lemon juice

2 teaspoons Dijon mustard

½ cup minced fresh parsley

1. Pat steaks dry with paper towels and sprinkle with ½ teaspoon salt and ¼ teaspoon pepper. Heat 1 tablespoon oil in 12-inch non-stick skillet over medium-high heat until just smoking. Add steaks and cook until well browned and meat registers 120 to 125 degrees (for medium-rare), 3 to 5 minutes per side. Transfer steaks to platter, tent with aluminum foil, and let rest while finishing dish.

2. Meanwhile, toss potatoes, 1 tablespoon oil, remaining ¾ teaspoon salt, and remaining ½ teaspoon pepper together in bowl. Microwave, covered, until tender, 4 to 7 minutes.

3. Heat remaining 1 tablespoon oil in now-empty skillet over medium-high heat until just smoking. Add potatoes and cook until browned, about 6 minutes. Stir in garlic and cook until fragrant, about 30 seconds. Off heat, stir in lemon juice and season with salt and pepper to taste.

4. Brush tops of steaks evenly with mustard and sprinkle with parsley. Serve with potatoes.

PREP AHEAD

- Cut potatoes
- Juice lemon
- Wash and pick parsley
- Trim and halve steaks

NOTES FROM THE TEST KITCHEN

- Sub Yukon Gold potatoes for red potatoes
- Sub spicy brown mustard for Dijon
- Sub basil or cilantro for parsley

GRILLED PORK TENDERLOIN *and* SUMMER SQUASH *with* CHIMICHURRI

SERVES 4 | ACTIVE TIME 30 MINUTES

6 tablespoons oil, divided

¼ cup minced fresh parsley

¼ cup minced fresh cilantro

3 tablespoons red wine vinegar

1 garlic clove, minced

½ teaspoon dried oregano

1 teaspoon table salt, divided

½ teaspoon pepper, divided

2 (12- to 16-ounce) pork tenderloins, trimmed and pounded ½ inch thick

1 tablespoon packed brown sugar

4 summer squashes, cut into ½-inch-thick lengths

1. FOR THE CHIMICHURRI Combine ¼ cup oil, parsley, cilantro, vinegar, garlic, oregano, ¼ teaspoon salt, and ¼ teaspoon pepper in bowl; set aside.

2. FOR THE PORK AND SQUASH Sprinkle pork with sugar, ½ teaspoon salt, and remaining ¼ teaspoon pepper. Brush squash with remaining 2 tablespoons oil and sprinkle with remaining ¼ teaspoon salt.

3. Place pork on grill over hot fire. Grill until pork is lightly browned and registers 135 to 140 degrees, about 2 minutes per side. Transfer pork to cutting board, tent with aluminum foil, and let rest while grilling squash.

4. Grill squash until charred and tender, 3 to 5 minutes per side; transfer to platter. Slice pork ½ inch thick on bias and transfer to platter with squash. Top with chimichurri and serve.

PREP AHEAD

- Wash and pick parsley
- Wash and pick cilantro
- Cut summer squashes
- Trim and pound pork tenderloins

MAKE AHEAD

- Refrigerate chimichurri for up to 1 day

NOTES FROM THE TEST KITCHEN

- We prefer a half-grill fire (page 25)
- Sub zucchini for summer squash

MEAL PLAN 19

WHY THIS MEAL PLAN WORKS

Super-healthy and hearty kale and butternut squash are spread creatively among three quite different meals in this week's plan to prevent leftover produce. The one-pan chicken breasts use both kale and squash; the vegetables can be prepped and assembled on the baking sheet and refrigerated until ready to bake, and the chicken can be seasoned ahead and then placed on the vegetables just before baking. The strip steaks make use of the remaining kale in a creamy, rich side dish, while the quesadillas incorporate the remaining squash—they're a delicious example of how only five ingredients (not counting oil and salt) can be transformed into a healthier version of a family favorite. And if you prep all of the vegetables and meat for the pork stir-fry ahead of time, the stir-frying itself goes very quickly.

GROCERY LIST

PROTEIN		Substitutions
☐ Bone-in split chicken breasts	4 (10 to 12 ounces each)	
☐ Strip steaks	2 (1 pound each), 1 inch thick	
☐ Pork tenderloins	2 (12 to 16 ounces each)	
PRODUCE		
☐ Butternut squash	3 pounds	*Sweet potatoes*
☐ Curly kale	2 pounds	*Lacinato kale*
☐ Eggplant	1 pound	
☐ Poblano chiles	4	*3 red bell peppers*
☐ Cilantro	1 bunch (enough for ½ cup chopped)	
DAIRY		
☐ Pepper Jack cheese	8 ounces	*Monterey Jack, cheddar, or a mix of cheeses*

PREP AHEAD

Peel and seed squash; cut 2 pounds into 1-inch pieces (6 cups), cut 1 pound into ½-inch pieces (3 cups)

Stem kale, then cut into 2-inch pieces

Cut eggplant into ¾-inch pieces

Stem, halve, and seed poblanos, then slice into ½-inch-wide strips

Mince 12 garlic cloves

Halve 8 shallots; thinly slice 1 shallot

Cut onion into ¼-inch-thick wedges

Grate lemon zest (1 teaspoon)

Juice lime (2 teaspoons)

Wash and pick cilantro

Shred pepper Jack cheese (2 cups)

Trim and halve chicken breasts

Trim and halve strip steaks

Trim pork tenderloins, then halve lengthwise and thinly slice crosswise

MAKE AHEAD

UP TO 3 DAYS	Microwave squash for quesadillas
	Prepare squash-poblano mixture for quesadillas
UP TO 2 DAYS	Blanch kale for steaks
UP TO 1 DAY	Make yogurt sauce for roast chicken
	Make and dress vegetable mixture for roast chicken
	Season chicken

PANTRY ITEMS

CUPBOARD & COUNTER

			Substitutions
☐ Oil	1 cup plus 2 teaspoons		
☐ Light brown sugar	2½ tablespoons packed		
☐ Cornstarch	1¾ teaspoons		
☐ Honey	2 teaspoons		
☐ Paprika	2 teaspoons		
☐ Garlic cloves	17 (2 heads)		
☐ Shallots	9		*2 onions (for roast chicken)*
☐ Onion	1 large		

REFRIGERATOR

☐ Heavy cream	1½ cups		
☐ Plain yogurt	¾ cup		
☐ Fish sauce	3 tablespoons		
☐ Soy sauce	3 tablespoons		*Tamari*
☐ Broth	2 tablespoons		
☐ Lime	1		
☐ Lemon	1		

FREEZER

☐ 10-inch flour tortillas	4		

ONE-PAN ROAST CHICKEN BREASTS *with* BUTTERNUT SQUASH *and* KALE

SERVES 4 | ACTIVE TIME 25 MINUTES

½ cup oil

2 teaspoons honey

1½ teaspoons table salt

¾ cup plain yogurt

1 tablespoon water

1 garlic clove, minced

1 teaspoon grated lemon zest

8 ounces curly kale, stemmed and cut into 2-inch pieces

2 pounds butternut squash, peeled, seeded, and cut into 1-inch pieces (6 cups)

8 shallots, halved

2 teaspoons paprika

4 (10- to 12-ounce) bone-in split chicken breasts, trimmed and halved crosswise

1. Adjust oven rack to upper-middle position and heat oven to 475 degrees. Whisk oil, honey, and salt together in large bowl until combined.

2. FOR THE YOGURT SAUCE In separate bowl, whisk yogurt, water, garlic, lemon zest, and 1 tablespoon oil mixture together; set yogurt sauce aside until ready to serve.

3. FOR THE DRESSED VEGETABLES Vigorously squeeze and massage kale with hands until leaves are uniformly darkened and slightly wilted, about 2 minutes. Toss massaged kale, squash, shallots, and ¼ cup oil mixture together on rimmed baking sheet.

4. FOR THE SEASONED CHICKEN Whisk paprika into remaining oil mixture, then add chicken and toss to coat.

5. TO FINISH Place chicken skin side up on top of vegetables and bake until chicken registers 160 degrees, 25 to 35 minutes, rotating sheet halfway through baking. Transfer chicken to serving platter, tent with aluminum foil, and let rest for 5 minutes. Transfer vegetables to platter with chicken, then drizzle with ¼ cup reserved yogurt sauce. Serve, passing remaining yogurt sauce separately.

PREP AHEAD

- Grate lemon zest
- Stem and cut kale
- Peel, seed, and cut butternut squash
- Halve shallots
- Trim and halve chicken breasts

MAKE AHEAD

- Refrigerate yogurt sauce for up to 1 day
- Refrigerate dressed vegetable mixture for up to 1 day
- Refrigerate seasoned chicken for up to 1 day

NOTES FROM THE TEST KITCHEN

- Sub Lacinato kale for curly kale
- Sub sweet potatoes for butternut squash
- Sub 2 large onions for shallots

STRIP STEAKS *with* CREAMED KALE

SERVES 4 | ACTIVE TIME 35 MINUTES

1½ pounds curly kale, stemmed and cut into 2-inch pieces

½ teaspoon table salt, plus salt for cooking kale

2 tablespoons oil, divided

4 garlic cloves, sliced thin

1 shallot, sliced thin

1½ cups heavy cream

½ teaspoon pepper, divided

2 (1-pound) strip steaks, 1 inch thick, trimmed and halved crosswise

Lemon wedges, for serving

1. FOR THE BLANCHED KALE Bring 4 quarts water to boil in Dutch oven over high heat. Add kale and 2 tablespoons salt and cook until wilted, about 2 minutes. Drain kale in colander, pressing with rubber spatula to remove excess water; set aside.

2. TO FINISH KALE Heat 1 tablespoon oil in now-empty pot over medium heat until shimmering. Add garlic and shallot and cook until just softened, about 2 minutes. Stir in kale and cook until any remaining water has evaporated, about 2 minutes. Add cream and ¼ teaspoon pepper and cook until cream is thickened and clings to kale, about 3 minutes. Remove pot from heat and cover to keep warm.

3. FOR THE STEAKS Pat steaks dry with paper towels and sprinkle with salt and remaining ¼ teaspoon pepper. Heat remaining 1 tablespoon oil in 12-inch nonstick skillet over medium-high heat until just smoking. Add steaks and cook, flipping every 2 minutes, until well browned and meat registers 120 to 125 degrees (for medium-rare), 10 to 12 minutes. Transfer steaks to platter, tent with aluminum foil, and let rest for 5 minutes. Serve steaks with kale and lemon wedges.

PREP AHEAD

- Stem and cut kale
- Slice shallot
- Trim and halve steaks

MAKE AHEAD

- Refrigerate blanched kale for up to 2 days

NOTES FROM THE TEST KITCHEN

- Flipping the steaks every 2 minutes increases their temperature gradually, allowing a crust to build up on the outside without overcooking the interior
- Sub Lacinato kale for curly kale

GARLICKY STIR-FRIED PORK, EGGPLANT, *and* ONIONS

SERVES 4 | ACTIVE TIME 45 MINUTES

12 garlic cloves, minced

¼ cup oil, divided

2 teaspoons pepper

3 tablespoons fish sauce, divided

3 tablespoons soy sauce, divided

2½ tablespoons packed light brown sugar

2 tablespoons broth

2 teaspoons lime juice

1¾ teaspoons cornstarch, divided

2 (12- to 16-ounce) pork tenderloins, trimmed, halved lengthwise, then sliced thin crosswise

1 pound eggplant, cut into ¾-inch pieces

1 large onion, cut into ¼-inch-thick wedges

¼ cup coarsely chopped fresh cilantro

1. Combine garlic, 1 tablespoon oil, and pepper in small bowl; set aside. Whisk 2½ tablespoons fish sauce, 2½ tablespoons soy sauce, sugar, broth, lime juice, and 1 teaspoon cornstarch in second small bowl until sugar has dissolved; set aside. Toss pork with remaining 1½ teaspoons fish sauce, 1½ teaspoons soy sauce, and ¾ teaspoon cornstarch until well combined.

2. Heat 2 teaspoons oil in 12-inch nonstick skillet over medium-high heat until just smoking. Add half of pork and increase heat to high. Cook, tossing pork slowly but constantly, until no longer pink, 2 to 6 minutes; transfer to large bowl. Repeat with 2 teaspoons oil and remaining pork.

3. Heat 1 tablespoon oil in now-empty skillet over high heat until just smoking. Add eggplant and cook, tossing slowly but constantly, until spotty brown, about 8 minutes; transfer to bowl with pork. Heat remaining 2 teaspoons oil in again-empty skillet over high heat until just smoking. Add onion and cook, tossing slowly but constantly, until just beginning to brown, about 2 minutes.

4. Push onion to one side of skillet and reduce heat to medium. Add garlic mixture to clearing and cook, mashing mixture into skillet, until fragrant, about 30 seconds. Stir garlic mixture into onion. Whisk fish sauce mixture to recombine, then add to skillet along with pork-eggplant mixture and any accumulated juices. Increase heat to high and cook, tossing constantly, until sauce has thickened, about 30 seconds. Sprinkle with cilantro and serve.

PREP AHEAD

- Mince garlic
- Juice lime
- Cut eggplant
- Cut onion
- Wash and pick cilantro
- Trim, halve, and slice pork

NOTES FROM THE TEST KITCHEN

- Instead of a 12-inch nonstick skillet, you can use a 14-inch flat-bottomed wok
- Serve with rice (pages 34–35), if you like
- Sub tamari for soy sauce

BUTTERNUT, POBLANO, *and* CHEESE QUESADILLAS

SERVES 4 | ACTIVE TIME 40 MINUTES

- 1 pound butternut squash, peeled, seeded, and cut into ½-inch pieces (3 cups)

- 2 tablespoons plus 2 teaspoons oil, divided

- 4 poblano chiles, stemmed, halved, seeded, and cut into ½-inch-wide strips

- ½ teaspoon table salt

- ¼ cup chopped fresh cilantro

- 8 ounces pepper Jack cheese, shredded (2 cups)

- 4 (10-inch) flour tortillas

1. FOR THE SQUASH Microwave squash in covered bowl until tender, 8 to 12 minutes, stirring halfway through. Drain squash well and return to bowl.

2. FOR THE SQUASH-POBLANO MIXTURE Meanwhile, heat 2 tablespoons oil in 12-inch nonstick skillet over medium heat until shimmering. Add poblanos and cook, stirring frequently, until spotty brown and tender, 10 to 12 minutes. Transfer to bowl with squash and stir in salt and cilantro. Wipe out skillet with paper towels.

3. FOR THE QUESADILLAS Sprinkle cheese evenly over half of each tortilla, leaving ½-inch border around edges. Top cheese with squash mixture, then fold tortillas over filling and press down firmly. Brush tops of quesadillas with 1 teaspoon oil. Place 2 quesadillas in now-empty skillet, oiled side down. Cook over medium heat until crispy and well browned, about 2 minutes. Brush tops of quesadillas in skillet with ½ teaspoon oil. Using two spatulas, carefully flip quesadillas and cook until second side is crispy and well browned, 1 to 2 minutes. Transfer to serving platter and repeat with remaining 2 quesadillas. Serve.

PREP AHEAD

- Peel, seed, and cut squash

- Stem, halve, seed, and slice poblanos

- Wash and pick cilantro

- Shred cheese

MAKE AHEAD

- Refrigerate microwaved squash for up to 3 days

- Refrigerate squash-poblano mixture for up to 3 days

NOTES FROM THE TEST KITCHEN

- Depending on the strength of your microwave, you may need to adjust the cooking time of the squash

- Serve with sour cream, salsa, guacamole, or any of your favorite quesadilla toppings

- Sub sweet potatoes for squash (microwave time may be shorter)

- Sub red bell peppers for poblanos

- Sub Monterey Jack, cheddar, or a mix of cheeses for pepper Jack

MEAL PLAN 20

MEAL 1 Pan-Seared Chicken Breasts with Chickpea Salad

MEAL 2 Pan-Seared Steak Tips with Roasted Potatoes and Horseradish Cream

MEAL 3 Spiced Pork Lettuce Wraps with Avocado and Mango

MEAL 4 Orecchiette with Broccoli, Currants, and Pine Nuts

MEAL 5 Choose a Pantry Recipe
(we suggest Kimchi Fried Rice with Shrimp)

WHY THIS MEAL PLAN WORKS

Only one of this week's meals clocks in with an active cooking time of more than half an hour; in fact, one dinner—the Spiced Pork Lettuce Wraps with Mango and Avocado—is a deliciously fun finger-food meal that will make you feel like a rock star when you're able to get it to the table in a mere 20 minutes. Some crispy oven-roasted potatoes and a versatile chickpea salad make up our crowd-pleasing sides this week. Try the salad another time with pork chops or stirred into rice for a hearty vegetarian dinner. And the orecchiette is a great one-dish meal that's really elevated by the addition of pine nuts and dried currants. The carton of sour cream on the grocery list gets all used up between the zesty, creamy horseradish sauce for the steak tips and the minty spiced sauce for the pork wraps.

GROCERY LIST

PROTEIN		Substitutions
☐ Boneless, skinless chicken breasts	4 (6 to 8 ounces each)	
☐ Sirloin steak tips	2 pounds	
☐ Ground pork	1 pound	
PRODUCE		
☐ Broccoli florets	1 pound	
☐ Bibb lettuce	1 head (8 ounces)	Green-leaf lettuce
☐ Avocado	1	
☐ Mango	1	
☐ Mint	1 bunch (enough for ½ cup chopped)	Cilantro (for chicken or pork); parsley (for chicken)
DAIRY		
☐ Sour cream	1 cup (8 ounces)	Greek yogurt
OTHER		
☐ Prepared horseradish	¼ cup	

PREP AHEAD

Halve potatoes

Separate and wash
Bibb lettuce leaves

Peel, pit, and finely chop mango

Thinly slice red onion

Wash and pick mint

Juice lemons (6 tablespoons)

Toast pine nuts

Grate Parmesan (1 cup)

Trim steak and cut into 2-inch pieces

MAKE AHEAD

UP TO 2 DAYS	Cook pork mixture for pork lettuce wraps (or freeze for up to 1 month)
UP TO 1 DAY	Season chicken breasts
	Make chickpea salad for chicken
	Make horseradish cream for steak tips
	Make sour cream sauce for pork lettuce wraps

PANTRY ITEMS

CUPBOARD & COUNTER		Substitutions
☐ Orecchiette	1 pound	Any short pasta
☐ Chickpeas	2 (15-ounce) cans	Small white beans
☐ Oil	⅔ cup	
☐ Honey	2 teaspoons	
☐ Ground cumin	2 teaspoons	
☐ Smoked paprika	1½ teaspoons	
☐ Small Yukon Gold potatoes (1- to 2-inch diameter)	1½ pounds	Small red potatoes
☐ Garlic cloves	6	
☐ Red onion	1	4 large shallots
☐ Dried currants	½ cup	Chopped raisins
REFRIGERATOR		
☐ Parmesan cheese	2 ounces	Pecorino Romano
☐ Broth	1 cup	
☐ Sriracha	1 tablespoon	Asian chili-garlic sauce
☐ Lemons	2	
FREEZER		
☐ Pine nuts	½ cup	Walnuts

PAN-SEARED CHICKEN BREASTS *with* CHICKPEA SALAD

SERVES 4 | ACTIVE TIME 30 MINUTES

6 tablespoons oil, divided

2 teaspoons honey

1½ teaspoons smoked paprika

1 teaspoon ground cumin

1 teaspoon table salt, divided

¾ teaspoon pepper, divided

¼ cup lemon juice (2 lemons)

2 (15-ounce) cans chickpeas, rinsed

½ red onion, sliced thin

4 (6- to 8-ounce) boneless, skinless chicken breasts, trimmed

¼ cup chopped fresh mint

1. FOR THE CHICKPEA SALAD Whisk 5 tablespoons oil, honey, paprika, cumin, ½ teaspoon salt, and ½ teaspoon pepper together in bowl. Measure out and reserve 2 tablespoons oil mixture in large bowl. Whisk lemon juice into remaining oil mixture, then stir in chickpeas and onion; set aside until ready to serve.

2. FOR THE CHICKEN Add chicken to 2 tablespoons reserved oil mixture in bowl and toss to coat; let sit for at least 20 minutes.

3. TO FINISH Pat chicken dry with paper towels and sprinkle with remaining ½ teaspoon salt and remaining ¼ teaspoon pepper. Heat remaining 1 tablespoon oil in 12-inch nonstick skillet over medium-high heat until just smoking. Add chicken and cook, turning as needed, until golden and chicken registers 160 degrees, about 12 minutes. Transfer chicken to large plate, tent with aluminum foil, and let rest for 5 minutes.

4. Stir mint into reserved chickpea mixture and season with salt and pepper to taste. Serve with chicken.

PREP AHEAD

- Juice lemons
- Slice onion
- Wash and pick mint

MAKE AHEAD

- Refrigerate chickpea salad for up to 1 day
- Refrigerate seasoned chicken for up to 1 day

NOTES FROM THE TEST KITCHEN

- Sub small white beans for chickpeas
- Sub 2 large shallots for red onion
- Sub cilantro or parsley for mint

PAN-SEARED STEAK TIPS
with ROASTED POTATOES *and* HORSERADISH CREAM

SERVES 4 | ACTIVE TIME 25 MINUTES

½ cup sour cream

¼ cup prepared horseradish

1½ teaspoon table salt, divided

¾ teaspoon pepper, divided

1½ pounds small Yukon Gold potatoes, unpeeled, halved

2 tablespoons oil, divided

2 pounds sirloin steak tips, trimmed and cut into 2-inch pieces

1. Adjust oven rack to lower-middle position and heat oven to 450 degrees.

2. FOR THE HORSERADISH CREAM Combine sour cream, horseradish, ½ teaspoon salt, and ¼ teaspoon pepper in bowl; set aside.

3. FOR THE POTATOES Toss potatoes, 1 tablespoon oil, ½ teaspoon salt, and ¼ teaspoon pepper together on rimmed baking sheet. Arrange potatoes cut side down on sheet and roast until tender and bottoms are well browned, about 25 minutes.

4. FOR THE STEAKS Meanwhile, pat steak tips dry with paper towels and sprinkle with remaining ½ teaspoon salt and remaining ¼ teaspoon pepper. Heat remaining 1 tablespoon oil in 12-inch nonstick skillet over medium-high heat until just smoking. Add steak tips and cook until well browned on all sides and meat registers 120 to 125 degrees (for medium-rare), about 7 minutes. Transfer to serving platter, tent with aluminum foil, and let rest for 5 minutes. Serve steak with potatoes and horseradish cream.

PREP AHEAD

- Halve potatoes
- Trim and cut steak tips

MAKE AHEAD

- Refrigerate horseradish cream for up to 1 day

NOTES FROM THE TEST KITCHEN

- Sub Greek yogurt for sour cream
- Sub red potatoes for Yukon Gold

SPICED PORK LETTUCE WRAPS
with AVOCADO *and* MANGO

SERVES 4 | ACTIVE TIME 20 MINUTES

½ cup sour cream

2 tablespoons chopped fresh mint

2 tablespoons water

1 teaspoon ground cumin, divided

1½ teaspoons table salt, divided

¾ teaspoon pepper, divided

1 pound ground pork

1 tablespoon sriracha

2 garlic cloves, minced

1 head Bibb lettuce (8 ounces), leaves separated

1 avocado, halved, pitted, and sliced thin

1 mango, peeled, pitted, and chopped fine

1. FOR THE SOUR CREAM SAUCE Whisk sour cream, mint, water, ¼ teaspoon cumin, ½ teaspoon salt, and ¼ teaspoon pepper together in bowl; set aside.

2. FOR THE COOKED PORK Cook pork in 12-inch nonstick skillet over medium-high heat, breaking up meat with wooden spoon, until no longer pink, about 4 minutes. Stir in sriracha, garlic, remaining 1 teaspoon salt, remaining ¾ teaspoon cumin, and remaining ½ teaspoon pepper and cook until fragrant, about 2 minutes.

3. TO FINISH Transfer pork to large serving platter with lettuce, avocado, and mango. Serve, passing sour cream sauce separately.

PREP AHEAD

• Wash and pick mint

• Separate and wash lettuce leaves

• Peel, pit, and chop mango

MAKE AHEAD

• Refrigerate cooked pork mixture for up to 2 days (or freeze for up to 1 month)

• Refrigerate sour cream sauce for up to 1 day

NOTES FROM THE TEST KITCHEN

• Serve with rice (pages 34–35), if you like

• Sub Greek yogurt for sour cream

• Sub green-leaf lettuce for Bibb

• Sub cilantro for mint

• Sub Asian chili-garlic sauce for sriracha

ORECCHIETTE *with* BROCCOLI, CURRANTS, *and* PINE NUTS

SERVES 4 | ACTIVE TIME 35 MINUTES

1 pound orecchiette

Table salt for cooking pasta

1 pound broccoli florets

2 tablespoons oil

½ red onion, sliced thin

½ cup pine nuts, toasted

4 garlic cloves, minced

1 cup broth

½ cup dried currants

2 ounces Parmesan cheese, grated (1 cup)

2 tablespoons lemon juice

1. Bring 4 quarts water to boil in large pot. Add pasta and 1 tablespoon salt and cook for 6 minutes. Add broccoli and cook until pasta is tender, broccoli is bright green, and florets start to break down, about 5 minutes. Reserve ½ cup cooking water, then drain pasta and broccoli and return them to pot.

2. Meanwhile, heat oil in 12-inch skillet over medium-high heat until shimmering. Add onion and cook until softened, about 3 minutes. Add pine nuts and garlic and cook until fragrant, about 30 seconds. Stir in broth and currants and simmer until reduced slightly, about 4 minutes.

3. Add sauce to pasta and toss to combine (broccoli should break up into bits). Stir in Parmesan and lemon juice and adjust consistency with reserved cooking water as needed. Season with salt and pepper to taste. Serve.

PREP AHEAD

- Slice red onion
- Toast pine nuts
- Grate Parmesan
- Juice lemon

NOTES FROM THE TEST KITCHEN

- Sub any short pasta for orecchiette
- Sub 2 large shallots for red onion
- Sub Pecorino Romano for Parmesan
- Sub walnuts for pine nuts
- Sub chopped raisins for currants

MEAL PLAN 21

WHY THIS MEAL PLAN WORKS

It's enormously satisfying to come home with a plentiful quantity of just a few different vegetables and then strategize successfully to finish them by week's end. Here we use refreshing, anise-y fennel twice, several zucchini all at once, and little red potatoes twice. You'll recognize one of our meal-prep secret weapons here: foil fish packets, which can be assembled completely ahead and then simply baked when you're ready to eat. We recommend cooking the fish within 2 days of purchase (or see page 14 for short-term freezing). The leftover canned coconut milk is delicious in smoothies or oatmeal, or freeze it for the next time you make the packets.

GROCERY LIST

PROTEIN		Substitutions
☐ Skinless halibut fillets	4 (6 to 8 ounces each), 1 inch thick	*Mahi-mahi, red snapper, striped bass, or swordfish*
☐ Bone-in chicken thighs	8 (5 to 7 ounces each)	
☐ Boneless pork chops	4 (6 to 8 ounces each), 1 inch thick	
PRODUCE		
☐ Fennel bulbs	3	
☐ Zucchini	4 (8 ounces each)	*Summer squash*
☐ Baby arugula	5 ounces (5 cups)	
☐ Cilantro	1 bunch (enough for ¼ cup chopped)	*Parsley or mint*
☐ Oregano	1 small bunch (enough for 2 tablespoons leaves)	*Basil*
☐ Ginger	1 knob (enough for 1 tablespoon grated)	
FROZEN		
☐ Pizza dough	1 pound	
OTHER		
☐ Dried figs	½ cup	*Pitted dates*

PREP AHEAD

Quarter 1½ pounds potatoes

Slice 1 pound potatoes ⅛ inch thick

Quarter zucchini lengthwise, then cut crosswise into 2-inch pieces

Halve and core 2 fennel bulbs, then cut into ½-inch-thick wedges

Halve, core, and thinly slice 1 fennel bulb

Mince 1 shallot

Thinly slice 1 shallot

Grate lemon zest (2 teaspoons)

Juice lemon (4 teaspoons)

Wash and pick cilantro

Wash and pick oregano

Stem and chop figs

Chop sun-dried tomatoes

Shave 2 ounces Parmesan

Grate 1½ ounces Parmesan (¾ cup)

Toast pine nuts

Bring pizza dough to room temperature

Chop bacon

MAKE AHEAD

UP TO 1 DAY	Make coconut sauce for fish packets
	Assemble fish packets
	Make pesto for pizza

PANTRY ITEMS

CUPBOARD & COUNTER

			Substitutions
☐	Couscous	1½ cups	
☐	Canned coconut milk	1 cup	
☐	Oil	¾ cup	
☐	Rice vinegar	2 tablespoons	Lime juice
☐	Dried oregano	2 teaspoons	
☐	Red pepper flakes	⅛ teaspoon	
☐	Dried rosemary	⅛ teaspoon	1½ teaspoons chopped fresh rosemary
☐	Small red potatoes (1- to 2-inch diameter)	2½ pounds	Small Yukon Gold potatoes
☐	Garlic cloves	6	
☐	Shallots	2	

REFRIGERATOR

☐	Parmesan cheese	3½ ounces	Pecorino Romano
☐	Feta cheese	2 ounces	Goat cheese
☐	Oil-packed sun-dried tomatoes	¼ cup	
☐	Oil from sun-dried tomatoes	3 tablespoons	Any oil
☐	Fish sauce	2 tablespoons	
☐	Madeira	¼ cup	Dry sherry
☐	Lemon	1	White wine vinegar (for pizza)

FREEZER

☐	Bacon	4 slices	4 ounces pancetta
☐	Pine nuts	¼ cup	Walnuts or almonds

HALIBUT *and* CREAMY COCONUT COUSCOUS PACKETS

SERVES 4 | ACTIVE TIME 25 MINUTES

2 cups boiling water plus ¼ cup room-temperature water

1 cup canned coconut milk

¼ cup chopped fresh cilantro

2 tablespoons fish sauce

1 tablespoon grated fresh ginger

3 garlic cloves, minced

⅛ teaspoon red pepper flakes

1½ cups couscous

4 (6- to 8-ounce) skinless halibut fillets, 1 inch thick

2 tablespoons rice vinegar

1. FOR THE COCONUT SAUCE Combine room-temperature water, coconut milk, cilantro, fish sauce, ginger, garlic, and pepper flakes in small bowl; set sauce aside.

2. FOR THE COUSCOUS Combine couscous and boiling water in bowl, cover with plastic wrap, and let sit until liquid is absorbed and couscous is tender, about 5 minutes. Fluff couscous with fork and season with salt and pepper to taste.

3. FOR THE PACKETS Adjust oven rack to middle position and heat oven to 400 degrees. Lay four 16 by 12-inch rectangles of aluminum foil on counter with short sides parallel to counter edge. Divide couscous evenly among foil rectangles, arranging in center of lower half of each sheet of foil. Pat halibut dry with paper towels, place on top of couscous, and spoon 1 tablespoon coconut sauce over top of each fillet; reserve remaining coconut sauce for serving. Fold top half of foil over fish and couscous, then tightly crimp edges into rough 9 by 6-inch packets, leaving as much headroom as possible so steam can circulate.

4. TO BAKE AND SERVE Place packets on rimmed baking sheet (they may overlap slightly) and bake until halibut registers 130 degrees, 15 to 18 minutes (insert thermometer through foil to check). Carefully open packets, allowing steam to escape away from you, then let halibut rest in packets for 10 minutes.

5. Microwave reserved coconut sauce until warmed through, about 1 minute, then stir in rice vinegar. Using thin metal spatula, gently slide halibut and couscous onto individual plates, drizzle with sauce, and serve.

PREP AHEAD

- Wash and pick cilantro

MAKE AHEAD

- Refrigerate coconut sauce for up to 1 day
- Refrigerate assembled packets for up to 1 day

NOTES FROM THE TEST KITCHEN

- Sub mahi-mahi, red snapper, striped bass, or swordfish for halibut
- Sub parsley or mint for cilantro
- Sub lime juice for rice vinegar

ROASTED CHICKEN THIGHS *with* POTATOES, FENNEL, *and* FIGS

SERVES 4 | ACTIVE TIME 35 MINUTES

1½ pounds small red potatoes, unpeeled, quartered

2 fennel bulbs, stalks discarded, bulbs halved, cored, and cut into ½-inch-thick wedges

4 slices bacon, chopped

2 tablespoons oil

1½ teaspoons table salt, divided

¾ teaspoon pepper, divided

8 (5- to 7-ounce) bone-in chicken thighs, trimmed

1 shallot, minced

⅛ teaspoon dried rosemary

½ cup dried figs, stemmed and chopped

¼ cup Madeira

1. Adjust oven rack to lowest position and heat oven to 475 degrees. Combine potatoes, fennel, bacon, oil, 1 teaspoon salt, and ½ teaspoon pepper in large bowl. Spread mixture in rimmed baking sheet and roast for 10 minutes.

2. Meanwhile, pat chicken dry with paper towels and sprinkle with remaining ½ teaspoon salt and remaining ¼ teaspoon pepper. Place chicken skin side down in 12-inch nonstick skillet. Cook over high heat until skin is deep golden brown, about 10 minutes. Transfer chicken skin side up to sheet with vegetables and continue to roast until chicken registers 175 degrees and vegetables are browned on bottoms, about 15 minutes longer.

3. Pour off all but 2 tablespoons fat from skillet and heat over medium-high heat until shimmering. Add shallot and rosemary and cook until shallot is softened, about 1 minute. Add figs and Madeira and cook until mixture is slightly thickened, about 3 minutes. Serve chicken and vegetables with fig sauce.

PREP AHEAD

• Quarter potatoes

• Halve, core, and cut fennel bulbs

• Mince shallot

• Stem and chop figs

• Chop bacon

NOTES FROM THE TEST KITCHEN

• If your fennel bulbs came with fronds, use them for garnish

• Sub Yukon Gold potatoes for red potatoes

• Sub 4 ounces pancetta for bacon

• Sub 1½ teaspoons chopped fresh rosemary for dried

• Sub pitted dates for dried figs

• Sub dry sherry for Madeira

OREGANO PORK CHOPS *with* WARM ZUCCHINI-FETA SALAD

SERVES 4 | ACTIVE TIME 35 MINUTES

4 zucchini (8 ounces each), quartered lengthwise and cut crosswise into 2-inch pieces

¼ cup oil-packed sun-dried tomatoes, chopped, plus 3 tablespoons sun-dried tomato oil, divided

1 shallot, sliced thin

1¼ teaspoons table salt, divided

2 garlic cloves, sliced thin

1¼ teaspoons pepper

4 (6- to 8-ounce) boneless pork chops, ¾ to 1 inch thick, trimmed

2 teaspoons grated lemon zest plus 1 teaspoon juice

2 teaspoons dried oregano

2 ounces feta cheese, crumbled (½ cup)

2 tablespoons fresh oregano leaves

1. Cook zucchini, 2 tablespoons tomato oil, shallot, ½ teaspoon salt, garlic, and ¼ teaspoon pepper in 12-inch nonstick skillet over medium-high heat until zucchini is just tender and lightly browned, 10 to 12 minutes. Transfer to serving bowl; set aside.

2. Pat pork dry with paper towels and sprinkle with lemon zest, dried oregano, remaining ¾ teaspoon salt, and remaining 1 teaspoon pepper, pressing to adhere. Heat remaining 1 tablespoon tomato oil in now-empty skillet over medium-high heat until just smoking. Add pork and cook, flipping every 2 minutes, until well browned and meat registers 140 to 145 degrees, 8 to 10 minutes. Transfer to cutting board, tent with aluminum foil, and let rest for 5 minutes.

3. Stir feta, fresh oregano, sun-dried tomatoes, and lemon juice into zucchini mixture and season with salt and pepper to taste. Serve.

PREP AHEAD

- Quarter and cut zucchini
- Chop sun-dried tomatoes
- Slice shallot
- Grate lemon zest and juice lemon
- Wash and pick oregano

NOTES FROM THE TEST KITCHEN

- Flipping the pork chops every 2 minutes increases their temperature gradually, allowing a crust to build up on the outside without overcooking the interior
- Sub summer squash for zucchini
- Sub any oil for sun-dried tomato oil
- Sub goat cheese for feta
- Sub basil for fresh oregano

ARUGULA PESTO *and* POTATO PIZZA *with* FENNEL SALAD

SERVES 4 | ACTIVE TIME 25 MINUTES

1 pound small red potatoes, unpeeled, sliced ⅛ inch thick

½ cup plus 1 tablespoon oil, divided

5 ounces (5 cups) baby arugula, divided

¼ cup pine nuts, toasted

1 garlic clove, minced

3½ ounces Parmesan cheese, 1½ ounces grated (¾ cup), 2 ounces shaved

1 pound pizza dough, room temperature

1 tablespoon lemon juice

1 fennel bulb, stalks discarded, bulb halved, cored, and sliced thin

1. Adjust oven rack to upper-middle position and heat oven to 500 degrees. Toss potatoes with 1 tablespoon oil in bowl, cover, and microwave until potatoes are just tender, 3 to 7 minutes; set aside.

2. FOR THE PESTO Process 2 cups arugula, pine nuts, and garlic in food processor until smooth, about 30 seconds. With processor running, slowly add ¼ cup oil until combined. Transfer to bowl, stir in grated Parmesan, and season with salt and pepper to taste.

3. FOR THE PIZZA Brush rimmed baking sheet with 1 tablespoon oil. Press and roll dough into 16 by 9-inch oval on lightly floured counter, then transfer to prepared sheet. Spread pesto over dough, leaving ½-inch border around edge. Shingle potatoes over pesto and top with shaved Parmesan. Bake until edges of pizza are well browned, about 15 minutes.

4. While pizza bakes, whisk lemon juice and remaining 3 tablespoons oil together in large bowl. Add fennel and remaining 3 cups arugula and toss to coat. Season with salt and pepper to taste. Serve with pizza.

PREP AHEAD

- Slice potatoes
- Toast pine nuts
- Grate and shave Parmesan
- Bring pizza dough to room temperature
- Juice lemon
- Halve, core, and thinly slice fennel

MAKE AHEAD

- Refrigerate pesto for up to 1 day

NOTES FROM THE TEST KITCHEN

- Use a mandoline or a food processor fitted with a slicing disk to prep the potatoes and fennel quickly
- Sub small Yukon Gold potatoes for red potatoes
- Sub walnuts or almonds for pine nuts
- Sub Pecorino Romano for Parmesan
- Sub white wine vinegar for lemon juice

MEAL PLAN 22

MEAL 1   Pan-Seared Cod with Blistered Green Beans and Red Pepper Relish

MEAL 2   Red Curry Coconut Chicken Soup

MEAL 3   Steak Tacos

MEAL 4   Parmesan Polenta with Eggplant Ragu

MEAL 5   Choose a Pantry Recipe *(we suggest Spaghetti with Bacon and Spicy Tomato Sauce)*

WHY THIS MEAL PLAN WORKS

Make-ahead potential abounds in this plan. You can make the zesty herb paste for marinating the Steak Tacos as well as marinate the meat itself ahead (and that herb paste would be equally delicious with pork). The Parmesan polenta is a terrific make-ahead meal: If you cook the polenta and the eggplant ragu ahead, all you'll have to do before serving is reheat and combine the two components. While we often turn to foil packets for prepping cod and cooking it to moist perfection, sometimes we crave a golden crisped exterior, and this week we achieve that by quickly searing the fish in a skillet (the accompanying green beans get the same treatment). And try that red pepper relish as a topping for chicken or stirred into cooked grains. We recommend cooking the fish within 2 days of purchase (or see page 14 for short-term freezing).

GROCERY LIST

PROTEIN		Substitutions
☐ Skinless cod fillets	4 (6 to 8 ounces each), 1 inch thick	*Black sea bass, haddock, hake, or pollack*
☐ Boneless, skinless chicken breasts	1 pound	
☐ Flank steak	1½ pounds	
PRODUCE		
☐ Green beans	1 pound	
☐ Eggplant	1 pound	
☐ White mushrooms	8 ounces	*Cremini mushrooms*
☐ Scallions	6	*Basil (for cod)*
☐ Lemongrass	3 stalks	
☐ Jalapeño chiles	2	*Serrano chiles*
☐ Cilantro	1 large bunch (enough for ¾ cup leaves plus 8 sprigs)	
☐ Basil	1 bunch (enough for ¼ cup chopped)	*Parsley*

PREP AHEAD

Trim green beans

Cut eggplant into ½-inch pieces

Trim and thinly slice mushrooms

Trim lemongrass stalks to bottom 6 inches, then mince

Coarsely chop shallots

Chop 3 scallions; thinly slice 2 on bias

Stem and seed jalapeños, then coarsely chop 1 and thinly slice 1

Juice limes (4 tablespoons)

Wash and pick cilantro and basil

Finely chop roasted red peppers

Grate Parmesan (1½ cups)

Toast and finely chop almonds

Trim chicken breasts, then halve lengthwise and slice ¼ inch thick

Trim flank steak, then cut lengthwise with grain into 4 pieces

MAKE AHEAD

UP TO 3 DAYS	Make eggplant ragu for polenta
	Make polenta
UP TO 2 DAYS	Make and strain soup broth
UP TO 1 DAY	Make red pepper relish for cod
	Make herb paste–lime juice mixture for tacos
	Marinate steak for tacos

PANTRY ITEMS

CUPBOARD & COUNTER

		Substitutions
☐ Coarse-ground polenta (not fine-ground, stone-ground, or instant)	1½ cups	
☐ Diced tomatoes with garlic, basil, and oregano	2 (14.5-ounce) cans	*Unflavored diced tomatoes*
☐ Coconut milk	2 (14-ounce) cans	*Light coconut milk*
☐ Oil	¾ cup	
☐ Sherry vinegar	1 teaspoon	*Red wine vinegar*
☐ Sugar	1 tablespoon plus ½ teaspoon	
☐ Ground cumin	½ teaspoon	
☐ Shallots	3 large	
☐ Garlic cloves	3	

REFRIGERATOR

☐ Parmesan cheese	3 ounces	Pecorino Romano
☐ Broth	4 cups	
☐ Jarred roasted red peppers	1 cup (16-ounce jar)	
☐ Fish sauce	3 tablespoons	
☐ Thai red curry paste	2 teaspoons	
☐ Limes	4	
☐ Lemon	1	

FREEZER

☐ Whole almonds	¼ cup	*Walnuts or pecans*
☐ Corn tortillas	12 (6-inch)	

PAN-SEARED COD *with* BLISTERED GREEN BEANS *and* RED PEPPER RELISH

SERVES 4 | ACTIVE TIME 35 MINUTES

1 cup jarred roasted red peppers, patted dry and chopped fine

¼ cup whole almonds, toasted and chopped fine

3 tablespoons oil, divided

1 scallion, green part only, sliced thin

1 teaspoon sherry vinegar

1½ teaspoons table salt, divided

⅛ plus ¼ teaspoon pepper, divided

1 pound green beans, trimmed

¼ cup water

4 (6- to 8-ounce) skinless cod fillets, 1 inch thick

Lemon wedges for serving

1. FOR THE RED PEPPER RELISH Combine red peppers, almonds, 1 tablespoon oil, scallion green, vinegar, ½ teaspoon salt, and ⅛ teaspoon pepper in bowl; set aside.

2. FOR THE GREEN BEANS Combine green beans, water, 1 tablespoon oil, remaining 1 teaspoon salt, and remaining ¼ teaspoon pepper in 12-inch nonstick skillet. Cover and cook over medium-high heat, shaking pan occasionally, until water has evaporated, 6 to 8 minutes. Uncover and continue to cook until green beans are blistered and browned, about 2 minutes longer. Transfer to serving platter.

3. FOR THE COD Heat remaining 1 tablespoon oil in now-empty skillet over medium-high heat until shimmering. Pat cod dry, add to skillet, and cook until both sides are lightly browned and cod registers 135 degrees, about 6 minutes per side. Serve cod with green beans, relish, and lemon wedges.

PREP AHEAD

- Chop roasted red peppers
- Toast and chop almonds
- Trim green beans

MAKE AHEAD

- Refrigerate red pepper relish for up to 1 day

NOTES FROM THE TEST KITCHEN

- You will need a 12-inch nonstick skillet with a tight-fitting lid
- Sub walnuts or pecans for almonds
- Sub basil for scallion
- Sub red wine vinegar for sherry vinegar
- Sub black sea bass, haddock, hake, or pollack for cod

RED CURRY COCONUT CHICKEN SOUP

SERVES 6 | ACTIVE TIME 30 MINUTES

1 tablespoon oil

3 stalks lemongrass, trimmed to bottom 6 inches and minced

3 large shallots, chopped coarse

8 sprigs fresh cilantro, chopped, plus extra fresh leaves for serving

4 cups broth

2 (14-ounce) cans coconut milk, divided

3 tablespoons fish sauce, divided, plus extra for seasoning

1 tablespoon sugar

8 ounces white mushrooms, trimmed and sliced thin

1 pound boneless, skinless chicken breasts, trimmed, halved lengthwise, and sliced ¼ inch thick

3 tablespoons lime juice (2 limes), plus lime wedges for serving

2 teaspoons Thai red curry paste

2 scallions, sliced thin on bias

1 jalapeño chile, stemmed, seeded, and sliced thin

1. FOR THE STRAINED BROTH Heat oil in large saucepan over medium heat until shimmering. Add lemongrass, shallots, and cilantro sprigs and cook, stirring often, until just softened but not browned, 2 to 5 minutes. Stir in broth, 1 can coconut milk, and 1 tablespoon fish sauce and bring to simmer. Reduce heat to low, cover, and cook until flavors meld, about 10 minutes. Strain broth through fine-mesh strainer into large bowl or container; discard solids.

2. FOR THE SOUP Return broth to now-empty saucepan. Stir in remaining 1 can coconut milk and sugar and bring to simmer over medium-high heat. Stir in mushrooms and cook until just tender, 2 to 3 minutes. Stir in chicken and cook until no longer pink, 1 to 3 minutes. Remove saucepan from heat.

3. Whisk lime juice, curry paste, and remaining 2 tablespoons fish sauce together in bowl to dissolve curry, then stir into soup. Season with extra fish sauce to taste. Sprinkle individual portions with scallions, jalapeño, and extra cilantro leaves before serving with lime wedges.

PREP AHEAD

- Trim and mince lemongrass
- Chop shallots
- Wash and pick cilantro
- Trim and slice mushrooms
- Juice limes
- Slice scallions
- Stem, seed, and slice jalapeño
- Trim, halve, and slice chicken

MAKE AHEAD

- Refrigerate strained broth for up to 2 days

NOTES FROM THE TEST KITCHEN

- Sub cremini mushrooms for white mushrooms
- Sub light coconut milk for coconut milk
- Sub serrano chile for jalapeño

STEAK TACOS

SERVES 4 TO 6 | ACTIVE TIME 30 MINUTES

½ cup packed fresh cilantro leaves, plus extra for serving

3 scallions, chopped coarse

1 jalapeño chile, stemmed, seeded, and chopped coarse

3 garlic cloves, chopped coarse

½ teaspoon ground cumin

6 tablespoons oil, divided

1 tablespoon lime juice, plus lime wedges for serving

1½ pounds flank steak, trimmed, cut lengthwise with grain into 4 pieces, poked all over with fork

1½ teaspoons table salt

½ teaspoon sugar

½ teaspoon pepper

12 (6-inch) corn tortillas, warmed

1. FOR THE HERB PASTE–LIME JUICE MIXTURE Pulse cilantro, scallions, jalapeño, garlic, and cumin in food processor until finely ground, 10 to 12 pulses, scraping down sides of bowl as needed. Add ¼ cup oil and process until combined, about 15 seconds. Transfer 2 tablespoons herb paste to large bowl and whisk in lime juice; set aside.

2. FOR THE MARINATED STEAK Rub steak with salt and remaining herb paste on large plate. Cover with plastic wrap and refrigerate for at least 30 minutes.

3. FOR THE TACOS Scrape herb paste off steak and sprinkle with sugar and pepper. Heat remaining 2 tablespoons oil in 12-inch nonstick skillet over medium-high heat until just smoking. Add steak and cook until well browned all over and meat registers 120 to 125 degrees (for medium-rare), 7 to 13 minutes. Transfer steak to cutting board, tent with aluminum foil, and let rest for 5 minutes.

4. Slice steak thin against grain, then transfer to bowl with reserved herb paste–lime juice mixture and toss to coat. Serve steak in warm tortillas with extra cilantro and lime wedges.

PREP AHEAD

- Wash and pick cilantro
- Chop scallions
- Stem, seed, and chop jalapeño
- Juice lime
- Trim and cut steak

MAKE AHEAD

- Refrigerate herb paste–lime juice mixture for up to 1 day
- Refrigerate marinated steak for up to 1 day

NOTES FROM THE TEST KITCHEN

- Serve with salsa, minced white onion, thinly sliced radishes or cucumber, or any of your favorite taco toppings
- Sub serrano chile for jalapeño

PARMESAN POLENTA *with* EGGPLANT RAGU

SERVES 4 | ACTIVE TIME 30 MINUTES

1 pound eggplant, cut into
  ½-inch pieces

1¼ teaspoons table salt, divided

2 tablespoons oil

2 (14.5-ounce) cans diced tomatoes
  with garlic, basil, and oregano,
  drained with juice reserved

5 cups water, divided

1¼ teaspoons pepper, divided

1½ cups coarse-ground polenta

3 ounces Parmesan cheese, grated
  (1½ cups), plus extra for serving

¼ cup chopped fresh basil

1. FOR THE EGGPLANT RAGU Line large plate with double layer of coffee filters and spray with vegetable oil spray. Toss eggplant with ½ teaspoon salt, then spread into even layer on plate. Microwave, uncovered, until eggplant is dry and slightly shriveled, 8 to 12 minutes, turning pieces halfway through cooking.

2. Heat oil in Dutch oven over high heat until shimmering. Add eggplant and cook until browned, about 2 minutes. Stir in tomatoes and cook until beginning to brown, about 5 minutes. Stir in reserved tomato juice, 1 cup water, ¼ teaspoon salt, and ½ teaspoon pepper, scraping up any browned bits, and bring to boil. Reduce heat to medium, cover, and simmer gently until eggplant is completely broken down, 20 to 25 minutes.

3. FOR THE POLENTA Meanwhile, bring remaining 4 cups water and remaining ½ teaspoon salt to boil in medium saucepan over medium-high heat. Slowly add polenta, whisking constantly in circular motion to prevent clumping. Bring to simmer, stirring constantly, about 1 minute. Reduce heat to low, cover, and cook for 5 minutes. Whisk polenta to smooth out lumps, then cover and continue to cook, without stirring, until polenta is tender but slightly al dente, about 20 minutes. Off heat, stir in Parmesan and remaining ¾ teaspoon pepper; cover and let sit for 5 minutes.

4. TO FINISH Stir basil into eggplant ragu and season with salt and pepper to taste. Serve ragu over polenta, passing extra Parmesan separately.

PREP AHEAD

- Cut eggplant
- Grate Parmesan
- Wash and pick basil

MAKE AHEAD

- Refrigerate eggplant ragu for up to 3 days
- Refrigerate polenta for up to 3 days

NOTES FROM THE TEST KITCHEN

- If the polenta bubbles or sputters even slightly after the first 10 minutes, lower the heat
- Sub unflavored diced tomatoes for diced tomatoes with garlic, basil, and oregano
- Sub Pecorino Romano for Parmesan
- Sub parsley for basil

MEAL PLAN 23

WHY THIS MEAL PLAN WORKS

Straightforward grocery and pantry items are transformed into so much more than the sum of their parts in this plan. For the chicken soup, though you could buy a rotisserie chicken to shred and add to the broth, it pays off in major flavor to poach chicken breasts in the broth (and it's mostly hands-off). And since that portion of the recipe is make-ahead, when it's time to serve you'll just have to cook the pasta in the simmering soup. For the pork loin, seasoning the pork and prepping the potatoes in advance means that you can simply pop them into the oven on a sheet pan the night you want to serve them. The only cooking for the hearty grain bowls involves the farro and mushrooms, so if you complete those tasks and prep the carrots ahead of time, you'll need only to whisk the dressing and combine the components before dinner is served.

GROCERY LIST

PROTEIN		Substitutions
☐ Bone-in chicken breasts	1½ pounds	*Bone-in chicken thighs*
☐ Sirloin steak tips	2 pounds	
☐ Boneless pork loin roast	1 (2½ to 3 pounds)	
PRODUCE		
☐ Cremini mushrooms	1 pound	*White or portobello mushrooms*
☐ Baby spinach	10 ounces (10 cups)	
☐ Pear	1	*Apple*
☐ Parsley	1 bunch (enough for ⅓ cup minced)	*Dill (for soup)*
DAIRY		
☐ Goat cheese	4 ounces	*Gorgonzola (for steak); feta (for steak or grain bowls)*

PREP AHEAD

Halve potatoes

Trim and thinly slice mushrooms

Peel carrots; shave 4 carrots into ribbons, cut 1 carrot into ½-inch pieces

Halve, core, and thinly slice pear

Mince 1 shallot

Halve and thinly slice 1 shallot

Chop onion

Cut celery into ½-inch pieces

Grate lemon zest (1½ teaspoons)

Juice lemons (5 tablespoons)

Wash and pick parsley

Break spaghetti into 1-inch pieces

Trim and cut steak tips into 2-inch pieces

Cut bacon into ½-inch pieces

MAKE AHEAD

UP TO 3 DAYS	Boil farro for grain bowls
	Cook mushrooms for grain bowls
UP TO 2 DAYS	Make soup base and poach chicken for soup (or freeze for up to 1 month)
UP TO 1 DAY	Rub pork loin with spices
	Prepare potato mixture for pork loin
	Make mustard sauce for pork loin

PANTRY ITEMS

CUPBOARD & COUNTER

		Substitutions
☐ Farro	2 cups	Pearl barley
☐ Spaghetti	5 ounces	Fideos or egg noodles
☐ Oil	1¼ cups	
☐ White wine vinegar	1½ tablespoons	Other vinegar, such as cider, red wine, or sherry
☐ Garlic powder	1½ teaspoons	
☐ Ground coriander	1½ teaspoons	
☐ Ground cumin	1½ teaspoons	
☐ Dried thyme	¾ teaspoon	2¼ teaspoons chopped fresh thyme
☐ Small red potatoes (1- to 2-inch diameter)	2½ pounds	Small Yukon Gold potatoes
☐ Shallots	2	3 tablespoons minced red onion (for pork)
☐ Garlic cloves	2	
☐ Onion	1	4 large shallots

REFRIGERATOR

☐ Broth	8 cups	
☐ Whole-grain mustard	2 tablespoons	
☐ Carrots	5	
☐ Lemons	2	2 tablespoons balsamic vinegar (for steak tips); red wine vinegar (for grain bowls)
☐ Celery rib	1	

FREEZER

☐ Bacon	4 slices	
☐ Pistachios	3 tablespoons	Pecans

CHICKEN NOODLE SOUP

SERVES 4 TO 6 | ACTIVE TIME 45 MINUTES

1½ pounds bone-in chicken
    breasts, trimmed

½ teaspoon table salt, divided

¼ teaspoon pepper

1 tablespoon oil

8 cups broth

1 onion, chopped

1 carrot, peeled and cut into
    ½-inch pieces

1 celery rib, cut into ½-inch pieces

½ teaspoon dried thyme

5 ounces spaghetti, broken into
    1-inch pieces (1½ cups)

1 tablespoon minced fresh parsley

1. FOR THE SOUP BASE AND SHREDDED CHICKEN Pat chicken dry with paper towels and sprinkle with ¼ teaspoon salt and pepper. Heat oil in Dutch oven over medium-high heat until shimmering. Cook chicken until well browned all over, 8 to 10 minutes.

2. Add broth, onion, carrot, celery, thyme, and remaining ¼ teaspoon salt, scraping up any browned bits. Bring to boil, cover, and reduce heat to low. Simmer until chicken registers 160 degrees, 14 to 17 minutes.

3. Remove pot from heat; transfer chicken to plate and let cool slightly. Using 2 forks, shred chicken into bite-size pieces; discard skin and bones.

4. TO FINISH Return soup to boil over medium-high heat and add pasta. Cook, uncovered, until pasta is tender, 9 to 11 minutes, stirring often. Stir in chicken and parsley and cook until chicken is warmed through, about 2 minutes. Season with salt and pepper to taste. Serve.

PREP AHEAD

- Chop onion
- Peel and cut carrot
- Cut celery
- Break spaghetti into pieces
- Wash and pick parsley

MAKE AHEAD

- Refrigerate soup base and poached, shredded chicken for up to 2 days (or freeze for up to 1 month)

NOTES FROM THE TEST KITCHEN

- Sub bone-in thighs for breasts (cook to 175 degrees)
- Sub 4 large shallots for onion
- Sub 1½ teaspoons fresh thyme for dried
- Sub fideos or egg noodles for spaghetti
- Sub dill for parsley

STEAK TIPS *with* WILTED SPINACH, GOAT CHEESE, *and* PEAR SALAD

SERVES 4 | ACTIVE TIME 30 MINUTES

2 pounds sirloin steak tips, trimmed and cut into 2-inch pieces

¾ teaspoon table salt, divided

¼ teaspoon plus ⅛ teaspoon pepper, divided

3 tablespoons oil, divided

6 ounces (6 cups) baby spinach

1 ripe but firm pear, halved, cored, and sliced thin

3 tablespoons chopped pistachios

1 shallot, halved and sliced thin

1 garlic clove, minced

¼ teaspoon dried thyme

½ teaspoon grated lemon zest plus 2 tablespoons juice

2 ounces goat cheese, crumbled (½ cup)

1. Pat steak tips dry with paper towels and sprinkle with ½ teaspoon salt and ¼ teaspoon pepper. Heat 1 tablespoon oil in 12-inch skillet over medium-high heat until just smoking. Add steak tips and cook until well browned all over and meat registers 120 to 125 degrees (for medium-rare), 6 to 10 minutes. Transfer to serving platter, tent with aluminum foil, and let rest for 5 minutes.

2. Combine spinach and pear in large bowl. Add pistachios, shallot, garlic, thyme, remaining 2 tablespoons oil, remaining ¼ teaspoon salt, and remaining ⅛ teaspoon pepper to now-empty skillet and cook over medium heat until pistachios are toasted and shallot is softened, about 2 minutes. Stir in lemon zest and juice and any accumulated meat juices. Immediately pour warm dressing over spinach and toss gently to wilt. Season with salt and pepper to taste. Sprinkle with goat cheese. Serve with steak tips.

PREP AHEAD

- Halve, core, and slice pear
- Halve and slice shallot
- Grate lemon zest and juice lemon
- Trim and cut steak tips

NOTES FROM THE TEST KITCHEN

- Sub apple for pear
- Sub pecans for pistachios
- Sub ¾ teaspoon chopped fresh thyme for dried
- Sub 2 tablespoons balsamic vinegar for lemon zest and juice
- Sub Gorgonzola or feta for goat cheese

ROASTED PORK LOIN *with* POTATOES *and* MUSTARD SAUCE

SERVES 6 | ACTIVE TIME 35 MINUTES

1½ teaspoons garlic powder

1½ teaspoons ground coriander

1½ teaspoons ground cumin

¾ teaspoon table salt, divided

½ teaspoon pepper

1 (2½- to 3-pound) boneless pork loin roast, trimmed

2½ pounds small red potatoes, unpeeled, halved

4 slices bacon, cut into ½-inch pieces

7 tablespoons oil, divided

¼ cup minced fresh parsley

1 shallot, minced

2 tablespoons whole-grain mustard

1½ tablespoons white wine vinegar

1. FOR THE SPICE-RUBBED PORK Combine garlic powder, coriander, cumin, ½ teaspoon salt, and pepper in bowl. Rub pork evenly with spice mixture, wrap with plastic wrap, and refrigerate for at least 1 hour.

2. FOR THE POTATO MIXTURE Toss potatoes, bacon, remaining ¼ teaspoon salt, and 2 tablespoons oil together in bowl.

3. FOR THE MUSTARD SAUCE In separate bowl, combine ¼ cup oil, parsley, shallot, mustard, and vinegar; set aside.

4. TO ROAST AND FINISH Adjust oven rack to upper-middle position and heat oven to 325 degrees. Line rimmed baking sheet with aluminum foil and brush with remaining 1 tablespoon oil. Pat pork dry with paper towels and place fat side up in center of prepared sheet. Place bacon and potatoes, cut side down, on sheet around roast.

5. Roast pork and potatoes until pork registers 130 degrees, 40 minutes to 1 hour, rotating sheet halfway through roasting. Remove pork and potatoes from oven, adjust oven rack 6 inches from broiler element, and heat broiler. Broil until pork is spotty brown and registers 135 to 140 degrees, 3 to 5 minutes.

6. Transfer pork to cutting board, tent with foil, and let rest for 10 minutes. Meanwhile, return potatoes to oven and continue to broil until lightly browned, 5 to 10 minutes. Slice pork ½ inch thick. Whisk sauce to recombine and serve with pork and potatoes.

PREP AHEAD

- Halve potatoes
- Wash and pick parsley
- Mince shallot
- Cut bacon

MAKE AHEAD

- Refrigerate spice-rubbed pork for up to 1 day
- Refrigerate uncooked potato mixture for up to 1 day
- Refrigerate mustard sauce for up to 1 day

NOTES FROM THE TEST KITCHEN

- Sub Yukon Gold potatoes for red potatoes
- Sub 3 tablespoons minced red onion for shallot
- Sub cider vinegar, red wine vinegar, or sherry vinegar for white wine vinegar

HEARTY GRAIN *and* VEGETABLE BOWLS *with* GOAT CHEESE

SERVES 4 | ACTIVE TIME 30 MINUTES

2 cups farro

¾ teaspoon table salt, divided, plus salt for cooking farro

6 tablespoons oil, divided

1 teaspoon grated lemon zest plus 3 tablespoons juice

1 garlic clove, minced

½ teaspoon pepper, divided

4 carrots, peeled and shaved into ribbons

4 ounces (4 cups) baby spinach

1 pound cremini mushrooms, trimmed and sliced thin

2 ounces goat cheese, crumbled (½ cup)

1. FOR THE FARRO Bring 2 quarts water to boil in large saucepan. Add farro and 1 tablespoon salt. Return to boil, reduce heat to medium-low, and simmer until farro is tender with slight chew, 15 to 20 minutes. Drain.

2. Whisk ¼ cup oil, lemon zest and juice, garlic, ½ teaspoon salt, and ¼ teaspoon pepper together in bowl. Add carrots, spinach, and farro and toss to combine.

3. FOR THE MUSHROOMS Heat remaining 2 tablespoons oil in 12-inch nonstick skillet over medium-high heat until shimmering. Add mushrooms, remaining ¼ teaspoon salt, and remaining ¼ teaspoon pepper and cook, covered, until mushrooms release their liquid, about 5 minutes. Uncover and continue to cook until mushrooms begin to brown, about 3 minutes longer.

4. TO FINISH Divide farro mixture evenly among 4 serving bowls. Top with goat cheese and mushrooms. Serve.

PREP AHEAD

- Grate lemon zest and juice lemon
- Peel and shave carrots
- Trim and slice mushrooms

MAKE AHEAD

- Refrigerate cooked farro for up to 3 days
- Refrigerate cooked mushrooms for up to 3 days

NOTES FROM THE TEST KITCHEN

- You will need a 12-inch skillet with a tight-fitting lid
- Use a vegetable peeler to shave the carrots into ribbons
- Sub pearl barley for farro
- Sub red wine vinegar for lemon zest and juice
- Sub white or portobello mushrooms for cremini
- Sub feta for goat cheese

MEAL PLAN 24

Cod Baked in Foil
with Potatoes,
Zucchini, and Sun-
Dried Tomatoes
(page 224)

Chicken, Sun-Dried
Tomato, and Goat
Cheese Burgers
(page 225)

Stir-Fried Pork
with Green Beans
and Cashews
(page 226)

Fennel, Olive, and
Goat Cheese Tarts
(page 227)

Choose a
Pantry Recipe
*(we suggest Fusilli
Salad with Spinach,
Artichokes, and
Sun-Dried Tomatoes,
page 255)*

WHY THIS MEAL PLAN WORKS

Burgers are a meal prepper's friend; the patties can often be shaped in advance and refrigerated, so all you have to do when you're ready to eat is cook them. Better yet, shape a double batch and freeze some so that they're ready to thaw and cook on demand for a quick meal. We've got another flavor take on fish packets this week featuring potatoes, zucchini, and sun-dried tomatoes—with multiple substitution options for the fish. If you do the prep-ahead for the creamy, rich puff pastry tarts, all that will be left on the day of serving is to assemble the tarts and bake them for 5 minutes. Goat cheese logs are sold in various sizes; we love to have extra for snacking, but if you would rather minimize leftovers, look for a 10-ounce size or two 5-ounce logs. We recommend cooking the fish within 2 days of purchase (or see page 14 for short-term freezing).

GROCERY LIST

PROTEIN		Substitutions
☐ Skinless cod fillets	4 (6 to 8 ounces each), 1 inch thick	*Black sea bass, haddock, hake, or pollack*
☐ Ground chicken (not 99 percent lean)	1 pound	*Ground turkey (not 99 percent lean)*
☐ Pork tenderloin	1 (12 to 16 ounces)	
PRODUCE		
☐ Green beans	8 ounces	
☐ Zucchini	2	*Summer squash*
☐ Fennel bulb	1 large	
☐ Basil	1 large bunch (enough for ⅔ cup chopped)	*Parsley; chives (for cod or burgers)*
☐ Ginger	1 knob (enough for 1 tablespoon grated)	
DAIRY		
☐ Goat cheese	10 ounces	*Feta (for chicken burgers); cream cheese (for tart)*

PREP AHEAD

Trim and cut green beans into
2-inch pieces

Slice zucchini into ½-inch-thick rounds

Halve, core, and thinly slice fennel bulb

Mince 1 shallot

Halve and thinly slice 1 shallot

Wash and pick basil

Mince sun-dried tomatoes (½ cup)

Coarsely chop sun-dried
tomatoes (⅓ cup)

Grate lemon zest (1 teaspoon)

Juice lemon (1 tablespoon)

Chop olives

Chop cashews

Thaw puff pastry sheet, then halve

Trim pork tenderloin, then halve
lengthwise and thinly slice crosswise

MAKE AHEAD

UP TO 2 DAYS	Parbake puff pastry for tarts
	Make fennel mixture for tarts
	Mix goat cheese mixture for tarts
UP TO 1 DAY	Assemble foil packets for cod
	Shape chicken burgers (or freeze for up to 1 month)

PANTRY ITEMS

CUPBOARD & COUNTER		Substitutions
☐ Oil	6 tablespoons	
☐ Mirin	¼ cup	Sweet sherry
☐ Cornstarch	3 tablespoons	
☐ Extra-small Yukon Gold potatoes (less than 1-inch diameter)	1 pound	Extra-small red potatoes
☐ Garlic cloves	9	
☐ Shallots	2	
REFRIGERATOR		
☐ Broth	1 cup	
☐ Soy sauce	¼ cup	Tamari
☐ Oil-packed sun-dried tomatoes	½ cup minced, ⅓ cup chopped	
☐ Sun-dried tomato oil	¼ cup	Any oil
☐ Pitted oil-cured black olives	½ cup	Kalamata olives
☐ Dry white wine	½ cup	Dry vermouth
☐ Lemons	2	
FREEZER		
☐ Hamburger buns	5	
☐ Puff pastry	1 sheet (9½ by 9 inches)	
☐ Frozen peas	½ cup	
☐ Roasted cashews	¼ cup	Peanuts

COD BAKED IN FOIL *with* POTATOES, ZUCCHINI, *and* SUN-DRIED TOMATOES

SERVES 4 | ACTIVE TIME 20 MINUTES

1 pound extra-small Yukon Gold potatoes, unpeeled

3 tablespoons sun-dried tomato oil, divided, plus ½ cup minced oil-packed sun-dried tomatoes

¾ teaspoon table salt, divided

½ teaspoon pepper, divided

2 zucchini, sliced into ½-inch-thick rounds

1 shallot, halved and sliced thin

½ cup frozen peas

4 (6- to 8-ounce) skinless cod fillets, 1 inch thick

2 tablespoons chopped fresh basil

Lemon wedges for serving

1. FOR THE POTATOES Adjust oven rack to lowest position and heat oven to 450 degrees. Line rimmed baking sheet with aluminum foil. Toss potatoes, 1 tablespoon tomato oil, ¼ teaspoon salt, and ¼ teaspoon pepper together on prepared sheet and arrange around perimeter of sheet. Roast until potatoes start to brown, about 10 minutes.

2. FOR THE PACKETS Arrange four 12-inch sheets foil flat on counter. Divide zucchini, shallot, and peas among foil sheets, arranging in center of each sheet. Place cod on top of vegetables and sprinkle with remaining ½ teaspoon salt and remaining ¼ teaspoon pepper. Top fillets with tomatoes and drizzle with remaining 2 tablespoons tomato oil.

3. Top each vegetable pile with 12-inch sheet foil and tightly crimp edges of foil together until packet is well sealed, leaving as much headroom as possible so steam can circulate. Transfer packets to center of sheet with potatoes.

4. TO FINISH Bake until cod registers 135 degrees, 15 to 17 minutes (insert thermometer through packet into thick part of fish). Carefully open packets, allowing steam to escape away from you. Using thin metal spatula, gently slide cod and vegetables, and any accumulated juices, onto individual plates. Sprinkle cod and vegetables with basil and serve with potatoes and lemon wedges.

PREP AHEAD

- Mince sun-dried tomatoes
- Slice zucchini
- Halve and slice shallot
- Wash and pick basil

MAKE AHEAD

- Refrigerate assembled packets for up to 1 day

NOTES FROM THE TEST KITCHEN

- Sub red potatoes for Yukon Gold
- Sub any oil for sun-dried tomato oil
- Sub summer squash for zucchini
- Sub black sea bass, haddock, hake, or pollack for cod
- Sub parsley or chives for basil

CHICKEN, SUN-DRIED TOMATO, *and* GOAT CHEESE BURGERS

SERVES 4 | ACTIVE TIME 25 MINUTES

5 hamburger buns (1 bun torn into 1-inch pieces, 4 buns toasted if desired)

2 tablespoons water

1 pound ground chicken

2 ounces goat cheese, crumbled (½ cup)

⅓ cup oil-packed sun-dried tomatoes, chopped coarse, plus 1 tablespoon sun-dried tomato oil

1 shallot, minced

2 tablespoons chopped fresh basil

½ teaspoon table salt

¼ teaspoon pepper

1. FOR THE BURGER PATTIES Using fork, mash bun pieces and water into paste in large bowl. Add chicken, goat cheese, tomatoes, shallot, basil, salt, and pepper and knead gently with your hands until combined. Divide mixture into 4 portions, form each into loose ball, then press gently into ¾-inch-thick patties.

2. TO FINISH Heat tomato oil in 12-inch nonstick skillet over medium-high heat until just smoking. Add patties and cook until lightly browned on first side, 2 to 4 minutes. Flip patties and continue to cook until second side is lightly browned, 2 to 4 minutes.

3. Reduce heat to low, partially cover, and continue to cook until meat registers 160 degrees, 8 to 10 minutes, flipping as needed. Place burgers on buns. Serve.

PREP AHEAD

- Chop sun-dried tomatoes
- Mince shallot
- Wash and pick basil

MAKE AHEAD

- Refrigerate shaped burger patties for up to 1 day (or freeze for up to 1 month)

NOTES FROM THE TEST KITCHEN

- This recipe is easily doubled
- Serve with Simplest Salad (page 32), if you like
- Sub ground turkey for ground chicken
- Sub feta for goat cheese
- Sub any oil for sun-dried tomato oil
- Sub parsley or chives for basil

STIR-FRIED PORK *with* GREEN BEANS *and* CASHEWS

SERVES 4 | ACTIVE TIME 30 MINUTES

1 cup broth

¼ cup mirin

¼ cup soy sauce

3 tablespoons cornstarch, divided

1 (12- to 16-ounce) pork tenderloin, trimmed, halved lengthwise, and sliced thin crosswise

3 tablespoons oil, divided

8 ounces green beans, trimmed and cut into 2-inch pieces

6 garlic cloves, minced

1 tablespoon grated fresh ginger

¼ cup roasted cashews, chopped coarse

1. Whisk broth, mirin, soy sauce, and 1 tablespoon cornstarch together in bowl; set aside. Toss pork, 1 tablespoon oil, and remaining 2 tablespoons cornstarch together in large bowl. Heat 2 teaspoons oil in 12-inch nonstick skillet over medium-high heat until just smoking. Add half of pork and cook, tossing slowly but constantly, until browned, 3 to 5 minutes; transfer to plate. Repeat with 2 teaspoons oil and remaining pork.

2. Add green beans and remaining 2 teaspoons oil to now-empty skillet and cook, tossing slowly but constantly, until bright green, about 1 minute. Add garlic and ginger and cook until fragrant, about 30 seconds. Whisk broth mixture to recombine and add to skillet. Cook until thickened, about 2 minutes. Return pork and any accumulated juices to skillet and cook until heated through, about 1 minute. Sprinkle with cashews and serve.

PREP AHEAD

- Trim and cut green beans
- Chop cashews
- Trim, halve, and slice pork

NOTES FROM THE TEST KITCHEN

- Instead of a 12-inch nonstick skillet, you can use a 14-inch flat-bottomed wok
- Serve with rice (pages 34–35), if you like
- Sub sweet sherry for mirin
- Sub tamari for soy sauce
- Sub peanuts for cashews

FENNEL, OLIVE, *and* GOAT CHEESE TARTS

SERVES 4 | ACTIVE TIME 35 MINUTES

- 1 (9½ by 9-inch) sheet puff pastry, thawed and halved
- 3 tablespoons oil, divided
- 1 large fennel bulb, stalks discarded, bulb halved, cored, and sliced thin
- 3 garlic cloves, minced
- ½ cup dry white wine
- ½ cup pitted oil-cured black olives, chopped
- 1 teaspoon grated lemon zest plus 1 tablespoon juice
- 8 ounces goat cheese, softened (2 cups)
- 5 tablespoons chopped fresh basil, divided
- ¼ teaspoon pepper

1. FOR THE PUFF PASTRY Adjust oven rack to middle position and heat oven to 425 degrees. Place puff pastry halves on parchment paper–lined rimmed baking sheet and poke all over with fork. Bake until puffed and golden brown, about 15 minutes, rotating sheet halfway through baking. Using paring knife, cut ½-inch-wide border around top edge of each pastry (without cutting through pastry), then press centers down with your fingertips.

2. FOR THE FENNEL MIXTURE While pastry bakes, heat 1 tablespoon oil in 12-inch skillet over medium-high heat until shimmering. Add fennel and cook until softened and browned, about 10 minutes. Stir in garlic and cook until fragrant, about 30 seconds. Add wine, cover, and cook for 5 minutes. Uncover and cook until liquid has evaporated and fennel is very soft, 3 to 5 minutes. Off heat, stir in olives and lemon juice and season with salt and pepper to taste.

3. FOR THE GOAT CHEESE MIXTURE Mix goat cheese, ¼ cup basil, remaining 2 tablespoons oil, lemon zest, and pepper together in bowl.

4. TO FINISH Spread goat cheese mixture evenly over center of pastry shells. Spoon fennel mixture over top. Bake tarts until cheese is warmed through and crust is deep golden, 5 to 7 minutes. Sprinkle with remaining 1 tablespoon basil and serve.

PREP AHEAD

- Thaw puff pastry, then halve
- Halve, core, and slice fennel
- Chop olives
- Grate lemon zest and juice lemon
- Wash and pick basil

MAKE AHEAD

- Store parbaked puff pastry for up to 2 days
- Refrigerate cooked fennel mixture for up to 2 days
- Refrigerate goat cheese mixture for up to 2 days

NOTES FROM THE TEST KITCHEN

- To thaw frozen puff pastry, let it sit in the refrigerator for 24 hours or on the counter for 30 minutes to 1 hour
- Sub dry vermouth for white wine
- Sub kalamata olives for oil-cured olives
- Sub cream cheese for goat cheese
- Sub parsley for basil

MEAL PLAN 25

WHY THIS MEAL PLAN WORKS

We crave comfort food year-round, not just in the wintertime; with that in mind, we designed this week's meal plan to be comfort food–focused but with a lighter touch, so that you can turn to this plan anytime the need or desire arises. The wedge salad in particular is a satisfying, seasonless classic that's always a favorite. There are only a couple of make-ahead meal component options this week, but the extensive prep-ahead choices will give you a major leg up on bringing the dinners to the table in a timely manner. There are also loads of flexible substitutions on the grocery list for customizing according to your taste preferences or whatever looks best at the grocery store. We recommend cooking the fish within 2 days of purchase (or see page 14 for short-term freezing).

GROCERY LIST

PROTEIN		Substitutions
☐ Skinless halibut fillets	4 (6 to 8 ounces each), 1 inch thick	*Mahi-mahi, red snapper, striped bass, or swordfish*
☐ Sirloin steak tips	1½ pounds	
☐ Boneless pork cutlets	8 (3 ounces each), ½ inch thick	*Chicken cutlets*
☐ Pancetta	2 ounces	*2 slices bacon*
PRODUCE		
☐ Iceberg lettuce	1 head (2 pounds)	*Romaine lettuce hearts*
☐ Leeks	2 pounds	
☐ Cherry tomatoes	10 ounces	*Grape tomatoes*
☐ Baby kale	5 ounces (5 cups)	*Baby spinach*
☐ Chives	1 bunch (enough for 2 tablespoons minced plus ½ cup chopped)	*Parsley*
DAIRY		
☐ Blue cheese	3 ounces	

PREP AHEAD

Slice 2 pounds potatoes ¼ inch thick

Halve 1½ pounds potatoes

Core iceberg lettuce, then cut into 8 wedges

Halve white and light green parts of leeks, then thinly slice and wash thoroughly

Grate lemon zest (5 teaspoons)

Juice lemon (2 teaspoons)

Halve cherry tomatoes

Toast panko

Grate Parmesan (2¾ cups)

Trim steak tips, then cut into 2-inch pieces

Cut pancetta into ½-inch pieces

Cut bacon into ½-inch pieces

MAKE AHEAD

UP TO 1 DAY	Make blue cheese dressing for wedge salad
	Bread pork cutlets

PANTRY ITEMS

CUPBOARD & COUNTER		Substitutions
☐ Bucatini	1 pound	*Any strand pasta*
☐ Panko bread crumbs	½ cup	
☐ Oil	½ cup plus 1 tablespoon	
☐ Red wine vinegar	1 teaspoon	*White wine vinegar*
☐ Cayenne pepper	¼ teaspoon	
☐ All-purpose flour	1 cup plus 2 tablespoons	
☐ Small red potatoes (1- to 2-inch diameter)	3½ pounds	*Small Yukon Gold potatoes*
☐ Garlic cloves	5	
REFRIGERATOR		
☐ Parmesan cheese	5½ ounces	*Pecorino Romano*
☐ Whole milk	1 cup	
☐ Plain yogurt	¾ cup	
☐ Unsalted butter	5 tablespoons	*Oil*
☐ Eggs	3 large	
☐ Broth	3 cups	
☐ Dry white wine	¾ cup	*Dry vermouth*
☐ Lemons	2	
FREEZER		
☐ Frozen peas	1 cup	
☐ Bacon	4 slices	*4 ounces pancetta*

POACHED HALIBUT *with* LEEK COMPOTE *and* RED POTATOES

SERVES 4 | ACTIVE TIME 30 MINUTES

1½ pounds small red potatoes, unpeeled, halved

2 tablespoons unsalted butter, melted, plus 3 tablespoons unsalted butter

1¼ teaspoons table salt, divided

3 tablespoons chopped fresh chives, divided

2 teaspoons grated lemon zest plus 2 teaspoons juice

4 (6- to 8-ounce) skinless halibut fillets, 1 inch thick

¼ teaspoon cayenne pepper, plus extra for seasoning

2 pounds leeks, white and light green parts only, halved lengthwise, sliced thin, and washed thoroughly (4½ cups)

2 garlic cloves, minced

¼ cup dry white wine

1 cup broth

1. Adjust oven rack to lowest position and heat oven to 425 degrees. Toss potatoes, 2 tablespoons melted butter, and ½ teaspoon salt together on rimmed baking sheet, then arrange cut side down in single layer. Roast until potatoes are tender, about 25 minutes.

2. While potatoes roast, combine 1 tablespoon chives and lemon zest in bowl; set aside. Sprinkle halibut with cayenne and ½ teaspoon salt. Melt remaining 3 tablespoons butter in 12-inch skillet over medium-high heat. Add leeks, garlic, and remaining ¼ teaspoon salt and cook until leeks have wilted, about 5 minutes. Add wine and cook until nearly evaporated, about 1 minute. Add broth and bring to simmer.

3. Reduce heat to medium-low. Place halibut on top of leek mixture and cook, covered, until fish registers 130 degrees, 13 to 15 minutes. Using spatula, transfer halibut to large plate and tent with aluminum foil. Stir lemon juice and remaining 2 tablespoons chives into leek mixture, then season with salt and extra cayenne to taste. Sprinkle halibut with lemon zest mixture and serve with leek compote and potatoes.

PREP AHEAD

- Halve potatoes
- Grate lemon zest and juice lemon
- Halve, slice, and wash leeks

NOTES FROM THE TEST KITCHEN

- You will need a 12-inch skillet with a tight-fitting lid
- Sub Yukon Gold potatoes for red potatoes
- Sub oil for butter
- Sub parsley for chives
- Sub mahi-mahi, red snapper, striped bass, or swordfish for halibut
- Sub dry vermouth for white wine

WEDGE SALAD *with* STEAK TIPS *and* BLUE CHEESE DRESSING

SERVES 4 | ACTIVE TIME 35 MINUTES

4 slices bacon, cut into ½-inch pieces

1½ pounds sirloin steak tips, trimmed and cut into 2-inch pieces

¾ teaspoon table salt, divided

½ teaspoon pepper, divided

¾ cup plain yogurt

1 teaspoon red wine vinegar

3 ounces blue cheese, crumbled (¾ cup), divided

1 garlic clove, minced

1 head iceberg lettuce (2 pounds), cored and cut into 8 wedges

10 ounces cherry tomatoes, halved

2 tablespoons minced fresh chives

1. FOR THE BACON Cook bacon in 12-inch skillet over medium heat until crispy, 5 to 7 minutes. Using slotted spoon, transfer bacon to paper towel–lined plate. Pour off all but 2 tablespoons fat from skillet (or add oil until it measures 2 tablespoons).

2. FOR THE STEAK TIPS Pat steak dry with paper towels and sprinkle with ½ teaspoon salt and ¼ teaspoon pepper. Heat bacon fat in skillet over medium-high heat until just smoking. Add steak tips and cook until well browned all over and meat registers 120 to 125 degrees (for medium-rare), 6 to 8 minutes. Transfer to plate, tent with aluminum foil, and let rest for 5 minutes.

3. FOR THE BLUE CHEESE DRESSING Whisk yogurt, vinegar, ½ cup blue cheese, garlic, remaining ¼ teaspoon salt, and remaining ¼ teaspoon pepper together in bowl.

4. TO FINISH Arrange lettuce wedges and steak tips on individual plates and drizzle with dressing. Top with tomatoes, chives, bacon, and remaining ¼ cup blue cheese. Serve.

PREP AHEAD

- Core and cut lettuce
- Halve cherry tomatoes
- Cut bacon
- Trim and cut steak tips

MAKE AHEAD

- Refrigerate blue cheese dressing for up to 1 day

NOTES FROM THE TEST KITCHEN

- Sub pancetta for bacon
- Sub white wine vinegar for red wine vinegar
- Sub romaine lettuce hearts for iceberg lettuce
- Sub grape tomatoes for cherry tomatoes
- Sub parsley for chives

PARMESAN-CRUSTED PORK CUTLETS *with* CHIVE SMASHED POTATOES

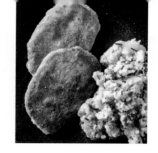

SERVES 4 | ACTIVE TIME 45 MINUTES

2 pounds small red potatoes, unpeeled, sliced ¼ inch thick

1 cup whole milk

½ cup oil, divided

2 teaspoons table salt, divided

¾ teaspoon pepper, divided

¼ cup chopped fresh chives

1 cup plus 2 tablespoons all-purpose flour, divided

3 large eggs

4 ounces Parmesan cheese, grated (2 cups)

8 (3-ounce) boneless pork cutlets, ½ inch thick, trimmed

1. FOR THE POTATOES Microwave potatoes, milk, ¼ cup oil, 1½ teaspoons salt, and ½ teaspoon pepper in covered bowl until potatoes are tender, about 15 minutes, stirring halfway through. Using potato masher, gently smash potatoes until nearly to desired consistency. Stir in chives and season with salt and pepper to taste; cover to keep warm and set aside until ready to serve.

2. FOR THE BREADED CUTLETS While potatoes cook, spread 1 cup flour in shallow dish. Beat eggs in second shallow dish. Combine Parmesan and remaining 2 tablespoons flour in third shallow dish. Pat pork dry with paper towels, then sprinkle with remaining ½ teaspoon salt and remaining ¼ teaspoon pepper. Working with 1 cutlet at a time, dredge cutlets in flour, dip in egg, then coat with Parmesan mixture; return to flour, pressing gently to adhere.

3. TO FINISH Heat 2 tablespoons oil in 12-inch nonstick skillet over medium heat until just smoking. Add 4 cutlets and cook until golden brown, 3 to 5 minutes per side. Transfer to paper towel–lined plate to drain. Wipe skillet clean with paper towels and repeat with remaining 2 tablespoons oil and remaining 4 cutlets. Serve cutlets with smashed potatoes.

PREP AHEAD

- Slice potatoes
- Grate Parmesan

MAKE AHEAD

- Refrigerate breaded cutlets for up to 1 day

NOTES FROM THE TEST KITCHEN

- Sub Yukon Gold potatoes for red potatoes
- Sub parsley for chives
- Sub Pecorino Romano for Parmesan
- Sub chicken cutlets for pork

BUCATINI *with* PEAS, KALE, *and* PANCETTA

SERVES 4 TO 6 | ACTIVE TIME 45 MINUTES

½ cup panko bread crumbs, toasted

1½ ounces Parmesan cheese, grated
    (¾ cup), divided

1 tablespoon oil

1 tablespoon grated
    lemon zest, divided

¼ teaspoon table salt

¼ teaspoon pepper

2 ounces pancetta, cut into
    ½-inch pieces

2 garlic cloves, minced

½ cup dry white wine

2½ cups water

2 cups broth

1 pound bucatini

5 ounces (5 cups) baby kale

1 cup frozen peas

1. Combine panko, ¼ cup Parmesan, oil, 1 teaspoon lemon zest, salt, and pepper in bowl; set aside. Cook pancetta in Dutch oven over medium heat until rendered and crispy, 6 to 8 minutes. Using slotted spoon, transfer pancetta to paper towel–lined plate.

2. Add garlic and remaining 2 teaspoons lemon zest to fat left in pot and cook until fragrant, about 30 seconds. Stir in wine, scraping up any browned bits, and cook until nearly evaporated, about 3 minutes. Stir in water, broth, and pasta and bring to vigorous simmer. Reduce heat to medium, cover, and cook, stirring often, until pasta is nearly tender, 8 to 10 minutes.

3. Uncover, stir in kale and peas, and simmer until pasta and kale are tender, about 4 minutes. Add remaining ½ cup Parmesan and stir vigorously until pasta is creamy and well coated, about 30 seconds. Season with salt and pepper to taste. Serve, sprinkling individual portions with pancetta and panko mixture.

PREP AHEAD

- Toast panko
- Grate Parmesan
- Grate lemon zest
- Cut pancetta

NOTES FROM THE TEST KITCHEN

- Sub Pecorino Romano for Parmesan
- Sub bacon for pancetta
- Sub dry vermouth for white wine
- Sub any strand pasta for bucatini
- Sub baby spinach for baby kale

Pantry
MEALS

AVGOLEMONO

SERVES 4 | ACTIVE TIME 35 MINUTES

8 cups broth

1 cup long-grain white rice

12 (4-inch) strips lemon zest plus
   ¼ cup juice (2 lemons)

4 green cardamom pods, crushed

1 bay leaf

1½ teaspoons table salt

2 large eggs plus 2 large yolks,
   room temperature

1. Bring broth to boil in medium saucepan over high heat. Stir in rice, lemon zest, cardamom pods, bay leaf, and salt. Reduce heat to medium-low and simmer until rice is tender and broth is aromatic, 16 to 20 minutes.

2. Whisk whole eggs, egg yolks, and lemon juice together gently in medium bowl until combined. Discard bay leaf, cardamom, and lemon zest. Reduce heat to low. Whisking constantly, slowly ladle 2 cups hot broth into egg mixture and whisk until combined. Pour egg mixture back into saucepan and cook, stirring constantly, until soup is slightly thickened and wisps of steam appear, about 5 minutes (do not simmer or boil). Serve immediately.

PREP AHEAD

- Zest and juice lemon

NOTES FROM THE TEST KITCHEN

- This soup does not reheat well
- Stir in shredded cooked chicken to make this soup heartier
- Garnish with scallions, mint, or chives, if you have any
- Sub 2 whole cloves for cardamom pods

SUN-DRIED TOMATO *and* WHITE BEAN SOUP *with* PARMESAN CRISPS

SERVES 6 | ACTIVE TIME 30 MINUTES

4 (15-ounce) cans small white beans, undrained

4 cups broth

¾ cup oil-packed sun-dried tomatoes, rinsed, patted dry, and chopped coarse

1 ounce Parmesan cheese, ½ ounce shredded (3 tablespoons) and ½ ounce grated (¼ cup)

1½ teaspoons lemon juice

1. FOR THE SOUP Bring beans and their liquid, broth, and tomatoes to boil in Dutch oven. Reduce heat to medium-low and simmer, covered, stirring occasionally, until beans begin to break down, 18 to 22 minutes.

2. Working in batches, process soup in blender until smooth, about 2 minutes; add grated Parmesan and lemon juice to last batch. Return soup to now-empty pot and adjust consistency with hot water as needed. Season with salt and pepper to taste.

3. FOR THE PARMESAN CRISPS While soup cooks, mound shredded Parmesan in 3 piles on large plate (1 tablespoon per mound), then spread each pile into 2½-inch-wide circle. Microwave until golden brown, about 2 minutes. Using thin metal spatula, carefully transfer wafers to wire rack and let cool, about 10 minutes. Once cool to touch, crumble into bite-size pieces; set aside until ready to serve. (If wafers aren't crisp after 2 minutes of cooling, blot dry with paper towels, then return wafers to microwave in 15-second bursts until crisp.)

4. TO FINISH Sprinkle individual portions with reserved crumbled Parmesan wafers and pepper to taste. Serve.

PREP AHEAD

- Rinse, pat dry, and chop sun-dried tomatoes

- Shred and grate Parmesan

- Juice lemon

MAKE AHEAD

- Refrigerate soup for up to 3 days (or freeze for up to 1 month)

- Refrigerate Parmesan crisps for up to 1 week

NOTES FROM THE TEST KITCHEN

- If you don't have a stand blender, you can use an immersion blender

- Garnish with basil, if you have it

- Sub Pecorino Romano for Parmesan

5-INGREDIENT BLACK BEAN SOUP

SERVES 6 | ACTIVE TIME 25 MINUTES

4 (15-ounce) cans black beans, undrained

4 cups broth

2–3 tablespoons minced canned chipotle chile in adobo sauce

½ cup plain Greek yogurt

1 teaspoon grated lime zest, plus lime wedges for serving

1. FOR THE SOUP Bring beans and their liquid, broth, and chipotle to boil in Dutch oven. Reduce heat to medium-low and simmer covered, stirring occasionally, until beans begin to break down, 20 to 25 minutes. Using potato masher, coarsely mash beans in pot. Adjust consistency with extra hot water as needed.

2. TO FINISH Stir in yogurt and lime zest and season with salt and pepper to taste. Serve with lime wedges.

PREP AHEAD

- Mince chipotle in adobo
- Grate lime zest

MAKE AHEAD

- Refrigerate soup for up to 3 days (or freeze for up to 1 month)

NOTES FROM THE TEST KITCHEN

- Garnish with any of these that you have on hand: tortilla strips, cotija or feta cheese, avocado, scallions, and/or cilantro
- Sub sour cream for yogurt
- Sub lemon zest for lime zest

WHITE BEAN SOUP *with* LEMON *and* OREGANO

SERVES 4 TO 6 | ACTIVE TIME 45 MINUTES

2 tablespoons extra-virgin olive oil, plus extra for drizzling

1 onion, chopped

4 celery ribs, chopped fine

½ teaspoon pepper

2 garlic cloves, minced

¾ teaspoon dried oregano

¼ teaspoon red pepper flakes

4 (15-ounce) cans cannellini beans, undrained

4 cups broth

3 tablespoons lemon juice

1. FOR THE SOUP Heat oil in Dutch oven over medium heat until shimmering. Add onion, celery, and pepper and cook until vegetables are softened and lightly browned, 7 to 9 minutes. Stir in garlic, oregano, and pepper flakes and cook until fragrant, about 30 seconds. Stir in beans and their liquid and broth and bring to boil. Reduce heat to medium-low and simmer covered, stirring occasionally, until beans begin to break down, 12 to 14 minutes. Using potato masher, coarsely mash beans in pot. Adjust consistency with extra hot water as needed.

2. TO FINISH Stir in lemon juice and season with salt and pepper to taste. Drizzle individual portions with extra oil and serve.

PREP AHEAD

- Chop onion
- Chop celery
- Juice lemon

MAKE AHEAD

- Refrigerate soup for up to 3 days
  (or freeze for up to 1 month)

NOTES FROM THE TEST KITCHEN

- Garnish with celery leaves, dill, parsley, or basil, if you have any
- Sub 4 large shallots for onion
- Sub 2¼ teaspoons fresh oregano leaves for dried

RED LENTIL SOUP *with* NORTH AFRICAN SPICES

SERVES 4 TO 6 | ACTIVE TIME 45 MINUTES

2 tablespoons extra-virgin olive oil, plus extra for drizzling

1 large onion, chopped fine

¾ teaspoon ground coriander

½ teaspoon ground cumin

¼ teaspoon ground ginger

¼ teaspoon pepper

⅛ teaspoon ground cinnamon

Pinch cayenne pepper

1 tablespoon tomato paste

1 garlic clove, minced

6 cups broth, plus extra hot broth as needed

10½ ounces (1½ cups) dried red lentils, picked over and rinsed

2 tablespoons lemon juice, plus extra for seasoning

1. FOR THE SOUP Heat oil in large saucepan over medium heat until shimmering. Add onion and cook until softened, about 5 minutes. Stir in coriander, cumin, ginger, pepper, cinnamon, and cayenne and cook until fragrant, about 2 minutes. Stir in tomato paste and garlic and cook for 1 minute.

2. Stir in broth and lentils and bring to boil. Reduce heat to medium-low and simmer covered, stirring occasionally, until lentils are soft and about half are broken down, about 15 minutes.

3. Off heat, whisk soup vigorously until broken down to coarse puree, about 30 seconds. Adjust consistency with extra hot broth as needed.

4. TO FINISH Stir in lemon juice and season with salt and extra lemon juice to taste. Drizzle individual portions with extra oil and serve.

PREP AHEAD

- Chop onion
- Juice lemon

MAKE AHEAD

- Refrigerate soup for up to 3 days (or freeze for up to 1 month)

NOTES FROM THE TEST KITCHEN

- Serve with Simplest Salad (page 32) and/or crusty bread
- Garnish with cilantro or dried mint, if you have any
- Sub 6 large shallots for onion
- Sub lime juice for lemon juice

GRILLED CHEESE *with* TOMATO SOUP

SERVES 4 | ACTIVE TIME 40 MINUTES

---

2 tablespoons unsalted butter, plus 4 tablespoons melted

1 large onion, chopped

½ teaspoon table salt

1 garlic clove, minced

1 (28-ounce) can whole peeled tomatoes

2 cups broth

1 tablespoon packed light brown sugar

9 slices hearty white sandwich bread, 1 slice torn into 1-inch pieces

8 ounces cheddar cheese, shredded (2 cups)

1. FOR THE SOUP Melt 2 tablespoons butter in large saucepan over medium-low heat. Add onion and salt and cook until softened, about 5 minutes. Stir in garlic and cook until fragrant, about 30 seconds. Stir in tomatoes and their juice, broth, sugar, and torn bread pieces, breaking up tomatoes with wooden spoon. Cook until bread pieces break down, about 5 minutes, stirring occasionally.

2. Working in batches, process soup in blender until smooth, about 2 minutes. Return soup to clean saucepan and season with salt and pepper to taste. Cover saucepan and place over low heat to keep warm while making sandwiches.

3. FOR THE SANDWICHES Brush 1 side of remaining 8 slices bread with melted butter. Heat 12-inch skillet over medium-low heat for 2 minutes. Place 4 slices prepared bread, buttered side down, in skillet (depending on size of bread, you may need to cook in 2 batches). Sprinkle cheddar evenly over bread in skillet, then top with remaining 4 slices prepared bread, buttered side up. Cover skillet and cook until sandwich bottoms are golden brown, 4 to 8 minutes, moving sandwiches as needed for even browning.

4. Using metal spatula, flip sandwiches and continue to cook, covered, until golden brown on second side and cheese is melted, about 3 minutes. Serve with soup.

PREP AHEAD
- Chop onion
- Shred cheddar

MAKE AHEAD
- Refrigerate soup for up to 3 days

NOTES FROM THE TEST KITCHEN
- If you don't have a stand blender, you can use an immersion blender
- Garnish soup with chives, if you have them
- Sub 6 large shallots for onion
- Sub granulated sugar for brown sugar
- Sub any sliced bread for white sandwich bread
- Sub any semisoft cheese for cheddar

CURRIED CHICKPEA SALAD SANDWICHES

SERVES 6 | ACTIVE TIME 15 MINUTES

2 (15-ounce) cans chickpeas, rinsed, divided

½ cup mayonnaise

¼ cup water

1 tablespoon lemon juice

1 tablespoon curry powder

½ teaspoon table salt

2 celery ribs, chopped fine

½ cup raisins

12 slices hearty bread, toasted

1. FOR THE CHICKPEA SALAD Process ¾ cup chickpeas, mayonnaise, water, lemon juice, curry powder, and salt in food processor until smooth, about 30 seconds, scraping down sides of bowl as needed.

2. Add remaining chickpeas to food processor and pulse until coarsely chopped with some larger pieces remaining, about 4 pulses.

3. Combine chickpea mixture, celery, and raisins in bowl and season with salt and pepper to taste.

4. TO FINISH Spread chickpea salad evenly over 6 bread slices. Top with remaining bread slices and serve.

PREP AHEAD

- Juice lemon
- Chop celery

MAKE AHEAD

- Refrigerate chickpea salad for up to 3 days

NOTES FROM THE TEST KITCHEN

- Serve with lettuce, tomato, sliced avocado, and/or sprouts, if desired
- Garnish with cilantro, parsley, chives, or scallions, if you have any
- Sub dried currants, dried cherries, or dried cranberries for raisins
- Sub naan, pita, or lettuce leaves for bread

LENTIL SALAD *with* ORANGES, CELERY, *and* FETA

SERVES 4 TO 6 | ACTIVE TIME 20 MINUTES

---

1 cup dried brown lentils, picked over and rinsed

¾ teaspoon table salt, divided, plus salt for brining

2 tablespoons cider vinegar

1 shallot, minced

1 tablespoon honey

½ teaspoon dried mint

¼ cup oil

1 orange, peel and pith cut away, fruit cut into 8 wedges, then sliced crosswise ¼ inch thick

2 celery ribs, sliced thin on bias, plus ¼ cup celery leaves

¼ cup pecans, toasted and chopped coarse, divided

1 ounce feta cheese, crumbled (¼ cup)

1. FOR THE BRINED LENTILS Place lentils and 1 teaspoon salt in bowl. Cover with 4 cups warm water (about 110 degrees) and soak for at least 1 hour or up to 1 day. Drain well.

2. FOR THE SALAD Adjust oven rack to middle position and heat oven to 325 degrees. Combine drained lentils, 4 cups water, and ½ teaspoon salt in medium ovensafe saucepan. Cover, transfer to oven, and bake until lentils are tender, 40 minutes to 1 hour. Drain lentils well.

3. Whisk vinegar, shallot, honey, mint, and remaining ¼ teaspoon salt together in large bowl. While whisking constantly, slowly drizzle in oil until combined. Add drained lentils, orange slices, celery and leaves, and 2 tablespoons pecans and toss to combine. Season with salt and pepper to taste.

4. TO FINISH Sprinkle with feta and remaining 2 tablespoons pecans. Serve warm or at room temperature.

PREP AHEAD

- Mince shallot
- Cut orange
- Slice celery and pick leaves
- Toast and chop pecans

MAKE AHEAD

- Refrigerate drained, brined lentils for up to 2 days
- Refrigerate salad for up to 3 days

NOTES FROM THE TEST KITCHEN

- Brining prevents the lentils from bursting as they cook, but you can skip it if you prefer
- Sub lentilles du Puy (French lentils) for brown lentils
- Sub white wine vinegar, sherry vinegar, red wine vinegar, or lemon juice for cider vinegar
- Sub dried oregano or 1½ teaspoons chopped fresh mint for dried mint
- Sub grapefruit, apple, or ½ cup pomegranate seeds for orange
- Sub 1 fennel bulb for celery
- Sub parsley for celery leaves
- Sub any nut for pecans
- Sub goat cheese for feta

BULGUR SALAD *with* SPINACH, CHICKPEAS, *and* APPLES

SERVES 4 | ACTIVE TIME 20 MINUTES

2¼ cups water

1½ cups medium-grind bulgur, rinsed

¾ teaspoon table salt, divided

5 tablespoons oil

1 shallot, minced

1 teaspoon smoked paprika

½ teaspoon grated lemon zest plus ¼ cup juice (2 lemons)

1 tablespoon honey

1 (15-ounce) can chickpeas, rinsed

10 ounces frozen chopped spinach, thawed and squeezed dry

2 apples, cored and cut into ½-inch pieces

½ cup walnuts, toasted and chopped

1. FOR THE BULGUR Combine water, bulgur, and ¼ teaspoon salt in medium saucepan and bring to simmer over medium heat. Reduce heat to low, cover, and simmer gently until bulgur is tender, 16 to 18 minutes. Spread bulgur over rimmed baking sheet and set aside to cool, about 15 minutes.

2. FOR THE VINAIGRETTE Meanwhile, whisk oil, shallot, paprika, and lemon zest in large bowl, then microwave until bubbling and fragrant, about 30 seconds. Whisk in lemon juice, honey and remaining ½ teaspoon salt.

3. FOR THE SALAD Add cooled bulgur, chickpeas, spinach, and apples to vinaigrette and toss to combine.

4. TO FINISH Season with salt and pepper to taste, and sprinkle with walnuts. Serve.

PREP AHEAD

- Mince shallot
- Grate lemon zest and juice lemon
- Thaw spinach and squeeze dry
- Core and cut apples
- Toast and chop walnuts

MAKE AHEAD

- Refrigerate cooked and cooled bulgur for up to 2 days
- Refrigerate vinaigrette for up to 2 days
- Refrigerate salad for up to 2 days

NOTES FROM THE TEST KITCHEN

- Do not use cracked wheat, which requires lengthier cooking than bulgur
- Sub couscous for bulgur (cooking time will be shorter)
- Sub 5 ounces (5 cups) fresh spinach for frozen
- Sub pears or 1 cup blueberries for apples
- Sub almonds or pecans for walnuts

FUSILLI SALAD *with* ARTICHOKES, SPINACH, *and* SUN-DRIED TOMATOES

SERVES 4 TO 6 | ACTIVE TIME 30 MINUTES

1 pound fusilli

½ teaspoon table salt, plus salt for cooking pasta

6 tablespoons oil

¼ cup red wine vinegar

1 garlic clove, minced

½ teaspoon pepper

6 ounces frozen chopped spinach, thawed and squeezed dry

2 cups jarred whole baby artichoke hearts packed in water, rinsed, patted dry, and quartered

1 cup oil-packed sun-dried tomatoes, rinsed, patted dry, and chopped

½ cup pitted kalamata olives, chopped coarse

½ cup pine nuts, toasted

1. FOR THE PASTA SALAD Bring 4 quarts water to boil in large pot. Add pasta and 1 tablespoon salt and cook, stirring often, until tender. Drain pasta, rinse with cold water, and drain again, leaving pasta slightly wet.

2. Whisk oil, vinegar, garlic, salt, and pepper together in large bowl. Add pasta, spinach, artichokes, sun-dried tomatoes, and olives and toss to combine. Cover and let sit for at least 15 minutes.

3. TO FINISH Stir in pine nuts and season with salt and pepper to taste. Serve.

PREP AHEAD

- Thaw spinach and squeeze dry
- Rinse, pat dry, and quarter artichokes
- Rinse, pat dry, and chop sun-dried tomatoes
- Toast pine nuts

MAKE AHEAD

- Refrigerate pasta salad for up to 3 days

NOTES FROM THE TEST KITCHEN

- Sub any short pasta for fusilli
- Sub white wine vinegar or cider vinegar for red wine vinegar
- Sub 3 ounces (3 cups) fresh spinach for frozen
- Sub any olives or pepperoncini for kalamata olives
- Sub walnuts or almonds for pine nuts

SPICY LINGUINE *with* OLIVES *and* GARLIC

SERVES 4 TO 6 | ACTIVE TIME 30 MINUTES

1 pound linguine

¾ teaspoon table salt, divided, plus salt for cooking pasta

1 tablespoon plus ½ cup oil, divided

½ cup panko bread crumbs

6 garlic cloves, sliced thin

1 teaspoon red pepper flakes

¼ teaspoon pepper

1 cup pitted green olives, halved

2 tablespoons lemon juice

1. FOR THE PASTA Bring 4 quarts water to boil in large pot. Add pasta and 1 tablespoon salt and cook, stirring often, until al dente. Reserve ½ cup cooking water, then drain pasta and return it to pot.

2. FOR THE PANKO TOPPING Combine 1 tablespoon oil, panko, and ¼ teaspoon salt in 12-inch nonstick skillet and cook over medium heat, stirring often, until panko is lightly toasted, about 3 minutes. Transfer topping to bowl.

3. TO FINISH Add remaining ½ cup oil, garlic, pepper flakes, remaining ½ teaspoon salt, and pepper to now-empty skillet and cook over medium heat until garlic begins to brown, about 4 minutes. Add olives, lemon juice, garlic oil, and ¼ cup reserved cooking water to pasta and toss to combine. Adjust consistency with remaining reserved cooking water as needed. Sprinkle with panko and serve.

PREP AHEAD

• Juice lemon

MAKE AHEAD

• Store panko topping in airtight container for up to 1 week

NOTES FROM THE TEST KITCHEN

• Garnish with parsley, if you have any, and Parmesan cheese, if desired

• Sub any strand pasta for linguine

• Sub any olives for green olives

GARLICKY SPAGHETTI *with* ARTICHOKES *and* HAZELNUTS

SERVES 4 TO 6 | ACTIVE TIME 35 MINUTES

¼ cup oil

6 garlic cloves, minced

1½ teaspoons fennel seeds, crushed

¼ teaspoon red pepper flakes

1 pound spaghetti

Table salt for cooking pasta

1½ cups jarred whole baby artichoke hearts packed in water, rinsed, patted dry, and chopped

1 tablespoon lemon juice

1 ounce Parmesan cheese, grated (½ cup), plus extra for serving

½ cup blanched hazelnuts, toasted and chopped

1. Cook oil and garlic in 8-inch nonstick skillet over low heat, stirring occasionally, until garlic is pale golden brown, 9 to 12 minutes. Off heat, stir in fennel seeds and pepper flakes; set aside.

2. Bring 2 quarts water to boil in large pot. Add pasta and 2 teaspoons salt and cook, stirring often, until al dente. Reserve 1 cup cooking water, then drain pasta and return it to pot. Add artichokes, lemon juice, reserved garlic-oil mixture, and reserved cooking water to pasta in pot. Stir until pasta is well coated with oil and no water remains in bottom of pot. Add Parmesan and hazelnuts and toss to combine. Season with salt and pepper to taste. Serve, passing extra Parmesan separately.

PREP AHEAD

- Rinse, pat dry, and chop artichokes
- Juice lemon
- Grate Parmesan
- Toast and chop hazelnuts

NOTES FROM THE TEST KITCHEN

- Cooking the pasta in a smaller amount of water makes for starchier cooking water, contributing body to the sauce
- Sub any strand pasta for spaghetti
- Sub Pecorino Romano for Parmesan
- Sub walnuts or almonds for hazelnuts

CACIO E PEPE

SERVES 4 TO 6 | ACTIVE TIME 25 MINUTES

1 pound spaghetti

Table salt for cooking pasta

6 ounces Pecorino Romano cheese, grated (3 cups), divided

2 tablespoons heavy cream

2 teaspoons extra-virgin olive oil

1½ teaspoons pepper

1. Set colander in large serving bowl. Bring 2 quarts water to boil in large pot. Add pasta and 2 teaspoons salt and cook, stirring often, until al dente. Drain pasta in prepared colander. Reserve 1½ cups cooking water in liquid measuring cup; discard remaining cooking water. Transfer pasta to now-empty bowl.

2. Place 2 cups Pecorino in medium bowl, then slowly whisk in 1 cup reserved cooking water until smooth. Whisk in cream, oil, and pepper. Gradually pour Pecorino mixture over pasta, tossing to coat. Let pasta rest for 1 to 2 minutes so sauce can thicken, tossing frequently and adjusting consistency with remaining reserved cooking water as needed. Serve immediately, passing remaining 1 cup Pecorino separately.

PREP AHEAD

• Grate Pecorino Romano

NOTES FROM THE TEST KITCHEN

• Cooking the pasta in a smaller amount of water makes for starchier cooking water, contributing body to the sauce

• Draining the pasta water into the serving bowl warms the bowl to help keep the dish hot until serving

• Sub any strand pasta for spaghetti

• Sub Parmesan for Pecorino Romano

CREAMY STOVETOP MACARONI *and* CHEESE

SERVES 4 | ACTIVE TIME 30 MINUTES

2 large eggs

1 (12-ounce) can evaporated milk, divided

1 teaspoon dry mustard

½ teaspoon table salt plus salt for cooking pasta

¼ teaspoon pepper

8 ounces (2 cups) elbow macaroni

4 tablespoons unsalted butter

12 ounces sharp cheddar cheese, shredded (3 cups), divided

1. Whisk eggs, half of evaporated milk, dry mustard, ½ teaspoon salt, and pepper together in bowl; set aside.

2. Bring 4 quarts water to boil in large pot. Add macaroni and 1 tablespoon salt and cook, stirring often, until al dente. Drain pasta and return it to pot. Add butter and cook over low heat until melted. Stir in egg mixture and half of cheddar. Cook, gradually stirring in remaining milk and cheddar, until mixture thickens and becomes hot and creamy, 5 to 7 minutes. Season with salt and pepper to taste, and serve.

PREP AHEAD

- Shred cheddar

MAKE AHEAD

- Refrigerate macaroni and cheese for up to 3 days

NOTES FROM THE TEST KITCHEN

- Top with toasted panko bread crumbs, if you have them

- Sub any short pasta for elbow macaroni

- Sub Monterey Jack or Colby for some or all of cheddar

SKILLET TORTELLINI SUPPER

SERVES 4 TO 6 | ACTIVE TIME 35 MINUTES

12 ounces dried cheese tortellini

Table salt for cooking pasta

4 slices bacon, cut crosswise into ¼-inch strips

4 garlic cloves, minced

1 cup heavy cream

½ teaspoon pepper

2 cups frozen peas, thawed

1 ounce Parmesan cheese, grated (½ cup), plus extra for serving

1 teaspoon grated lemon zest plus 2 teaspoons juice

1. Bring 4 quarts water to boil in large pot. Add pasta and 1 tablespoon salt and cook, stirring frequently, until not quite al dente, about 8 minutes. Reserve 1 cup cooking water, then drain pasta; set aside.

2. Meanwhile, cook bacon in 12-inch skillet over medium heat until crispy, 5 to 7 minutes. Using slotted spoon, transfer bacon to paper towel–lined plate.

3. Pour off all but 1 teaspoon fat from skillet. Add garlic and cook until fragrant, about 30 seconds. Stir in cream, pepper, pasta, and ½ cup reserved cooking water, and bring to simmer over medium heat. Cook, stirring often, until tortellini is al dente and sauce has thickened and coats pasta, 4 to 7 minutes. Stir in peas, Parmesan, and lemon zest and juice and cook until warmed through, about 1 minute, adjusting consistency with remaining reserved cooking water as needed. Season with salt and pepper to taste. Sprinkle with reserved bacon and serve, passing extra Parmesan separately.

PREP AHEAD

- Grate Parmesan
- Grate lemon zest and juice lemon
- Cut bacon

NOTES FROM THE TEST KITCHEN

- Cooking time for the tortellini will vary depending on brand and size; be sure to undercook it slightly in step 1, as it will continue to cook in the cream sauce
- Add some halved cherry tomatoes before serving, if you have them
- Garnish with chives, parsley, and/or basil, if you have any
- Sub 4 ounces prosciutto or pancetta for bacon
- Sub frozen corn for frozen peas
- Sub Pecorino Romano for Parmesan

PASTA and CHICKPEAS with TOMATO and PARMESAN

SERVES 4 TO 6 | ACTIVE TIME 30 MINUTES

- 2 tablespoons extra-virgin olive oil, plus extra for serving
- 1 onion, chopped fine
- 4 garlic cloves, minced
- ¼ teaspoon red pepper flakes
- ¾ teaspoon dried rosemary, crumbled
- 2 cups water, plus extra as needed
- 2 (15-ounce) cans chickpeas, undrained
- 1 (14-ounce) can diced tomatoes
- 1 teaspoon table salt
- 8 ounces (1½ cups) small shells
- 1 ounce Parmesan cheese, grated (½ cup)

1. FOR THE PASTA AND CHICKPEAS Heat oil in Dutch oven over medium heat until shimmering. Add onion and cook until softened and just beginning to brown, 5 to 7 minutes. Stir in garlic, pepper flakes, and rosemary and cook until fragrant, about 1 minute. Stir in water, chickpeas and their liquid, tomatoes and their juice, and salt and bring to boil. Reduce heat to medium-low and simmer for 10 minutes.

2. Add pasta and cook, stirring frequently, until tender, 10 to 12 minutes. Adjust consistency with extra hot water as needed and season with salt and pepper to taste.

3. TO FINISH Serve, passing Parmesan and extra oil separately.

PREP AHEAD

- Chop onion
- Grate Parmesan

MAKE AHEAD

- Refrigerate pasta and chickpeas for up to 3 days

NOTES FROM THE TEST KITCHEN

- Sub 4 large shallots for onion
- Sub 2¼ teaspoons chopped fresh rosemary for dried
- Sub ditalini or elbow macaroni for small shells (sub by weight, not volume)
- Sub Pecorino Romano for Parmesan

PASTA *with* TUNA *and* CRISPY BREAD CRUMBS

SERVES 4 TO 6 | ACTIVE TIME 45 MINUTES

---

1 pound farfalle

Table salt for cooking pasta

2 tablespoons oil, divided

½ cup panko bread crumbs

3 tablespoons capers, rinsed

1 teaspoon grated lemon zest,
  plus lemon wedges for serving

4 garlic cloves, minced

¼ teaspoon red pepper flakes

1 (28-ounce) can crushed tomatoes

½ cup pitted kalamata olives, chopped

12 ounces olive oil–packed tuna,
  drained

1. FOR THE PASTA Bring 4 quarts water to boil in large pot. Add pasta and 1 tablespoon salt and cook, stirring often, until al dente. Reserve ½ cup cooking water, then drain pasta and return it to pot.

2. FOR THE PANKO TOPPING Heat 1 tablespoon oil in 12-inch nonstick skillet over medium heat until shimmering. Add panko and capers and cook, stirring frequently, until panko is golden brown and capers have darkened and shrunk, 3 to 5 minutes. Stir in lemon zest and cook until fragrant, about 1 minute. Transfer topping to bowl.

3. TO FINISH Wipe skillet clean with paper towels. Heat remaining 1 tablespoon oil in now-empty skillet over medium heat until shimmering. Add garlic and pepper flakes and cook until fragrant, about 30 seconds. Stir in tomatoes and simmer until thickened slightly, about 10 minutes. Stir in olives and remove from heat.

4. Add sauce to pasta in pot and stir until pasta is well coated. Fold in tuna gently until combined but chunks still remain. Season with salt and pepper to taste, and adjust consistency with reserved cooking water as needed. Sprinkle with reserved panko mixture. Serve with lemon wedges.

PREP AHEAD
- Grate lemon zest

MAKE AHEAD
- Store panko topping in airtight container for up to 1 week

NOTES FROM THE TEST KITCHEN
- Be sure to fold in the tuna gently, so that it doesn't break apart too much
- Garnish with basil or parsley, if you have any
- Sub any short pasta for farfalle
- Sub any olives for kalamata olives

SPAGHETTI *with* BACON *and* SPICY TOMATO SAUCE

SERVES 4 TO 6 | ACTIVE TIME 35 MINUTES

6 slices bacon, cut crosswise into ¼-inch strips

Oil, as needed

1 onion, chopped fine

3 garlic cloves, minced

¼ teaspoon red pepper flakes

1 (28-ounce) can diced tomatoes

1 pound spaghetti

Table salt for cooking pasta

1 ounce Parmesan cheese, grated (½ cup), plus extra for serving

1. Cook bacon in 12-inch skillet over medium heat until crispy, 5 to 7 minutes. Using slotted spoon, transfer bacon to paper towel–lined plate.

2. Pour off all but 2 tablespoons fat from skillet (or add oil until it measures 2 tablespoons). Add onion and cook until softened, about 5 minutes. Stir in garlic and pepper flakes and cook until fragrant, about 30 seconds. Stir in tomatoes and their juice and cook until thickened, about 10 minutes.

3. Meanwhile, bring 4 quarts water to boil in large pot. Add pasta and 1 tablespoon salt and cook, stirring frequently, until al dente. Reserve ½ cup cooking water, then drain pasta and return it to pot. Add sauce to pasta in pot and stir until pasta is well coated. Add Parmesan and toss to combine. Season with salt and pepper to taste, and adjust consistency with reserved cooking water as needed. Sprinkle with reserved bacon and serve, passing extra Parmesan separately.

PREP AHEAD

- Chop onion
- Grate Parmesan
- Cut bacon

NOTES FROM THE TEST KITCHEN

- Sub 6 ounces pancetta, guanciale, or salt pork for bacon
- Sub 4 large shallots for onion
- Sub chopped canned whole peeled tomatoes or crushed tomatoes for diced tomatoes
- Sub any strand pasta for spaghetti
- Sub Pecorino Romano for Parmesan

CORIANDER-SPICED COUSCOUS
with CHICKPEAS

SERVES 4 TO 6 | ACTIVE TIME 30 MINUTES

¼ cup oil, divided

1½ cups couscous

2 carrots, peeled and chopped fine

1 onion, chopped fine

1 teaspoon table salt

3 garlic cloves, minced

1 teaspoon ground coriander

1 teaspoon ground ginger

1¾ cups broth

1 (15-ounce) can chickpeas, rinsed

1½ cups frozen peas

Lemon wedges for serving

1. FOR THE COUSCOUS MIXTURE Heat 2 tablespoons oil in 12-inch skillet over medium-high heat until shimmering. Add couscous and cook, stirring frequently, until grains are just beginning to brown, 3 to 5 minutes. Transfer to bowl and wipe skillet clean with paper towels.

2. Heat remaining 2 tablespoons oil in now-empty skillet over medium heat until shimmering. Add carrots, onion, and salt and cook until softened and just beginning to brown, 5 to 7 minutes. Stir in garlic, coriander, and ginger and cook until fragrant, about 30 seconds. Stir in broth and chickpeas and bring to simmer.

3. Stir in peas and couscous. Cover, remove skillet from heat, and let sit until couscous is tender, about 7 minutes.

4. TO FINISH Fluff with fork and season with salt and pepper to taste. Serve with lemon wedges.

PREP AHEAD

- Peel and chop carrots
- Chop onion

MAKE AHEAD

- Refrigerate couscous, chickpea, and vegetable mixture for up to 2 days

NOTES FROM THE TEST KITCHEN

- Garnish with cilantro or mint, if you have any
- Sub 2 celery ribs for carrots
- Sub 4 large shallots for onion
- Sub small white beans or black-eyed peas for chickpeas

RED CURRY RICE NOODLES
with **SHALLOTS** *and* **CASHEWS**

SERVES 4 | ACTIVE TIME 35 MINUTES

12 ounces (¼-inch-wide) rice noodles

2 tablespoons oil

6 shallots, quartered

¼ cup Thai red curry paste

1 (14-ounce) can coconut milk

2 tablespoons fish sauce

¼ cup roasted cashews, chopped

Lime wedges for serving

1. Bring 4 quarts water to boil in large pot. Remove from heat, add noodles, and let sit, stirring occasionally, until soft and pliable but not fully tender, 8 to 10 minutes. Drain noodles, rinse with cold water, and drain again; set aside.

2. Heat oil in 12-inch nonstick skillet over medium heat until shimmering. Add shallots and cook until softened and beginning to brown, about 5 minutes. Stir in curry paste and cook until shallots are well coated, about 2 minutes.

3. Whisk in coconut milk and fish sauce and bring to simmer. Add drained rice noodles and cook, tossing gently, until noodles are well coated and tender and sauce has thickened slightly, about 3 minutes. Adjust consistency with hot water as needed and season with salt and pepper to taste. Sprinkle with cashews. Serve with lime wedges.

PREP AHEAD

- Quarter shallots
- Chop cashews

NOTES FROM THE TEST KITCHEN

- Top with fried or scrambled eggs or stir in chopped cooked shrimp to make this more substantial
- Garnish with cilantro, mint, or basil, if you have any
- Sub ⅜-inch-wide rice noodles for ¼-inch-wide rice noodles
- Sub Thai green curry paste for red curry paste
- Sub peanuts for cashews

SPICY PEANUT RICE NOODLES *with* SHRIMP

SERVES 4 | ACTIVE TIME 40 MINUTES

---

2 carrots, peeled and shredded

5 tablespoons seasoned rice vinegar, divided

12 ounces (¼-inch wide) rice noodles

12 ounces extra-large shrimp (21 to 25 per pound), thawed, peeled, and deveined

¼ cup oil, divided

1 cup frozen edamame, thawed

⅓ cup crunchy or smooth peanut butter

2 tablespoons soy sauce

1 tablespoon sugar

1 tablespoon sriracha

3 garlic cloves, minced

1. FOR THE PICKLED CARROTS Combine carrots and 2 tablespoons vinegar in small bowl; set aside until ready to serve.

2. Bring 4 quarts water to boil in large pot. Remove from heat, add noodles, and let sit, stirring occasionally, until soft and pliable but not fully tender, 8 to 10 minutes. Drain noodles, rinse with cold water, and drain again; set aside.

3. FOR THE SHRIMP Meanwhile, pat shrimp dry with paper towels. Heat 1 tablespoon oil 12-inch nonstick skillet over medium-high heat until just smoking. Add shrimp and cook, stirring constantly, until just opaque, about 2 minutes; transfer to plate.

4. FOR THE EDAMAME Heat 1 tablespoon oil in now-empty skillet over medium-high heat until just smoking. Add edamame and cook until spotty brown but still bright green, about 2 minutes; transfer to plate.

5. TO FINISH Whisk 1½ cups water, peanut butter, remaining 3 tablespoons vinegar, soy sauce, remaining 2 tablespoons oil, sugar, sriracha, and garlic together in bowl. Add peanut sauce, drained noodles, and shrimp mixture to again-empty skillet and bring to simmer over medium-high heat. Cook, tossing gently, until noodles are coated and tender and sauce has thickened slightly, about 3 minutes. Adjust consistency with hot water as needed and season with salt and pepper to taste. Serve, passing carrot mixture separately.

PREP AHEAD

- Peel and shred carrots
- Thaw, peel, and devein shrimp

MAKE AHEAD

- Refrigerate pickled carrots for up to 5 days
- Refrigerate cooked shrimp for up to 2 days
- Refrigerate cooked edamame for up to 2 days

NOTES FROM THE TEST KITCHEN

- You can cook the edamame straight from frozen, but the cooking time will be longer
- Garnish with cilantro, mint, or basil, if you have any
- Sub 1 cup shredded cabbage for carrots
- Sub tamari for soy sauce
- Sub brown sugar for granulated sugar

KIMCHI FRIED RICE *with* SHRIMP

SERVES 4 | ACTIVE TIME 30 MINUTES

2 tablespoons oil, divided

1 onion, chopped

1 pound extra-large shrimp
  (21 to 25 per pound), thawed,
  peeled, deveined, and cut
  crosswise into thirds

2 garlic cloves, minced

1 recipe White Rice Pilaf
  (page 34), chilled

2 cups kimchi, drained

1 cup frozen edamame, thawed

½ cup oyster sauce

1. Heat 1 tablespoon oil in 12-inch nonstick skillet over medium-high heat until shimmering. Add onion and cook until softened and just beginning to brown, 5 to 7 minutes. Add shrimp and cook, stirring constantly, until just opaque, about 2 minutes. Add garlic and cook until fragrant, about 30 seconds; transfer to bowl.

2. Break up any large clumps of rice with your fingers. Heat remaining 1 tablespoon oil in now-empty skillet over medium heat until shimmering. Add rice, kimchi, edamame, oyster sauce, and shrimp mixture along with any accumulated juices and increase heat to high. Cook, tossing rice constantly, until mixture is thoroughly combined and warmed through, about 3 minutes. Serve.

PREP AHEAD

- Chop onion
- Thaw, peel, devein, and cut shrimp

MAKE AHEAD

- Refrigerate White Rice Pilaf for at least 1 day and up to 5 days
- Refrigerate fried rice for up to 3 days

NOTES FROM THE TEST KITCHEN

- Cooking the white rice ahead and chilling it ensures that the grains stay distinct and don't break down when you fry them
- Garnish with sriracha and/or scallions, if you have any
- Sub frozen peas for frozen edamame

GARLICKY WHITE BEANS *with* SHRIMP

SERVES 4 TO 6 | ACTIVE TIME 45 MINUTES

¼ cup oil, divided

1 pound large shrimp (26 to 30 per pound), thawed, peeled, deveined, and shells reserved

1 cup water

1 onion, chopped fine

4 garlic cloves, sliced thin

2 anchovy fillets, rinsed, patted dry, and minced

¼ teaspoon red pepper flakes

⅛ teaspoon pepper

2 (15-ounce) cans cannellini beans, undrained

1 (14.5-ounce) can diced tomatoes, drained

½ teaspoon grated lemon zest plus 1 tablespoon juice

1. FOR THE SHRIMP STOCK Heat 1 tablespoon oil in 12-inch skillet over medium heat until shimmering. Add shrimp shells and cook, stirring frequently, until spotty brown, 2 to 4 minutes. Off heat, carefully add water, scraping up any browned bits. Return skillet to medium heat and simmer gently, stirring occasionally, for 5 minutes. Strain mixture through fine-mesh strainer set over large bowl, pressing on solids to extract as much liquid as possible. Discard shells and reserve stock (you should have about ¼ cup).

2. FOR THE SHRIMP AND BEANS Wipe skillet clean with paper towels. Cook 2 tablespoons oil, onion, garlic, anchovies, pepper flakes, and pepper in now-empty skillet over medium-low heat until onion is softened, about 5 minutes. Stir in beans and their liquid, tomatoes, and reserved shrimp stock, bring to simmer, and cook for 15 minutes.

3. Reduce heat to low, stir in shrimp, cover, and cook until shrimp are just opaque, 5 to 7 minutes. Off heat, stir in lemon zest and juice and season with salt and pepper to taste. Drizzle with remaining 1 tablespoon oil. Serve.

PREP AHEAD
- Chop onion
- Grate lemon zest and juice lemon
- Thaw, peel, and devein shrimp, reserving shells

MAKE AHEAD
- Refrigerate shrimp stock for up to 2 days

NOTES FROM THE TEST KITCHEN
- Garnish with basil or parsley, if you have any
- Sub 4 large shallots for onion
- Sub 1 teaspoon anchovy paste for anchovies
- Sub small white beans for cannellini beans

SHRIMP SCAMPI

SERVES 4 | ACTIVE TIME 35 MINUTES

2 tablespoons oil, divided

1½ pounds extra-large shrimp (21 to 25 per pound), thawed, peeled, deveined, and shells reserved

1 cup dry white wine

¼ teaspoon dried thyme

3 tablespoons lemon juice, plus lemon wedges for serving

1 teaspoon cornstarch

8 garlic cloves, sliced thin

½ teaspoon red pepper flakes

¼ teaspoon pepper

4 tablespoons unsalted butter, cut into ½-inch pieces

1. FOR THE SHRIMP STOCK Heat 1 tablespoon oil in 12-inch skillet over medium heat until shimmering. Add shrimp shells and cook, stirring frequently, until spotty brown, 2 to 4 minutes. Off heat, carefully add wine and thyme, scraping up any browned bits. Return skillet to medium heat and simmer gently, stirring occasionally, for 5 minutes. Strain mixture through fine-mesh strainer set over large bowl, pressing on solids to extract as much liquid as possible. Discard shells and reserve stock (you should have about ⅔ cup).

2. FOR THE SCAMPI Wipe skillet clean with paper towels. Combine lemon juice and cornstarch in small bowl. Cook remaining 1 tablespoon oil, garlic, pepper flakes, and pepper in now-empty skillet over medium-low heat until garlic is fragrant and just beginning to brown at edges, 3 to 5 minutes. Add reserved shrimp stock, increase heat to high, and bring to simmer. Reduce heat to low, stir in shrimp, cover, and cook until shrimp are just opaque, 4 to 6 minutes. Off heat, transfer shrimp to bowl using slotted spoon.

3. Return skillet to medium heat, add lemon juice–cornstarch mixture, and cook until slightly thickened, about 1 minute. Remove from heat and whisk in butter until combined. Return shrimp and any accumulated juices to skillet and toss to combine. Serve, passing lemon wedges separately.

PREP AHEAD

- Juice lemon
- Thaw, peel, and devein shrimp, reserving shells

MAKE AHEAD

- Refrigerate shrimp stock for up to 2 days

NOTES FROM THE TEST KITCHEN

- Serve with crusty bread
- Garnish with basil or parsley, if you have any
- Sub dry vermouth for dry white wine
- Sub ¾ teaspoon fresh thyme leaves for dried

BLACK BEANS *and* RICE *with* EGGS

SERVES 4 TO 6 | ACTIVE TIME 35 MINUTES

---

2 slices bacon, chopped

2 tablespoons oil, divided

1 small onion, chopped fine

3 garlic cloves, minced

1 teaspoon dried oregano

¾ teaspoon ground cumin

1½ cups long-grain white rice, rinsed

2¼ cups broth

1 (15-ounce) can black beans, undrained

2 tablespoons red wine vinegar

6 large eggs

1. FOR THE BEANS AND RICE Cook bacon and 1 tablespoon oil in 12-inch nonstick skillet over medium heat until crispy, 5 to 7 minutes. Stir in onion and cook until softened and just beginning to brown, 5 to 7 minutes. Stir in garlic, oregano, and cumin and cook until fragrant, about 30 seconds. Stir in rice and cook until edges begin to turn translucent and rice is fragrant, about 2 minutes. Stir in broth, beans and their liquid, and vinegar and bring to boil. Cover, reduce heat to low, and simmer, without stirring, until liquid is absorbed and rice is tender, 20 to 25 minutes.

2. Remove from heat and let sit, covered, for 10 minutes. Fluff rice with fork, season with salt and pepper to taste, transfer to serving dish, and cover with aluminum foil to keep warm.

3. TO FINISH Crack eggs into 2 small bowls (3 eggs per bowl). Wipe skillet clean with paper towels. Heat remaining 1 tablespoon oil in now-empty skillet over medium-high heat until shimmering. Working quickly, pour 1 bowl of eggs in 1 side of skillet and second bowl of eggs in other side. Cover and cook for 1 minute. Remove skillet from heat and let sit, covered, for 15 to 45 seconds for runny yolks (white around edge of yolk will be barely opaque), 45 to 60 seconds for soft but set yolks, and about 2 minutes for medium-set yolks. Serve rice with eggs.

PREP AHEAD

- Chop onion
- Chop bacon

MAKE AHEAD

- Refrigerate cooked beans and rice for up to 3 days

NOTES FROM THE TEST KITCHEN

- You will need a 12-inch skillet with a tight-fitting lid
- Garnish with hot sauce, if you like
- Sub 2 ounces salt pork for bacon
- Sub 3 shallots for onion
- Sub kidney beans or red beans for black beans
- Sub white wine vinegar or cider vinegar for red wine vinegar

EGGS *in* PURGATORY

SERVES 4 | ACTIVE TIME 45 MINUTES

3 tablespoons extra-virgin olive oil, plus extra for drizzling

1 shallot, minced

4 garlic cloves, sliced thin

1 tablespoon tomato paste

½ teaspoon red pepper flakes

½ teaspoon dried oregano

1 teaspoon table salt, divided

1 (28-ounce) can crushed tomatoes

8 large eggs

¼ teaspoon pepper

¼ cup grated Parmesan cheese

1. FOR THE TOMATO SAUCE Heat oil in 12-inch skillet over medium heat until shimmering. Add shallot and garlic and cook until softened and beginning to brown, about 3 minutes. Stir in tomato paste, pepper flakes, oregano, and ¾ teaspoon salt and cook until rust-colored, about 4 minutes. Stir in tomatoes and bring to simmer. Reduce heat to medium-low and simmer gently, stirring occasionally, until thickened slightly, about 15 minutes. Remove skillet from heat.

2. TO FINISH Using back of spoon, make 8 shallow indentations in sauce (7 around perimeter and 1 in center). Crack 1 egg into bowl and pour into 1 indentation (it will hold yolk but not fully contain white). Repeat with remaining 7 eggs. Spoon sauce over edges of egg whites so that whites are partially covered and yolks are exposed. Sprinkle eggs with pepper and remaining ¼ teaspoon salt.

3. Bring to simmer over medium heat, cover, and cook until egg whites are set and egg yolks film over, 5 to 7 minutes. Off heat, sprinkle with Parmesan and drizzle with extra oil. Serve.

PREP AHEAD

- Mince shallot
- Grate Parmesan

MAKE AHEAD

- Refrigerate tomato sauce for up to 2 days

NOTES FROM THE TEST KITCHEN

- You will need a 12-inch skillet with a tight-fitting lid
- Serve with crusty bread
- Garnish with basil, chives, parsley, mint, or dill, if you have any
- Sub dried rosemary, thyme, or herbes de Provence for oregano
- Sub feta, goat cheese, or Pecorino Romano for Parmesan

FRIED EGGS *with* POTATO *and* PARMESAN PANCAKE

SERVES 4 | ACTIVE TIME 35 MINUTES

2½ pounds Yukon Gold potatoes, peeled and shredded

1½ teaspoons cornstarch

1¼ teaspoons table salt, divided

Pinch plus ⅛ teaspoon pepper, divided

¼ cup plus 2 teaspoons oil, divided

8 large eggs

1 ounce Parmesan cheese, grated (½ cup)

1. Place potatoes in large bowl and fill bowl with cold water. Using hands, swirl to remove excess starch, then drain, leaving potatoes in colander. Wipe bowl dry. Working in batches, squeeze potatoes dry in clean dish towel. Transfer potatoes to now-empty bowl and repeat with remaining potatoes. Sprinkle cornstarch, 1 teaspoon salt, and pinch pepper over potatoes in bowl and toss until well combined.

2. Heat 2 tablespoons oil in 12-inch nonstick skillet over medium heat until shimmering. Add potato mixture to skillet in even layer, cover, and cook for 6 minutes. Uncover, press potatoes gently into even layer, and cook until bottom is deep golden brown, 8 to 10 minutes, pressing potatoes as needed.

3. Slide potato pancake onto large plate, browned side down, using spatula for guidance. Add 2 tablespoons oil to now-empty skillet and swirl to coat. Invert potato pancake onto second plate and slide potato pancake, browned side up, back into skillet. Cook, pressing pancake occasionally, until bottom is well browned, 8 to 10 minutes. Transfer pancake to cutting board and set aside while preparing eggs.

4. Crack eggs into 2 small bowls (4 eggs per bowl) and sprinkle with remaining ¼ teaspoon salt and remaining ⅛ teaspoon pepper. Wipe skillet clean with paper towels. Heat remaining 2 teaspoons oil in again-empty skillet over medium-high heat until shimmering. Working quickly, pour 1 bowl of eggs in 1 side of skillet and second bowl of eggs in other side. Cover and cook for 1 minute. Remove skillet from heat and let sit, covered, for 15 to 45 seconds for runny yolks (white around edge of yolk will be barely opaque), 45 to 60 seconds for soft but set yolks, and about 2 minutes for medium-set yolks. Sprinkle pancake with Parmesan, cut into wedges, and serve with eggs.

PREP AHEAD

- Peel and shred potatoes
- Grate Parmesan

NOTES FROM THE TEST KITCHEN

- You will need a 12-inch nonstick skillet with a tight-fitting lid
- Shred the potatoes on the large shredding disk of a food processor, or use a box grater to cut the potatoes lengthwise so you get long shreds
- Garnish with parsley or chives, if you have any
- Sub Pecorino Romano for Parmesan

SAVORY CREPES

SERVES 4 | ACTIVE TIME 40 MINUTES

---

4 ounces cream cheese

8 ounces frozen chopped spinach, thawed and squeezed dry

4 ounces feta cheese, crumbled (1 cup)

½ cup oil-packed sun-dried tomatoes, patted dry and chopped coarse

⅛ teaspoon pepper

½ teaspoon oil

1 cup (5 ounces) all-purpose flour

¼ teaspoon table salt

1½ cups whole milk

7 large eggs, divided

3 tablespoons unsalted butter, melted and cooled, divided

1. FOR THE FILLING Microwave cream cheese in large bowl at 50 percent power until softened, about 30 seconds. Add spinach, feta, sun-dried tomatoes, and pepper and mix until thoroughly combined; set filling aside.

2. FOR THE CREPES Heat oil in 12-inch nonstick skillet over low heat for at least 10 minutes. While oil is heating, whisk flour and salt together in medium bowl. Whisk milk and 3 eggs together in second bowl. Add half of milk mixture and 2 tablespoons melted butter to dry ingredients and whisk until smooth. Whisk in remaining milk mixture until smooth. Adjust oven rack to middle position and heat oven to 450 degrees. Line rimmed baking sheet with parchment paper and spray with vegetable oil spray.

3. Wipe skillet with paper towels, leaving thin film of oil on bottom and sides of pan. Increase heat to medium and heat skillet for 1 minute. Test heat of skillet by placing 1 teaspoon batter in center of pan and cooking for 20 seconds. If mini crepe is golden brown on bottom, skillet is properly heated; if it is too light or too dark, adjust heat accordingly and retest.

4. Off heat, pour ½ cup batter into far side of skillet, then swirl gently in clockwise direction until batter evenly covers bottom of skillet. Return skillet to heat and cook crepe, without moving, until surface is dry and crepe starts to brown at edges, 35 to 40 seconds. Gently slide heat-resistant rubber spatula underneath edge of crepe, grasp edge with your fingertips, and flip crepe. Cook until second side is lightly spotted, about 20 seconds. Transfer crepe to wire rack. Return skillet to heat for 10 seconds and repeat with remaining batter.

5. TO FINISH Arrange crepes on prepared sheet (they will hang over edge and overlap). Working with 1 crepe at a time, place ¼ of spinach mixture in center of crepe. Using back of spoon, press and spread mixture gently into 5-inch circle, then make well in center of filling. Crack 1 egg into well, then fold in 4 sides of crepe, leaving egg yolk exposed, pressing at corners to adhere.

6. Brush crepe edges with remaining 1 tablespoon melted butter and transfer sheet to oven. Bake until egg whites are uniformly set and yolks have filmed over but are still runny, 10 to 12 minutes. Serve immediately.

PREP AHEAD

- Thaw spinach and squeeze dry
- Pat dry and chop sun-dried tomatoes

MAKE AHEAD

- Refrigerate filling for up to 3 days
- Refrigerate unfilled crepes for up to 3 days (or freeze for up to 1 month)

NOTES FROM THE TEST KITCHEN

- The batter yields enough for 1 "practice" crepe (5 total); only 4 are needed for the filling
- Serve with Simplest Salad (page 32)
- Garnish with basil, chives, parsley, mint, or dill, if you have any
- Sub goat cheese, shredded Parmesan, or shredded cheddar for feta

VINDALOO-STYLE POTATOES

SERVES 4 TO 6 | ACTIVE TIME 45 MINUTES

2 tablespoons oil

1 onion, chopped

1½ teaspoons table salt

6 garlic cloves, minced

4 teaspoons paprika

2 teaspoons ground cumin

½ teaspoon ground cardamom

½ teaspoon cayenne pepper

⅛ teaspoon ground cloves

2½ cups water

2 pounds red potatoes, unpeeled and cut into ½-inch pieces

1 (28-ounce) can diced tomatoes

1 tablespoon red wine vinegar

Plain yogurt for serving

1. Heat oil in Dutch oven over medium heat until shimmering. Add onion and salt and cook until softened, about 5 minutes. Stir in garlic, paprika, cumin, cardamom, cayenne, and cloves and cook until fragrant, about 2 minutes. Gradually stir in water, scraping up any browned bits, then add potatoes and bring to simmer. Cover, reduce heat to medium-low, and cook until potatoes are tender, 15 to 20 minutes.

2. Stir in tomatoes and their juice and vinegar and continue to simmer, uncovered, until sauce has thickened slightly, about 15 minutes. Season with salt and pepper to taste. Serve with yogurt.

PREP AHEAD

- Chop onion
- Cut potatoes

MAKE AHEAD

- Refrigerate braised potatoes for up to 3 days

NOTES FROM THE TEST KITCHEN

- Serve over White Rice Pilaf (page 34), if desired
- Sub 4 large shallots for onion
- Sub sweet potatoes or Yukon Gold potatoes for red potatoes
- Sub chopped canned whole peeled tomatoes or crushed tomatoes for diced tomatoes
- Sub white wine vinegar or cider vinegar for red wine vinegar

CHEESE ENCHILADAS

SERVES 4 | ACTIVE TIME 35 MINUTES

2 tablespoons oil

1 onion, chopped fine, divided

3 tablespoons chili powder

4 teaspoons tomato paste

4 garlic cloves, minced

3 tablespoons all-purpose flour

3 cups broth

12 (6-inch) corn tortillas, warmed

1 pound Monterey Jack cheese, shredded (4 cups), divided

Lime wedges for serving

1. Adjust oven rack to middle position and heat oven to 450 degrees. Heat oil in 12-inch skillet over medium heat until shimmering. Add ¾ of onion and cook until softened, 3 to 5 minutes. Stir in chili powder, tomato paste, and garlic and cook until fragrant, about 30 seconds. Stir in flour and mash into skillet with wooden spoon until well combined, about 30 seconds. Gradually add broth, whisking constantly to smooth out any lumps. Bring to simmer and cook until thickened slightly, about 4 minutes. Remove from heat.

2. Spread 1 cup sauce in bottom of 13 by 9-inch baking dish. Working with one warm tortilla at a time, spread ¼ cup cheese across center of tortilla, tightly roll tortilla around filling, then place seam side down in prepared dish. Repeat with remaining 11 tortillas (2 columns of 6 tortillas will fit neatly across width of dish).

3. Pour remaining sauce over top of enchiladas and sprinkle with remaining 1 cup cheese. Cover dish with lightly greased aluminum foil and bake until cheese is melted, about 10 minutes. Uncover and continue to bake until sauce is bubbling around edges, about 5 minutes. Let cool for 10 minutes, then sprinkle with remaining ¼ of onion. Serve with lime wedges.

PREP AHEAD

- Chop onion
- Shred Monterey Jack

MAKE AHEAD

- Refrigerate enchiladas for up to 2 days (or freeze for up to 1 month)

NOTES FROM THE TEST KITCHEN

- Serve with whatever toppings you have on hand, such as salsa, diced onion, chopped avocado, sour cream, and/or cilantro
- Corn tortillas are traditional for enchiladas, but you can substitute flour tortillas
- Sub red onion for onion
- Sub chipotle chile powder for chili powder
- Sub any semisoft cheese for Monterey Jack

NUTRITIONAL INFORMATION *for* OUR RECIPES

To calculate the nutritional values of our recipes per serving, we used The Food Processor SQL by ESHA research. When using this program, we entered all the ingredients, using weights for important ingredients such as most vegetables. We also used our preferred brands in these analyses. Any ingredient listed as "optional" was excluded from the analyses. We did not include salt or pepper for food that's "seasoned to taste." If there is a range in the serving size, we used the highest number of servings to calculate the nutritional values.

	CALORIES	TOTAL FAT (G)	SAT FAT (G)	CHOL (MG)	SODIUM (MG)	TOTAL CARB (G)	DIETARY FIBER (G)	TOTAL SUGARS (G)	PROTEIN (G)
Getting Started									
Make-Ahead Vinaigrette	210	22	2.5	0	200	2	0	2	0
Classic Basil Pesto	220	23	3	0	45	2	0	0	2
Garlic-Herb Compound Butter	100	11	7	30	0	0	0	0	0
Mustard-Chive Compound Butter	120	11	7	30	230	0	0	0	0
White Rice Pilaf	180	2.5	0	0	200	36	0	0	4
Boiled Brown Rice	150	2	0	0	390	35	3	0	3
Big-Batch Baked White Rice	190	2	1.5	5	240	38	0	0	4
Big-Batch Baked Brown Rice	190	4	1	5	240	42	4	0	4
Meal Plan 1									
Skillet Turkey Burgers with Tomato and Arugula Salad	690	41	10	80	1180	43	2	7	40
Roasted Chicken Breasts with Green Pearl Couscous	790	33	13	175	1460	61	2	4	59
Pork Milanese with Arugula and Parmesan Salad	930	68	8	150	760	45	1	1	32
Bucatini with Eggplant and Tomatoes	540	13	1.5	0	590	93	8	8	16
Meal Plan 2									
Pan-Seared Chicken Breasts with Artichokes and Spinach	460	24	13	170	990	11	4	2	43
Quick White Wine–Braised Chicken and Potatoes	990	60	23	285	610	54	7	12	46
Flank Steak with Farro and Mango Salsa	870	33	9	155	1000	85	9	7	61
Shrimp and White Bean Salad with Garlic Toasts	500	20	3	145	990	50	8	7	28

	CALORIES	TOTAL FAT (G)	SAT FAT (G)	CHOL (MG)	SODIUM (MG)	TOTAL CARB (G)	DIETARY FIBER (G)	TOTAL SUGARS (G)	PROTEIN (G)
Meal Plan 3									
Cod Baked in Foil with Leeks and Carrots	340	18	11	120	560	11	2	3	32
Skirt Steak with Pinto Bean Salad	590	32	10	110	1030	33	9	2	45
Roasted Pork Tenderloin with Apples and Shallots	440	21	5	120	390	27	5	18	37
Shrimp and Orzo Risotto	440	9	4	230	1270	55	1	6	34
Meal Plan 4									
Salmon, Grapefruit, and Avocado Salad	660	47	8	95	730	23	11	11	39
Pan-Roasted Chicken Thighs with Fennel-Apple Slaw	650	46	12	240	960	19	3	14	41
Balsamic Steak Tips with Tomato Salad	650	45	16	155	870	16	3	12	45
Grilled and Glazed Pork Chops with Radicchio Salad	670	43	10	95	880	35	3	27	36
Meal Plan 5									
Chicken and Leek Soup with Parmesan Dumplings	610	30	13	255	2720	31	1	4	53
Garlicky Strip Steaks with Cauliflower	670	40	17	165	960	23	8	8	59
Pork Chops with Chorizo Rice	840	41	13	175	1420	44	2	4	69
Orzo Primavera with Feta	450	10	7	40	860	72	5	12	20
Meal Plan 6									
Chicken Curry with Tomatoes and Ginger	330	16	3	165	870	10	3	5	36
Ground Beef Tacos	380	17	6	65	600	34	2	6	24
Honey-Mustard Pork Tenderloin with Egg Noodles	670	16	8	230	1420	70	0	11	52
Spicy Corn and Tomato Soup	260	11	6	25	1730	32	3	10	9
Meal Plan 7									
Skillet Chicken with Spicy Red Beans and Rice	650	23	5	160	1740	52	5	4	57
Lemon-Herb Pork Tenderloin with Green Beans	340	16	3	105	820	13	5	6	37
Pork Chops with Cauliflower and Roasted Red Pepper Sauce	540	35	6	75	940	22	6	7	36
Shiitake Mushroom Frittata with Pecorino Romano	360	23	8	575	860	10	3	4	27
Meal Plan 8									
Bibb Lettuce and Chicken Salad with Peanut Dressing	490	28	4.5	125	1260	15	3	8	44
Rib-Eye Steaks with Roasted Vegetables and Sage Butter	630	36	18	180	1690	27	5	7	49
Seared Scallops with Squash Puree and Sage Butter	400	20	13	95	1260	34	5	6	23
Spinach-Stuffed Portobello Caps	460	29	10	45	1010	35	4	7	16

	CALORIES	TOTAL FAT (G)	SAT FAT (G)	CHOL (MG)	SODIUM (MG)	TOTAL CARB (G)	DIETARY FIBER (G)	TOTAL SUGARS (G)	PROTEIN (G)
Meal Plan 9									
Parmesan Chicken with Cherry Tomato Salad	760	37	8	190	1120	49	2	4	47
Chicken and Rice with Chorizo and Artichokes	690	32	10	135	1870	51	4	5	47
Prosciutto-Wrapped Pork with Lemony Broccolini	340	14	3	135	1750	6	3	1	47
Skillet Tortellini with Sausage and Tomatoes	570	26	8	85	1970	54	1	5	32
Meal Plan 10									
Foil-Baked Chicken with Sweet Potatoes and Radishes	410	19	3	125	560	19	3	6	40
Beef and Bean Chili	390	19	7	75	760	28	9	8	28
Maple Pork Chops with Sweet Potato–Bacon Hash	860	33	11	220	910	53	4	32	82
Sesame Noodles with Snow Peas, Radishes, and Bell Peppers	350	20	3	15	620	33	3	23	12
Meal Plan 11									
Glazed Strip Steaks with Roasted Broccoli Rabe	620	36	10	135	1130	18	5	11	58
Italian Sausages with Balsamic Stewed Tomatoes	560	23	7	50	1610	43	5	13	36
Penne with Fresh Tomato Sauce	360	9	1	0	300	61	5	6	11
Broccoli Rabe and Portobello Melts	520	25	10	40	1340	47	4	11	23
Meal Plan 12									
Coriander Chicken with Cauliflower and Yogurt Sauce	690	49	13	240	1300	18	6	8	46
One-Pan Steak with Potatoes, Mushrooms, and Asparagus	600	28	14	165	1130	30	3	6	60
Foil-Baked Cod with Black Beans and Corn	380	13	7	105	1230	30	1	3	37
Tortellini Salad with Asparagus and Mint	560	35	7	50	1140	50	3	6	16
Meal Plan 13									
Steak, Mushroom, and Spinach Rice Bowl	770	32	7	265	1820	81	5	6	44
Roasted Pork Tenderloin with Asparagus Salad	700	44	11	130	2070	24	5	8	51
Tortellini and Vegetable Soup with Pesto	360	16	4	25	1120	37	4	9	15
Shrimp Burgers	460	19	2.5	215	840	40	0	4	30
Meal Plan 14									
Herb-Poached Salmon with Cucumber-Dill Salad	480	33	8	100	590	7	1	3	37
Crispy Chicken with Carrot, Orange, and Chickpea Salad	730	38	12	195	1280	30	8	13	65

	CALORIES	TOTAL FAT (G)	SAT FAT (G)	CHOL (MG)	SODIUM (MG)	TOTAL CARB (G)	DIETARY FIBER (G)	TOTAL SUGARS (G)	PROTEIN (G)
Meal Plan 14 *(cont.)*									
Meatballs and Lemon Orzo with Mint and Dill	930	53	17	130	910	63	1	6	46
Teriyaki Stir-Fried Beef with Green Beans	460	25	7	115	860	18	4	12	40
Meal Plan 15									
Green Chicken Chili	540	22	6	180	2670	32	9	7	54
Pan-Seared Chicken with Warm Bulgur Pilaf	580	23	7	150	850	45	8	3	50
Chorizo and Bell Pepper Tacos with Salsa Verde	690	48	18	105	1890	34	1	6	31
Spaghetti with Spring Vegetables	460	17	3	5	360	64	6	5	15
Meal Plan 16									
Roasted Salmon and Broccoli Rabe with Gremolata	510	36	7	95	580	6	4	1	40
Chicken with Parsley Sauce and Celery Root Slaw	530	25	6	180	560	21	3	9	55
Chicken Thighs with White Beans, Pancetta, and Kale	750	47	13	245	1320	27	8	3	53
Ground Beef Stroganoff with Egg Noodles	630	32	11	150	1290	52	1	6	33
Meal Plan 17									
Curried Chicken Sandwiches with Apple-Yogurt Slaw	660	26	8	95	1250	66	2	10	41
Spicy Beef Lettuce Wraps with Oyster Sauce	290	17	7	75	700	8	2	2	24
Spicy Pork Chops with Summer Vegetable Sauté	330	15	3.5	75	400	17	4	7	34
Soba Noodles with Roasted Eggplant and Sesame	710	28	3	0	2090	99	9	32	20
Meal Plan 18									
Salmon Burgers with Asparagus and Lemon Mayo	560	34	7	70	890	31	2	6	31
Chicken with Spring Vegetables, Capers, and Lemon	710	49	10	145	1390	13	4	4	52
Herbed Steaks with Lemon-Garlic Potatoes	520	22	6	120	950	24	3	2	55
Grilled Pork Tenderloin and Summer Squash with Chimichurri	430	25	4	110	680	11	2	8	38
Meal Plan 19									
One-Pan Roast Chicken Breasts with Butternut Squash and Kale	840	51	11	150	1070	43	8	15	55
Strip Steaks with Creamed Kale	780	53	26	220	510	20	7	7	62
Garlicky Stir-Fried Pork, Eggplant, and Onions	480	20	3	125	640	26	4	14	48
Butternut, Poblano, and Cheese Quesadillas	580	33	13	50	1310	52	3	6	22

	CALORIES	TOTAL FAT (G)	SAT FAT (G)	CHOL (MG)	SODIUM (MG)	TOTAL CARB (G)	DIETARY FIBER (G)	TOTAL SUGARS (G)	PROTEIN (G)
Meal Plan 20									
Pan-Seared Chicken Breasts with Chickpea Salad	530	27	4	125	980	26	6	6	45
Pan-Seared Steak Tips with Roasted Potatoes and Horseradish Cream	650	33	11	170	780	33	1	2	52
Spiced Pork Lettuce Wraps with Avocado and Mango	480	37	12	95	1030	17	4	3	22
Orecchiette with Broccoli, Currants, and Pine Nuts	740	25	4	10	570	106	9	17	27
Meal Plan 21									
Halibut and Creamy Coconut Couscous Packets	520	15	11	85	480	54	3	0	42
Roasted Chicken Thighs with Potatoes, Fennel, and Figs	1040	66	17	295	1380	52	9	18	56
Oregano Pork Chops with Warm Zucchini-Feta Salad	420	21	6	125	250	13	3	6	44
Arugula Pesto and Potato Pizza with Fennel Salad	830	48	9	20	1170	79	5	12	24
Meal Plan 22									
Pan-Seared Cod with Blistered Green Beans and Red Pepper Relish	300	16	2	75	1130	4	1	2	32
Red Curry Coconut Chicken Soup	430	33	26	55	870	13	1	5	23
Steak Tacos	450	25	5	75	680	29	0	4	27
Parmesan Polenta with Eggplant Ragu	570	13	4	15	1590	89	10	9	18
Meal Plan 23									
Chicken Noodle Soup	290	12	3	60	1030	22	2	3	24
Steak Tips with Wilted Spinach, Goat Cheese, and Pear Salad	600	38	12	160	650	12	3	6	52
Roasted Pork Loin with Potatoes and Mustard Sauce	630	32	7	130	630	32	4	3	49
Hearty Grain and Vegetable Bowls with Goat Cheese	630	27	5	5	580	85	11	10	18
Meal Plan 24									
Cod Baked in Foil with Potatoes, Zucchini, and Sun-Dried Tomatoes	390	14	2	75	580	30	3	4	36
Chicken, Sun-Dried Tomato, and Goat Cheese Burgers	400	19	6	80	720	31	1	5	27
Stir-Fried Pork with Green Beans and Cashews	330	16	2	55	1340	20	2	8	23
Fennel, Olive, and Goat Cheese Tarts	540	38	17	25	560	36	3	4	16
Meal Plan 25									
Poached Halibut with Leek Compote and Red Potatoes	560	17	9	120	1060	61	7	12	39
Wedge Salad with Steak Tips and Blue Cheese Dressing	570	31	16	160	920	12	3	8	48
Parmesan-Crusted Pork Cutlets with Chive Smashed Potatoes	890	42	11	275	1880	63	4	6	62
Bucatini with Peas, Kale, and Pancetta	430	9	2.5	10	600	66	5	4	19

	CALORIES	TOTAL FAT (G)	SAT FAT (G)	CHOL (MG)	SODIUM (MG)	TOTAL CARB (G)	DIETARY FIBER (G)	TOTAL SUGARS (G)	PROTEIN (G)
Pantry Meals									
Avgolemono	280	5	1.5	185	1930	41	1	3	16
Sun-Dried Tomato and White Bean Soup with Parmesan Crisps	300	4.5	1	5	1550	50	14	3	19
5-Ingredient Black Bean Soup	270	3.5	2	5	1430	52	0	4	18
White Bean Soup with Lemon and Oregano	300	5	0.5	0	1120	47	14	6	18
Red Lentil Soup with North African Spices	240	6	0.5	0	600	34	8	3	13
Grilled Cheese with Tomato Soup	710	38	23	105	1420	67	2	16	23
Curried Chickpea Salad Sandwiches	490	18	2	5	890	68	5	16	11
Lentil Salad with Oranges, Celery, and Feta	260	14	2.5	5	350	26	6	6	8
Bulgur Salad with Spinach, Chickpeas, and Apples	600	30	3.5	0	780	74	15	16	15
Fusilli Salad with Artichokes, Spinach, and Sun-Dried Tomatoes	540	26	3	0	440	65	5	2	14
Spicy Linguine with Olives and Garlic	520	25	3	0	620	63	3	2	10
Garlicky Spaghetti with Artichokes and Hazelnuts	450	18	2.5	5	270	60	4	2	14
Cacio e Pepe	350	8	3	20	210	57	3	2	13
Creamy Stovetop Macaroni and Cheese	670	42	26	215	1020	44	2	1	32
Skillet Tortellini Supper	500	31	15	95	820	40	2	5	16
Pasta and Chickpeas with Tomato and Parmesan	350	10	1.5	5	1020	52	9	3	15
Pasta with Tuna and Crispy Bread Crumbs	460	9	1	25	710	70	5	7	26
Spaghetti with Bacon and Spicy Tomato Sauce	450	14	4.5	20	670	64	5	6	16
Coriander-Spiced Couscous with Chickpeas	340	11	1.5	0	710	49	7	4	11
Red Curry Rice Noodles with Shallots and Cashews	670	34	20	0	970	86	2	5	11
Spicy Peanut Rice Noodles with Shrimp	730	29	3.5	105	1290	93	2	15	27
Kimchi Fried Rice with Shrimp	520	14	1.5	145	2180	69	0	3	31
Garlicky White Beans with Shrimp	300	10	1	95	850	32	9	6	21
Shrimp Scampi	350	20	8	245	260	7	0	1	24
Black Beans and Rice with Eggs	380	14	3	190	610	51	4	2	16
Eggs in Purgatory	350	23	6	375	1250	19	4	10	19
Fried Eggs with Potato and Parmesan Pancake	560	28	6	375	1010	52	0	0	22
Savory Crepes	610	37	20	415	810	39	2	7	26
Vindaloo-Style Potatoes	200	5	0	0	920	34	6	6	5
Cheese Enchiladas	730	48	21	100	1440	53	3	8	32

CONVERSIONS *and* EQUIVALENTS

Some say cooking is a science and an art. We would say that geography has a hand in it, too. Flours and sugars manufactured in the United Kingdom and elsewhere will feel and taste different from those manufactured in the United States. So we cannot promise that the loaf of bread you bake in Canada or England will taste the same as a loaf baked in the States, but we can offer guidelines for converting weights and measures. We also recommend that you rely on your instincts when making our recipes. Refer to the visual cues provided. If the dough hasn't "come together in a ball as described, you may need to add more flour—even if the recipe doesn't tell you to. You be the judge.

The recipes in this book were developed using standard U.S. measures following U.S. government guidelines. The charts below offer equivalents for U.S. and metric measures. All conversions are approximate and have been rounded up or down to the nearest whole number.

EXAMPLE

1 teaspoon	=	4.9292 milliliters, rounded up to 5 milliliters
1 ounce	=	28.3495 grams, rounded down to 28 grams

VOLUME CONVERSIONS

U.S.	METRIC
1 teaspoon	5 milliliters
2 teaspoons	10 milliliters
1 tablespoon	15 milliliters
2 tablespoons	30 milliliters
¼ cup	59 milliliters
⅓ cup	79 milliliters
½ cup	118 milliliters
¾ cup	177 milliliters
1 cup	237 milliliters
1¼ cups	296 milliliters
1½ cups	355 milliliters
2 cups (1 pint)	473 milliliters
2½ cups	591 milliliters
3 cups	710 milliliters
4 cups (1 quart)	0.946 liter
1.06 quarts	1 liter
4 quarts (1 gallon)	3.8 liters

WEIGHT CONVERSIONS

OUNCES	GRAMS
½	14
¾	21
1	28
1½	43
2	57
2½	71
3	85
3½	99
4	113
4½	128
5	142
6	170
7	198
8	227
9	255
10	283
12	340
16 (1 pound)	454

CONVERSIONS FOR COMMON BAKING INGREDIENTS

Baking is an exacting science. Because measuring by weight is far more accurate than measuring by volume, and thus more likely to produce reliable results, in our recipes we provide ounce measures in addition to cup measures for many ingredients. Refer to the chart below to convert these measures into grams.

INGREDIENT	OUNCES	GRAMS
Flour		
1 cup all-purpose flour*	5	142
1 cup cake flour	4	113
1 cup whole-wheat flour	5½	156
Sugar		
1 cup granulated (white) sugar	7	198
1 cup packed brown sugar (light or dark)	7	198
1 cup confectioners' sugar	4	113
Cocoa Powder		
1 cup cocoa powder	3	85
Butter†		
4 tablespoons (½ stick or ¼ cup)	2	57
8 tablespoons (1 stick or ½ cup)	4	113
16 tablespoons (2 sticks or 1 cup)	8	227

* U.S. all-purpose flour, the most frequently used flour in this book, does not contain leaveners, as some European flours do. These leavened flours are called self-rising or self-raising. If you are using self-rising flour, take this into consideration before adding leaveners to a recipe.

† In the United States, butter is sold both salted and unsalted. We generally recommend unsalted butter. If you are using salted butter, take this into consideration before adding salt to a recipe.

OVEN TEMPERATURES

FAHRENHEIT	CELSIUS	GAS MARK
225	105	¼
250	120	½
275	135	1
300	150	2
325	165	3
350	180	4
375	190	5
400	200	6
425	220	7
450	230	8
475	245	9

CONVERTING TEMPERATURES FROM AN INSTANT-READ THERMOMETER

We include doneness temperatures in many of the recipes in this book. We recommend an instant-read thermometer for the job. Refer to the table above to convert Fahrenheit degrees to Celsius. Or, for temperatures not represented in the chart, use this simple formula:

Subtract 32 degrees from the Fahrenheit reading, then divide the result by 1.8 to find the Celsius reading.

EXAMPLE
"Roast chicken until thighs register 175 degrees."

To convert:

$175°F - 32 = 143°$

$143° ÷ 1.8 = 79.44°C$, rounded down to 79°C

INDEX

Note: Page references in *italics* indicate photographs.